Please return/renew this item by the last date shown.
Items may also be renewed by the internet*

https://library.eastriding.gov.uk

* Please note a PIN w... ...service
- this can be obtained

D1420141

A JOURNEY THROUGH BOXING'S WASTELANDS

Tris Dixon

First published by Pitch Publishing, 2014
Softback edition, 2016

Pitch Publishing
A2 Yeoman Gate
Yeoman Way
Durrington
BN13 3QZ
www.pitchpublishing.co.uk

© Tris Dixon, 2014

A CIP catalogue record is available for this book
from the British Library.

ISBN 978 1-78531-143-7

Typesetting and origination by Pitch Publishing

Printed by Bell & Bain, Glasgow, Scotland

Contents

Acknowledgements

I T'S been a gruelling journey through boxing's wastelands. Although a lot of work went into finding the fighters and putting their stories together, without them, of course, this book could never have happened.

Several took me out to dinner. Micky Ward, Gene Fullmer, Chico Vejar, Chuck Wepner and Joey Giardello all treated their poor British friend to good food; valuable fuel for the long bus rides that lay ahead.

Other boxers welcomed me as a guest in their homes, allowing me to see behind the scenes and really find out where they are now.

My old friend, the late Phil Rooney, made the call to then *Boxing News'* assistant editor Tony Connolly to let him know what I was doing in the US. Without that, the ball would never have started to roll.

Special thanks, also, goes to my great friend George Zeleny, a true boxing historian, for his constant encouragement. Two of my favourite writers today, Donald McRae and Elliot Worsell, have been patient and generous with ideas when providing their eloquent counsel on this book.

My *Boxing News* team, too, of Danny Flexen, Matt Christie, Nick Bond, John Dennen and Paul Wheeler have all lent appreciated support.

Thanks also to Claude Abrams, Daniel Herbert, Tony and Steve Connolly and to Mary Payne, Kevin Mitchell (*Observer/ Guardian*), Jeff Powell, Dominic Calder-Smith, Nigel Collins, Bill Browne, Chris Mardell, Kit Neilson, the late Mike Biggs and Greg Juckett.

Of course, there was a mini-network of contacts helping throughout, made up of my friends Tom Jess, Jim Carlin and Jeff

Brophy and the late International Boxing Hall of Fame historian Hank Kaplan and Brad Berkwitt.

Without their help I would still be in the USA trying to find a starting point.

Many thanks to the team at Pitch Publishing, led by Paul Camillin, for taking a chance on me, and following *The Road to Nowhere*.

Duncan Olner, who has produced a fabulous cover, was a pleasure to work with.

The president of the Boxing Writers' Association of America, Jack Hirsch, deserves credit for planting an early seed about turning my travels into a book and my old journalism lecturer at Falmouth, the late Jim Hall, made it seem no one was out of reach.

It's fair to say my father was always sceptical about my 'American jaunts' and I wish he was alive to read this.

Thanks also to my brother, Justin, who sacrificed his J-reg Ford Escort to fund one of my early trips.

My beautiful girlfriend Amy has given me the time and space to finish this large project but there is, however, one person who actually inspired me to put a metaphorical pen to a metaphorical piece of paper to write these memoirs.

When I moved house in July 2006, I was floating down memory lane with dozens of pictures of the fighters on these pages when I wondered whether my newborn son would ever want to know how I found these old warriors and why I looked for them.

It was only then that, rather than years from now through faded memories, I decided to bring my thoughts and feelings to book. I hope he will enjoy them when he is older.

It was my boy, Benjamin, who made me write this and I owe him – and my precious daughter Lois – everything.

Preface

IT wasn't the road to nowhere and I knew where we were going. I just had no idea where we were or whether we would reach our intended destination. It was getting dark and the rickety old two-tone Cadillac with scraped blue doors and a battered grey hood boasted tyres that looked flat to the untrained eye but somehow kept us chugging from Atlantic City in the general direction of New York City.

The driver and car owner, former world light-heavyweight champion Matthew Saad Muhammad, reassured me he knew where we were going and offered kind words of support when he erratically swerved away from cars, the central reservation and anything else we nearly collided with. However, not even my favourite fighter could make the trip any easier.

I did not have a great deal of faith in his driving.

He'd had a long, hard career and the physical signs would tell you as much.

His words were slurred. He walked with a lurching stagger. This was one of my more dangerous assignments. The first of many, yes, and one that would give me a taste of the future, but one that would, as is often the case in boxing, leave me shocked, amazed and devastated, yet somehow wanting more.

Over the last few months Matthew and I had often talked at length but I said very little on this road trip. My tensed knuckles glowed white as I clawed to my seat, my eyes were like saucers and said more than I could. If that wasn't a giveaway about anxiety levels, perhaps the sweaty brow was.

It seemed like a lifetime but it was not too long before the hazy neons of New York could be seen from the Garden State.

A little further and we could make out the Empire State Building and the Chrysler, but the gap where the World Trade Center had stood proudly little more than a fortnight earlier left a raw scar.

There had been doubts about whether the fight we were going to see, the middleweight title clash between hot favourite Felix Trinidad and Philadelphia veteran Bernard Hopkins, would go ahead. It had been originally scheduled for 15 September, but the horrific events of 9/11 had forced it back to the 29th.

Miraculously we made it to the Garden and found a place at street level to park.

There was not much chance of anyone taking the car. It looked like an abandoned vehicle, it was so decrepit.

I was a 20-something wannabe boxing guy, Saad was an ex-champion who'd stumbled upon hard times.

He had been living a nondescript existence in a rundown part of Atlantic City. He didn't have his own place. He slept in a friend's living room and either took the small single bed at the foot of the apartment's one window or he slept on the couch.

We'd known one another for little more than a year. I'd stayed with a mutual friend on the outskirts of Atlantic City but eventually Matthew invited me to move in with his buddy in that downtrodden section. It was an offer I couldn't refuse.

He and I would alternate sleeping on the spare bed or the couch in a bland, unattractive two-room apartment.

I will never forget Matthew's beaming smile at the Hall of Fame when we first met, nor will I forget the shock I felt at finding him in his all-too-real surroundings when I visited him in Atlantic City later that summer.

The memorabilia from his career had gone and friends of his had told me he had pawned his world title belt and International Boxing Hall of Fame ring.

Daily, he was faced with the stark reality of his life as it was now.

As I followed my dreams of becoming a fighter, he trained me in the Atlantic City Police Athletic League gym, working on the pads, moving with me in the ring, supervising my skipping and other exercises. To thank him for taking me, I bought him and I matching navy training T-shirts.

He had always said how much he missed not having his own equipment anymore, although he maintained it was safely in storage with friends in New Orleans.

I doubted it.

The T-shirts sported Team Saad across the back in gold and MSM with some boxing gloves, also in gold, on the chest.

His face lit up when I presented him with it just before we left for the fights.

'Are these for me, man?' he smiled, with his full set of teeth on display.

'One each,' I said.

He hugged me tightly, almost lifting me off the floor.

He even welled up a bit but was too happy to let the water settle in his eyes.

He proudly wore the $20 T-shirt to the Garden and despite his smart new appearance he couldn't bluff his way beyond all of Don King's men.

Instead, I had to let my MasterCard flex its flimsy muscles and purchased the two cheapest seats left.

They were $75 apiece.

Saad was deflated as we scaled the zig-zagging escalators to take our seats in the nosebleeds. He was even more dejected when we sat down and could see the preliminary fighters the size of pinpricks in the distance.

'Are you OK?' I asked, knowing he was disappointed.

'Yes, thanks Tris. I'm fine. Thank you very much,' he lied.

Usually, despite everything, you couldn't shift that grin.

I was content to be a part of the big fight atmosphere from the peripheries but Saad wasn't accustomed to being so far from the action.

As the bouts progressed we tended to watch them on the huge screens above the ring rather than observe the dot-like participants far beneath us. I went to use the toilet.

When I came back, Saad was wearing a checked shirt with long sleeves.

There was no sign of the top I had bought.

He wouldn't look at me.

Before the main event, former champions including Iran Barkley, Chuck Wepner and Jake LaMotta were introduced from their ringside seats.

'I'm a champion, too,' Matthew mumbled, just loud enough for me to hear.

We rose for the national anthems and when Hopkins took to the ring Saad and I whooped and hollered.

'That's my friend,' he barked proudly.

'Down there, Bernard Hopkins is my friend, man. We both Philadelphia, you know?'

'Yeah, I know Saad.'

As excited as he was, he knew he belonged in the thick of it. He wished he was ringside.

Hopkins started to surprisingly dictate the pace against his fancied opponent. We stood to cheer on Bernard but as his dominance grew through the rounds, so did Saad's frustration.

'I should be down there, man. Instead I'm up here and I can't even see anything.'

He shook his head, putting his face in his hands so he could watch between his fingers.

'Do you think I can still get down there?' he asked, halfway through.

'There must be a way,' he said, trying to think of how he could join the other former champions who had unobstructed views of the action.

He didn't go, though. He didn't want to miss the action and he wouldn't leave me because he had to take me back to Atlantic City.

Fight scribe AJ Liebling had always written about the benefits of being at the fights in person and as I read his work I often nodded in agreement. On this occasion there were no benefits. We should have stayed in Atlantic City with our friends and watched it on their illegal cable.

Hopkins won with a 12th round knockout and as he did a victorious forward roll Saad and I embraced and jumped for joy at the birth of another Philadelphia underdog story.

But instead of feeling like I had gone with a friend it felt as though I had made him realise how far he had fallen.

On the long, silent ride as we swerved back to Atlantic City I asked him about the new shirt.

There had been a long, uncomfortable quiet before I eventually spoke.

'What happened with the T-shirt?'

He paused. He sighed. He pushed his lips together and looked out at the empty road ahead.

'A guy came up to me and said he'd give me $15 for it, I had to take it. I couldn't eat that shirt, could I?' he snapped, clearly disappointed I had pushed him for an admission.

'I've got to eat,' he said.

He sold the shirt off his back and was so ashamed he could not look at me. I wouldn't have been as upset had he at least made back the $20 I had spent.

With that out of the way, and us at least on talking terms once more, we dropped the subject.

As always, I would ask him about his favourite fights, the wars with Marvin Johnson, Richie Kates, Billy Douglas and Yaqui Lopez to get him started.

Only this time I moved on to asking him about what happened to all of the hangers-on I had seen in the ring after his hand was raised in victory.

'Listen, man,' he said sharply. 'When you're there and you're on top, everybody is everywhere. Now I'm broke I can't even find those guys. I fed them, I gave them places to stay, bought them cars and now I can't even find them.'

From our room in the high-storey block of flats in Atlantic City we sometimes looked out over the ghetto, heard police and ambulance sirens and even, on occasion, gunshots. We could see the bright lights of the Boardwalk on the not too distant horizon but for Matthew they were in the very distant past.

He offered me the single bed. I took the two-seater sofa, which meant my feet dangled over the edge. My wafer-thin bed sheet wasn't keeping me warm so I put a jumper on.

'You OK?' he asked, as the lights of the Trump Plaza and Caesars Palace flickered in the window above his bed.

I told him I was fine but was missing England after a few months away.

'Do you have any regrets?' I asked him, the same question he answered positively at the Hall of Fame months earlier.

'I wish I had been a singer or a movie star,' he said, changing the answer from the previous time. 'Then things wouldn't be like this.' His life had come full circle. The boy who had been abandoned by his parents, who became a multi-millionaire and won the respect of millions, had nothing again.

The name on his reissued driving licence even read Maxwell Antonio Loach, the name his parents had given him before the family spat him out on to a Philadelphia sidewalk when he was just five.

I was mesmerised by his sadness and amazed he could still sometimes smile.

Why I was hooked on boxing from the start I don't know. I had no idea how I could make a difference, either. I was due to head home but America was calling me back before I'd even left.

'Night, buddy,' said Saad.

'Night, Champ.'

Introduction

THE explosive punches came in thick, fast and were extraordinarily heavy. I felt my brain rattle from one particular dynamite right hand that looped around my left and I did not see coming. I froze but my head pivoted on my neck so I was left looking up at the light above the ring thinking how my grey matter had just been partially crushed.

Once I escaped that violent trance, and the subsequent ambush, I held on and threw hard shots to keep my antagoniser at bay for the rest of the round. We did one more, but I don't remember anything about it other than feeling like I had won a world title when the bell sounded. Survival was a victory of sorts, I guess.

Lenord Pierre was a pure puncher. He was being trained by Kevin Rooney and I was sharing the gym in Catskill with them. I'd been in town a few weeks and in the USA for a few days longer.

The next afternoon, I was terrified as I waited for Pierre at the gym. He did not show for the morning run and, as I gasped through the mountains, I could still feel my brain rolling around. It was agony. Perhaps it was a concussion. It hurt. The pain did not subside properly for weeks.

It didn't matter, of course. We were always going to spar again the following day so I got to the gym 15 minutes early.

In many ways the wait for Lenord was worse than the anxious hours before an amateur fight because I *knew* I was going to get a beating. I figured I was game, had a hard head and could punch a bit, which generally saw me getting hit a lot and landing rarely, but Pierre was class. He would go on to box future middleweight champion Kelly Pavlik and, in the pros, he knocked more than one man silly in less than three minutes.

But, at 3pm, he was not around. My heart was thumping and each time I heard a car pull up my mind was coated with a thick veil of dread. It was no fun waiting for a whipping. Twenty minutes after our agreed meeting time had passed, Lenord emerged. I wanted to run like the wind but he said he couldn't spar because his back was sore.

Relieved, I was left to contemplate an extraordinary few weeks.

With my trusty J-reg Ford Escort sold – meaning I was only slightly in the red instead of on the wrong end of a £2,000 overdraft – I'd left England. The plan was to stay in the USA for six months and learn about the sport from the best.

For someone who had less than a penny to his name, six months seemed an awfully ambitious amount of time to spend dawdling in America. In the first few hours after landing in New York there had been train tickets, food and the subway. I knew I would not be earning for some time.

It was five o'clock in the morning when I arrived in Syracuse after an overnight bus ride from the city and no one there had heard of Canastota, let alone the International Boxing Hall of Fame. Surprised and disappointed, I stumbled wearily to a taxi rank and after striking a deal for $30 I was on my way, petrified that I would be home within a week as I plunged further into debt.

It was dawn at the Hall and everything was shut when I arrived. I knew it would not be open for a while – several hours at least – so I paced through the tidy, old-fashioned town as day broke. I eventually came out the other side, walking up and down the hills that lead to Oneida, the next town along. Shattered, I strolled up to a billboard that warned me of black bears living nearby, walked a hundred yards or so from the roadside verge and tossed my rucksack lazily on to the parched grass.

My head nestled on the padded part of a sparring glove.

A couple of hours later, I retraced my footsteps but felt like a vagrant when I returned to the Hall of Fame with all of my worldly possessions hanging off one shoulder. I scurried to join growing crowds in anticipation of meeting some past greats of the game.

Within two hours I had talked to several old champions.

I spoke with former light-heavyweight champion Matthew Saad Muhammad, ex-heavyweight king Leon Spinks, Scotland's Ken Buchanan, one of the hardest punchers of all time Earnie

Shavers, the still-fearsome Iran Barkley and Philadelphia's George Benton, a good middleweight who later became an excellent trainer. A day later I was sat at a table with legendary trainers Eddie Futch, Angelo Dundee and Lou Duva. I could never have done that in England but after a few hours in Canastota I had.

Within a day or so, legendary faces had become familiar and friendly ones and featured smiles I'd see over and over for the remainder of the weekend.

Only Barkley proved the exception.

A polite request for a photo saw him try to shake me down for $10.

The makeshift photographer behind the lens said Iran should have asked me before doing the picture. Barkley looked blank, as if to say, 'Oh yeah.'

Later on I found him and gave him the $10. I felt sorry for him.

This was a sad business at times. It was called the hurt business and sometimes it did hurt. Considerably. What also hurt was the feeling of money running through my fingers and having very little to show for it.

I'd walk the 30-or-so minutes back to the black bear billboard each night to sleep under the warm blanket of stars, but never once did I see a bear. I don't think I even heard one. There were always plenty of deer around, though.

I shaved in the disabled toilet at the Hall of Fame museum.

And then Sunday afternoon came. The induction ceremonies took place and it was splendid. Among others, Philadelphia bantamweight great Jeff Chandler and Scottish boxing legend Buchanan were enshrined and gave moving speeches. Then they left. Everyone left. Finally, even I was gone.

I was the first person at the Hall of Fame that weekend and the last to leave. I had made one or two friends but as the crowds dispersed I was by myself.

I hitched a ride to Syracuse and jumped on a bus to Catskill. I was on my way to Mike Tyson's old town.

His old trainer, Kevin Rooney, had been expecting me. I had called before I left England and he seemed happy to take a look at me as a fighter even though I admitted to being average at best.

'Let's see,' he said, happily enough.

That was weeks ago, however, and it came as no surprise when I called to remind him of our chat that he didn't recall it.

He said he would send someone to meet me when I arrived.

Andre Kopilov was a giant Russian heavyweight. He was 6ft 9in or thereabouts, had a black flat-top, a gold Honda 4x4 and didn't provide much change out of 19 stone. His flash vehicle, he told me, had been bought for him by his manager, Bill Cayton, who used to look after Tyson.

Kopilov took me to see Rooney, who was at the local OTB (Off-Track Betting) shop. Andre went in alone and emerged alone. Kevin was gambling and couldn't leave, apparently. But the Russian behemoth had been instructed to take me to the Catskill Motel, as bog-standard a place as you could hope to temporarily reside, and I bartered passionately for them to accept $150 for the week. Even so, this six months of mine was getting shorter by the hour.

The weeks sped by in Catskill. I moved into a family-run resort, called Forlinis, and helped around the place, taking ice to the bar, cutting the grass and running errands whenever I wasn't training in the once-famous gym above the police station. In exchange, I stayed for a peppercorn rent. They treated me like one of the family and allowed me to share mealtimes, most of which consisted of wonderful old-school Italian delicacies.

In time, I became a familiar face about town and had my hair cut by Bobby Meo, who owned a private barbershop on the main drag and who used to cut Tyson's hair when he lived there. Tyson, he said, was always courteous and used to bring his amateur trophies into the shop to show Bobby's father before he passed away.

I trained with Andre every day. He had a big fight coming up in New York and I was either in the gym or out on the road running with a couple of Kevin's other prospects, a welterweight from New Orleans called Jay Krupp and a Haitian middleweight named Lenord Pierre. Lenord was the one to watch. There were stories around town that he had recently knocked out three cruiserweights in three rounds of sparring. He had that Tyson look, the peekaboo style where you attack and defend from bobbing and weaving positions.

Rooney taught me some of the basics. He did not do pads any longer on account of old injuries. Frankly, aside from drinking, which he did habitually, he did not appear to be in good enough shape to do all that much. He was three times the man he used to be but only half the trainer. The boxers, all trying to follow in Mike Tyson's footsteps, had to motivate themselves to train and Kevin was only there when we sparred or if he brought guys in from out of town to work with his men.

Frequently I would bump into him around Catskill – when he was not in OTB and I was not in the gym – and he would be walking with his two giant golden retrievers and a bottle of the hard stuff in a paper bag. He seemed to sweat buckets no matter what time of day it was and regardless of the temperature.

Sure, on the rare occasions when we were in the gym he showed me some things but by then Lenord had taught me almost all of the moves Kevin would demonstrate. In fact, Lenord Pierre took me under his wing. He had an enormous, but affectionate, slobbering Rottweiler and I think Pierre liked me because I was the only one in the gym as often as him.

The others? Well, Jay was in with a bad crowd and Andre seemed homesick. Lenord, though, enjoyed running, training and performing the drills with me.

Everything we did was what Tyson used to do. We sparred in the same dilapidated ring, hit the same dusty old bags and even listened to the same tape in the gym. No, it was not 80s music from back in the day but a cassette created by Tyson's trainer and mentor Cus D'Amato.

It would be played after we'd aligned ourselves with the wall-mounted bags and then Cus, the man responsible for Tyson's incredibly swift ascent to the top, would call out combinations from beyond the grave for us to practise. In the days and weeks there I learned the punches, numbered from one to eight, to an obsessive degree. I had practised the footwork daily and whenever a number was called I knew exactly what to throw. It became an auto-pilot function and doing it two or three times a day allowed it to sink in deeply.

Sometimes it helped but one day Lenord beat me black and blue in the gym and hurt me worse than anyone ever had in the past or would do in the future.

As I waited for him that day, eventually delighted he wouldn't spar because he'd strained his lower back walloping me, the pain in my head did not stop me from reflecting on the best few weeks of my life.

I knew I wanted to be involved in boxing.

The following day we ran together and I'd help Lenord with exercises for his back as I had my own lingering lumbar injuries.

Sightings of Kevin in the gym were scarce, and Jay's attendance was hit and miss. Andre had been chinned badly in Coney Island but Lenord and I were there every day, more often than not in the morning and the afternoon. One weekend, we got some cleaning kit and polished the whole place down. Every piece of wood flooring, every bag, every bit of kit was meticulously scrubbed. It took hours. I was under the impression it was the first time the gym had ever been cleaned.

It was still more museum than fitness facility. The old yellow clippings on the wall documented Tyson's time there. Rooney's own decent career was also on the equally faded and torn pieces of paper, so were articles on other fighters who had passed through, like Vinny Pazienza and Omar Sheika.

There was press on all of them. But those days were in the past, where this gym seemed to survive from.

After a couple of months or so, Kevin was in the gym one day. I had done some rounds with Lenord, got my ass kicked as normal, and then the trainer called Jay in, not for Lenord but for me.

I was in a dizzy haze and merely greeted Jay's arrival with a shrug. He had the same dip-and-weave style but was not the explosive or powerful hitter Lenord was. He was not the dedicated trainer Pierre was, either, and stood more upright, which suited me. I also knew the fighting style like a cabbie knows a shortcut.

For three rounds, Kevin called out the numbered combinations to Jay and for three rounds I hit him with them before he could get me. I boxed better than I could ever imagine. Better than I dreamt I could.

The numbers were called out and the shots came tumbling from my gloves. Not Jay's, though. He was waiting too long to get his punches off and, of course, I knew what was coming when he did shoot, having learned the codes.

Rooney was pissed off. Jay went back to his corner between rounds and Kevin screamed at him. 'He's only been here a few weeks and he's doing what *you* should be doing.'

I wanted some praise. I had been there, running out of money, training with his guys and trying to keep them motivated when he was not around. I was there whenever they wanted to train or spar and had scrubbed those filthy floorboards until my back was stiff and my knees were red raw. Jay was given water between rounds. Rooney, trying to ignite something, cursed him.

Tumbleweed swept through my corner. No one was there. I wanted this to be my home, too, but I was very much the 'away' fighter. Dejected if not heartbroken, at least I knew where I stood.

Round two opened up and despite assuming Jay would come out bombing, the same thing happened. Kevin called the numbers and I let the punches go. Round three, same thing. That was the last round I sparred at Catskill and, at its conclusion, I felt absolutely worthless, despite boxing better than I ever thought I could.

While Rooney tore into Jay, he could barely manage a cursory 'well done' nod in my direction. Lenord patted me on the back and Krupp embraced me as most fighters do following a good spar. Still, I had gone from camp insider to camp outsider in three short rounds.

I had learned their techniques and felt ready to move on to another city and another gym where I could use that system to my benefit. I decided to leave, telling the guys I was going to Atlantic City and a day or so later Kevin was drinking in Forlinis. I was bringing some ice into the bar when he said, 'I hear you're leaving town.'

I nodded coldly, fearing he would demand an explanation.

'Where are you going?' he asked.

'Atlantic City,' I said.

'Do you gamble?'

'No.'

'Well, why are you going there? There's nothing there but gambling.'

I knew there were boxing gyms there. I also knew Matthew Saad Muhammad had said he'd train me if I could get there.

'For a change of scene,' I squirmed, avoiding confrontation.

And that was about it. I left the next day.

Atlantic City was a hell hole, really, but it was home to me for a while and I consequently developed a strange, sickly affinity with it. At first I trained at the Police Athletic League Gym with lightweight contender Leavander Johnson and up-and-coming welterweight Shamone Alvarez, then, a year later, I was over at the Pleasantville Rec Center with Ray Mercer, Virgil Hill and Al Cole.

During different stints on the East Coast I had been to train at Joe Frazier's Gym in Philadelphia, Gleason's in New York and scores of other smaller, lesser-known haunts where I found the Catskill style did not work as well as I hoped it might.

Annoyingly, other trainers tried to 'correct' the way I had been taught in Catskill. They reckoned I was too flat-footed and generally too square on, rendering Rooney's part-time teachings redundant.

I worked with Bill Johnson, Leavander's dad, and a few of the other trainers at the PAL.

As he promised, Saad Muhammad coached me several times. Saad had done quite well as a trainer but couldn't hold on to the guys he was bringing through. They left for bigger if not necessarily better things. Besides, Saad, one the most exciting fighters the sport had seen, was a local celebrity and it's hard to get quality gym time with someone who is constantly harassed for old war stories.

I was meeting lots of people and making some good connections but making little progress from a career perspective. I had lived the dream and survived for so long with so little, experiencing genuine hardship as a homeless and hungry traveller.

I had slept in boxing gymnasiums, in fields in Mark Twain country in upstate New York, on river banks in the Hudson Valley, at the top of the Rocky steps of the famous art museum in Philadelphia, on the beach and beneath the Boardwalk in Atlantic City, in Central Park, Internet cafes and in countless train and bus stations.

I had trained fighters, carried spit buckets, cleaned gyms, penned articles for Internet boxing sites and was even a round card guy for women's fights – all with the objective of somehow making a life in boxing.

And I suppose that was the bizarre part; I had explored so many avenues I no longer had a grasp on what it was exactly I should focus on.

Wherever I was going, I wasn't going anywhere fast.

I was patient, of course. I had no choice. Time was not really an issue but considering it had been my brother's turn to sell his car for me to return to Atlantic City a few months later I really needed a result.

And that was when the phone rang...

Chapter 1

CRITICS dismissed Micky Ward as a clubfighter. Worse still, he had been referred to as a journeyman. If it took the amount of heart he had to be a clubfighter or journeyman then where did I have to sign? He was a warrior among warriors.

Better than that, he was one of the sport's stars in the aftermath of his exhilarating Fight of the Year win over fans' favourite Arturo Gatti.

It had thrust him into the limelight and at the International Boxing Hall of Fame weekend, a fortnight after their war, he had been the man everyone, fighters included, wanted to be seen with.

I wanted to learn his unforgiving left hook to the liver and inherit every piece of knowledge I could.

We had agreed that I'd visit Lowell in Massachusetts to train with him but Tony Connolly at *Boxing News* had other ideas. He'd heard about my plans and called, asking me to write a feature with 'Irish' Micky. In an instant everything changed. My sole focus was writing the piece and filing it rapidly.

I travelled through the night from Atlantic City on a Greyhound bus and was turfed out in New York for a couple of hours in the early stages of the morning, well before daybreak.

With two hours to kill, I threw my bag over my shoulder and explored. It was around 4am on Saturday night and Times Square was heaving. The bright flashing lights from illuminated advertising boards beamed in the intoxicated eyes of entranced tourists and loitering gangs.

My bag kept swinging into people and the humidity bothered me. After around 40 uncomfortable minutes I headed back to the cool surroundings of the deepest and darkest section of the enormous Port Authority bus terminal.

I sat at my departure gate for a while and began to get nervous as the queue of people waiting for the ride to Boston grew. By the time I finally decided to join, it must have been about 30 strong and was quickly piling up behind me.

I knew I wouldn't have the luxury of a seat to myself.

It was this part of waiting I particularly hated. You started to eye up who you might sit next to and wrote mental shortlists about who you didn't want to be with and why. Very large people used more than their share of the seat. Tall folks required lots of leg room. Those wearing headphones played music too loudly. This was before you got on to any of the unsavoury-looking characters.

More often than not, the queue to board Greyhound buses looked like a police line-up.

On this occasion I was fortunate enough to get a window seat and it wasn't too near the toilets at the back. They had to be avoided at all costs if the odd whiff was anything to go by.

I had a student-type next to me. I didn't make eye contact with him to let him know I wouldn't be talking for the six-or-so-hour journey.

I would be trying to get some rest.

There was another two-hour layover in Boston, where I moved on to a Peter Pan bus for the final leg of the trip.

That final section of the journey, which took around three-quarters of an hour, wasn't as busy and there was some room to manoeuvre courtesy of a seat to myself; a welcome coup.

I wrote some questions down for 'Irish' Micky and called him to come and collect me from the bus station when I arrived at mid-morning. The sky was grey and drizzle filled the warm, moist air. Lowell was an industrial town that thrived in the fifties but had become run down. There were still nice areas but the mean streets more than lived up to their reputation.

Ward's gleaming black BMW pulled up, leaving a gentle spray of fresh rain in its wake. It was a smart-looking car, not flashy as you might expect of a boxer who had been a TV idol for a decade and who, for two years running, had been involved in *The Ring* magazine's Fight of the Year.

I'd met fighters who had frittered hard-earned funds on garages filled with needlessly fast cars, mansions, exotic pets and extravagant entourages made up of bumbling and largely disloyal hangers-on. I had seen images of Mike Tyson and his fleets of expensive vehicles. Zab Judah and Floyd Mayweather haemorrhaged millions on designer clothes and excessive bling.

Ward wore a plain long-sleeved grey Nike T-shirt, navy tracksuit bottoms and he had a baseball cap on back to front. The cut over his left eye, which he had sustained in his ferocious battle with his new friend Gatti, had healed and his bruised right hand was able to shake mine firmly. He greeted me with a warm smile and tossed my bag in the trunk of his car by its shoulder strap.

No one seemed to recognise him at the station and as we left I asked if that was normal.

'I used to get stopped all the time,' he smiled, obviously pleased to be given his own space. 'But they're used to me around here now.'

It was 18 May 2002, and I'd visited the Mohegan Sun in Uncansville, Connecticut, as a fight fan looking for kicks and expecting a war.

What actually happened exceeded my own heightened prophecies. Micky Ward and Arturo Gatti tore into one another like lions quarrelling over a steak.

For ten ferocious rounds they planted their feet and swung their fists. They banged each other's bodies until they were red and sent litres of sweat flying from their faces as they repeatedly rocked their heads back with wild lefts and rights.

The ninth round, 'The round of the century' as the great trainer Emanuel Steward roared while broadcasting from ringside, was magnificent. It was the ultimate guilty pleasure. Ward was under the heaviest of fire but turned the tide with his patented left hook to the body.

Gatti was downed, agony finally etched on a previously stoic and unflinching face.

He'd cracked first.

Some wondered whether the Canadian hero would survive. Those who knew the warrior within had no doubt he would try to make it back to his feet.

He did, only for an avalanche of leather to fly his way and he was in dire straits once more.

Meanwhile, in my cheap seat, fans who were standing on their chairs and leaping up and down, were high-fiving complete strangers. In the arena they were sharing something as unique as the fighters were in the ring. A bond had formed while the violence was unfolding, and two men smashing into one another, reversing and then doing it over and over was linking them all in one hedonistically exciting brotherhood.

Gatti somehow saw out the ninth round. He survived and, incredibly, they both pulled through to hear the final bell after the tenth.

The fighters were exhausted. The fans were left sweaty and hyperventilating. The atmosphere buzzed and Ward won by the narrowest of margins, that brutal knockdown being the punctuation mark that made the difference on the scorecards.

Less than a month later I was in Micky's front room and he was reliving it, saying he wanted to go through it all again with his new friend, Gatti.

'It's only another 40 minutes of torture,' he reasoned, a sickly grin creasing the cheeks of his unmarked face.

Those ten three-minute rounds had gone into the history books as one of the definitive ring struggles of the modern era, a throwback fight to the days of smaller gloves, longer fights and fewer medical provisions. Ward had endured his fair share of thrillers before, but the struggles with Emanuel Augustus, Antonio Diaz and Shea Neary had been wonderfully eclipsed. He was an uncomplicated, mellow man who could transform into a disturbed grizzly bear at the sound of the bell.

He was, in the business, labelled a warrior and that's all he really wanted.

'That means more to me than anything,' he said. 'I want to be remembered as someone who's honest, fought tough and never disrespected anyone.'

Now 36, he was prepared to quit fighting had he lost to Gatti. Instead, there was speculation over a world title fight with Kostya Tszyu although he was closer to landing a lucrative return with Gatti.

'Me and him, you know, it was supposed to be a great fight and it ended up being one. I always knew it would be exciting. He banged me around pretty good but I was so focused and if we fight again I'm just going to drag him right back into it, into the pain. I'm going to start fast and come out swinging from round one.'

It had been so close – and so viciously good – that the clamour for the rematch had intensified.

Ward said he'd drawn confidence from experiences earlier in his career, and that lessons learned from previous losses helped earn him his biggest win.

'I look at it like it could have gone either way. Some rounds could have gone his way and some mine,' he explained of the outcome. 'People lose and they fall apart like it's the end of the world. They're never the same. But if you take a loss like a win and learn from it you come back stronger and it makes you a better fighter and person. I should know, I've had 11 of them.'

Micky showed me around his home, introducing me to his dogs, a Pekinese, a St Bernard and an English mastiff. His brother Dicky, a former fighter, lived in Lowell too, as did Micky's seven sisters.

The Gatti fight had been so well received Ward had even had a personal invitation to meet President George Bush at the White House.

'I live in a white house here,' he joked, 'but it's not as big. It's kind of unreal,' he added.

Ward realised, however, that the end game was nearing. The veteran's weary legs were growing older. The career had been hard.

'Two more fights at the most,' he shrugged. 'If everything goes well with this Gatti fight again and then one more big one, then we'll see. I take one fight at a time because any one could be my last.'

He knew the game. There are only so many last hurrahs a fighter can produce.

Several hours later, after taking the tour of Micky's home, meeting his fiancée Charlene, daughter Kasie and playing with the hounds, and after a quick lunch in a roadside sandwich bar, I was back at the station.

I completed the 700-mile round trip to Atlantic City on the buses, stopping once again in New York and when I arrived back in New Jersey I went to the library to type up and file the feature I had hand-written on the bus.

Tony at *Boxing News* seemed pleased enough.

'Oh, and by the way, Tris,' he said, his voice lifting towards the end of a brief chat. 'While you're out there, who else will you see?'

Just like that, my new journey had begun.

Chapter 2

ROCKY Castellani was a middleweight contender from the 1950s. He became a referee and boxing judge after his stellar career ended, retiring in Atlantic City and living on the outskirts.

He was not in the phonebook and I'd been unable to find an address but an acquaintance in New Jersey, Tom Jess, once said he could help me find old fighters who had slipped off the radar. Within minutes of calling I had an address for Castellani, just no phone number.

Tom, an autograph collector, said he had been to Rocky's place a few times but warned he had rarely found him at home.

I hadn't heard anything about Castellani for years and couldn't find any up-to-date stories about him online. He had seemingly sunk without trace.

As Tom and I talked about other fighters I could interview, the name of 1980s bantamweight Jeff Chandler caught my attention.

So, too, did Joey Giardello's.

The film *Hurricane* had recently been released and controversy surrounded Giardello's portrayal in it. The movie showed him winning a disputed decision over Rubin 'Hurricane' Carter with the guys in Hollywood making it look like Joey had received a favour from the judges because of his skin colour.

I knew it wasn't true. I'd seen a tape of the fight and read about it in grainy old magazines from the time. Joey had outboxed Carter and later settled out of court with the producers for their inaccuracies. Those were the three fighters I decided on and I was going to try and interview them all in a day.

Starting with Rocky in Atlantic City, I would go on to meet Giardello in Cherry Hill, a few miles on the New Jersey side of Philly, then visit Chandler in the City of Brotherly Love.

I was going to find boxers with stories to tell, preferably untold tales, and I wanted to find those who had been forgotten. I felt certain that the more obscure the names were the better my chances of having some work published became. The logic doesn't make sense now but it did at the time.

I located Rocky's street on a map of Atlantic City and spent around 45 minutes walking up the packed Boardwalk and into Ventnor in the summer heat, eventually arriving a little after ten in the morning.

Rocky would be 76 now. He fought a who's who of contenders and champions, including Cuban legend Kid Gavilan and the great Sugar Ray Robinson. He'd lost those but had given both good contests and was one of more than a dozen excellent boxers in the division at the time. Unannounced, I arrived on his doorstep and rung the bell.

His home was a large, detached white building. It was impressive, with pleasant views over the tidal waters and calm pools on the other side of the city to the casino-lined beach and Atlantic Ocean.

I knocked on the door and a lady with neat, strawberry-blonde, parted hair answered. She had a warm, rosy face yet her expression was initially curious, hesitant, the blank way a dog might look if you showed it a card trick.

'I'm trying to find Rocky Castellani,' I said, explaining why.

I was enthused by her positive response and radiant smile. She looked over my shoulder to see where I had parked and asked where my vehicle was.

I told her I was travelling on a budget and had walked there from the city. She introduced herself as Mary, Rocky's wife. She smiled again, lighting up her pinkish cheeks, and invited me in.

'Rocky doesn't have a very good memory,' she cautioned, as we moved into the living room. She said she might have to help him along the way if my questions posed him trouble.

Rocky was sat at the dining table playing with a puzzle.

He looked up, smiled briefly and winked his left eye. Then he looked back down and continued trying to put the pieces together.

He wore a green and blue checked lumberjack shirt over a white vest and on top of his round face was a light sprinkling of white hair, combed smartly to one side. He had the friendliest eyes I had seen but they wouldn't look at me for long.

He gently told me his memory wasn't what it was, reiterating Mary's initial warning, as we sat down, but whenever he couldn't finish a story Mary would help. She sat beside him and they held hands.

I thought I would try and lighten a slightly awkward mood by saying I was planning on meeting Rocky's former foe, Joey Giardello, later in the day.

'He's a very good friend of ours,' Mary smiled.

'Nice guy,' Rocky added, beaming happily.

'He really is,' Mary went on. 'He looks a little like Rocky and you'll really enjoy talking to him.'

'Did you beat him or did he beat you?' she asked her husband.

'I beat him,' Rocky shot back, starting to focus on me a little more.

Within moments we were transported to long before I was born and the start of Castellani's career in 1944.

'We had no money at the time so I did it just to raise a couple of bucks,' he explained.

'I never fought in the amateurs. I fought strictly pro.'

Mary stepped in, trying to get his momentum going so he could take over the sentence.

'His father wouldn't let him fight so Rocky fought under the name Roxy Wargo and then he went into the Marines.'

'I was only 17 years old then,' Rocky began again.

Rocky fought in the Korean War and was part of the Iwo Jima invasion during which almost 20,000 soldiers were injured and more than 6,000 killed. A lot of fighters from his era were called up to serve at the time and I asked what he thought of Muhammad Ali's choice years later not to go to Vietnam.

'I didn't like Ali,' Rocky snarled.

'He wouldn't fight for his country. I was involved in the invasions in Guam and Iwo Jima when I was just a teenager.'

He recalled stories from his service before Mary went upstairs and returned with an engraved wooden plaque with an outlined sketch of Rocky in his prime and his proud career record upon it. A fan had lovingly crafted it, presenting it to him when he retired in 1957. I looked at the names on the wooden display and asked him to flesh out details from some of his contests.

'What was it like to fight Kid Gavilan?' I asked of the 1949 bout that took place 53 years before I had turned up at their usually quiet homestead. Rocky lost on points in Madison Square Garden, New York, and was down in the second and third rounds.

'Great fighter,' he quickly responded.

'You lost to him, didn't you?' Mary offered.

'Only on points,' I interrupted, trying to let Rocky avoid the confirmation.

'How about Bobo Olson? You fought him for the middleweight title.'

Mary answered in a way that suggested she had told and heard the story many times about how he and Olson floored one another before the champion retained his title courtesy of a 15-round decision.

'When he fought for the championship people thought he won but they gave it to Bobo Olson. Do you remember, honey?' Mary asked.

'Do you remember Bobo Olson?'

'I thought I beat him.' Rocky again answered rapidly.

Mary went further, 'But they gave him a small ring, is that what it was?'

'They gave him a small ring so I couldn't move,' said Rocky, who would usually use the whole canvas for his artistry, jabbing and staying out of trouble.

'If they had given me a bigger ring I would have beaten him so bad they would have had to give me the fight because he couldn't catch me.'

'Rocky is a boxer,' Mary added, now holding on to her man's arm. 'He's a dancer.'

'Hit and move, hit and move,' Rocky chimed in and confirming stylistically he was the antithesis of his Hollywood namesake, stopping just 16 of his 84 foes.

'Hit a guy and move, you don't stay there for him,' he added, with the boxing buzz surging back through his blood.

'He was a good fighter, Rocky was,' Mary said proudly.

'Look at the names on his record, they are unbelievable,' I agreed.

'How about Gene Fullmer?' I tried.

'Fullmer,' Rocky exclaimed. 'He was a good puncher.'

'He beat you though, didn't he?' Mary boldly stepped in.

'I don't know,' Rocky answered, struggling to recall a 1956 scrap that saw two judges score for Fullmer and one for Castellani.

'Giardello,' Rocky said, with his eyes lighting up as he looked at the names on his ledger. 'I beat him once and he beat me once. They were close fights.'

I double-checked but knew he fought Giardello only once, and Rocky had beaten him.

'I was very happy with what boxing did for me,' Castellani went on, contemplating a career that concluded with 66 wins, 14 losses and four draws.

Mary again interjected, 'He had a nice life. He really did.

'While he was boxing he was so sincere. He never did anything wrong. He trained hard. He ran every day at five o'clock in the morning with Marine boots on and where we lived there was nothing but hills and he would run five miles of those hills every morning.

'He would eat a big steak every night, carrots and salad with no dressing and that was it. All the time he trained. He never cheated. He never went out. He didn't smoke, didn't drink. He was so, so strict.'

'Now I drink but I don't smoke,' Rocky laughed, brightening a mood that had become a little solemn.

'He will have a glass of red wine once in a while,' Mary added, dryly. 'Then, the first thing he would do when he was through training was to get a banana split. He loved ice cream but his favourite was a big banana split with chocolate fudge and stuff like that. That was his one luxury. That's why he never got hurt, because he was so strict in his training.'

'So you liked the hard work and the training?' I asked him.

By now, Rocky was looking at me the whole time.

He clearly liked talking boxing and enjoyed revisiting a place and era I could only suggest he hadn't been to for a long time.

'I loved it,' he said, his passion surfacing. 'I used to say I never wanted to get old because I didn't want to stop training.'

'You fought so many top guys, is there anyone you didn't fight you would have liked to?'

He didn't even need time to think about an answer.

'Jake LaMotta,' came his now customarily quick response. 'But he would never fight me. I had the style to beat him so easy. Forget about it. I wanted to fight him but he wouldn't fight me.'

'Rocky Graziano wouldn't fight you either,' Mary offered.

'They couldn't beat me, neither of them,' Rocky reckoned.

'Because they were brawlers?' I suggested.

'I had the style to beat them,' he beamed, shoulders now hunched looking as though he was ready to jump up and throw some punches to prove he still had it.

'I would have just punched and run,' he grinned.

'When I fought Sugar Ray Robinson I had him down and everything else. I was all over him. I lost a split decision. He fought LaMotta so many times but Jake wouldn't fight me so I had to fight Robinson. I had Ray down in our fight. I caught him with a left hook and dropped him.'

Rocky quit the sport when he turned 30, the highlight arguably being his knockdown of the great Ray Robinson. Shortly after, he married Mary.

'Just when he had placed the ring on my finger the phone rang,' she happily laughed.

Rocky smiled, knowing where the conversation was leading but not letting on.

'It was his manager, Tommy Ryan, and he said, "Rocky, we've got Kid Gavilan."'

Rocky smirked cheekily and interrupted, 'I told him, "Then we've got a fight,"' stealing the punchline and Mary's carefully concocted thunder.

The mood was again light. I was thoroughly enjoying the visit yet could not help feeling for Rocky because a once superb fighter was now so frail.

I was sure I could see signs of Alzheimer's in Rocky, who had been born in May 1927, but didn't press the matter. There were indications that 84 pro fights and more than 700 rounds boxed had taken a physical toll, not least his poor memory. There were scars over his eyes from more than a hundred stitches that had plugged numerous leaks.

He had also clocked up a high mileage after boxing.

He stayed in the sport as a judge when he hung his gloves up, becoming a respected official.

'On one trip,' he smiled, 'it took me 28 hours to get to Taiwan to judge a fight and the guy was knocked down and out in a minute.

'Twenty-eight hours for one minute. I got on the plane and came straight home. Can you believe it?'

He also became a restaurateur in Atlantic City, eventually closing his joint down in around 2000 to retire in peace.

Still, he appeared happy, even if he was a little bewildered that a young Brit with a notepad, tape recorder and camera had turned up out of the blue.

'I don't think he looks the same but people still remember him and he still gets fan mail,' Mary smiled, looking deeply and proudly into her man's eyes.

She said he kept his mind and body active playing board games, cards, puzzles and solitaire. They also went for long daily walks on the Boardwalk. Mary teased that her husband had outgrown the middleweight division by staying up eating late-night snacks.

'I don't know how he's putting weight on,' she said, bemused. 'After breakfast we walk four miles and after dinner we walk three. We are active and I watch what I cook.

'I think he probably waits until I go to bed, then he eats ice cream.'

A knowing expression spread across Rocky's face, as if the little boy had been found with his fingers in the proverbial cookie jar.

'I'm very happy,' Rocky said, looking around his front room and out towards the sea. 'Boxing was good to me. It gave me nice things. It gave us a nice house when I had no education.

'I had three boys and one girl and managed to put them all through school. The girl married a millionaire so that took care of one of them!

'I fought Gavilan, had Sugar Ray down and fought a lot of great fighters.'

'The house is beautiful,' I added in complimentary fashion as we now stood shoulder to shoulder, gazing out of a large bay window across the water.

'What's good about the house is I have a nice wife.

'She's real good to me.'

I asked them to pose for some pictures.

Mary declined, saying she hadn't had time to get ready.

Rocky tried to persuade her. 'I don't know what's wrong with you, you're still good-looking.'

'No, I'm not,' she protested.

'But I still love you,' Rocky tried again.

Our combined flattering worked and she finally clung to Rocky's side for a single shot.

'Before you go, we have something for you,' she said, disappearing upstairs again.

She returned with a copy of *Young Rocky*, Castellani's autobiography and a 10x8 shot of Rocky in his fighting prime. He insisted on signing both.

He wrote, 'To Tris, a great fight fan, your pal, Rocky Castellani.'

I hugged and kissed Mary goodbye and shook Rocky's hand gently.

He winked again at me as he had done at the start and asked where I was going next, forgetting I was heading towards Philadelphia to see Giardello.

'Tell him I'm making a comeback,' Rocky smiled.

'I want to fight him again.'

Chapter 3

THE train ran from the station at Atlantic City to Cherry Hill without any changes and I made it to the Diamond Diner just five minutes before I was due to meet Joey Giardello, the former middleweight champion of the world.

The skies were still blue, yet the temperature remained pleasantly cool inland.

The station was a few hundred yards and a hazardous double road crossing from the diner where we were due to meet.

'Are you looking for me?' said a short, elderly man with a flat nose as I entered the diner.

'Joey?' I asked.

'That's me,' he said, like an East Coast gangster from a 1930s film.

'I've got someone I'd like you to meet,' he went on, introducing me to a tall man, around 6ft 4in, who wore a thick, woolly, cream jumper and brown cords.

'Peter Green,' he said, in a quintessentially and surprisingly English accent as we shook hands.

'It's always nice to meet another Englishman,' he smiled. 'There aren't too many around here.'

He was the first Brit I had seen in months.

'I thought you would have something in common,' Joey smiled, as if he had set up some sort of blind date.

Peter and Joey had been friends for years and the three of us took our seats.

Joey might have looked like an old man now, aged 72 and in poor health with a leg that required yet another operation, but Mary Castellani was right, Joey did look similar to her Rocky, although his features were more rugged. His sharper eyes were not as kind as Rocky's, and his blunt nose made him look more like an ex-fighter. His conk had been spread over both cheeks in some of the fights I had seen on various tapes in my VHS collection.

He had a similar haircut to Castellani too, but a thicker mop. His soft edges made him look like the grandpa everyone loves.

He was 5ft 10in but well rounded. Not plump, cuddly.

He wore a soft, black polo-neck sweater and it seemed impossible to shake the smile from his face.

Whatever he once was, he was now one of the good guys.

He must have had dirt on just about every racket-run fighter from the 1940s to the time he retired in 1967, following an incredible 135 fights.

I told Joey I had just visited Castellani and passed on the message that he wanted to make a comeback for a rematch.

'Is that what he said?' Joey smiled. 'He's going to come back?'

He shook his head.

'When I fought him I was so disappointed because I beat the shit out of him,' he muttered. 'I beat him but I didn't get the decision.'

'But it's a long time ago now,' he conceded.

His memory was clearly superior to Rocky's and, considering he'd had surgery just ten days earlier, he seemed in decent shape.

'It's a little better now,' he said of his leg, in his gruff Italian-American accent.

Waitress Beryl came over to our table to take our food order.

I was too excited to be hungry. I should have been starving because it was early in the afternoon and I hadn't eaten since before daybreak.

'I'm OK thanks,' I told her, clearly embarrassed and perhaps even more obviously broke.

'What did you say, kid?' Joey asked, incredulous.

'I said, "I'm fine, thanks."'

'You've got to eat something,' he said.

'It's on me,' Peter stepped in. 'Do you drink coffee?'

'Yes.'

Rarely.

'Then we will have three coffees.'

'Joe, what do you want to eat?'

'Something sweet,' he said, smiling at Beryl the same way he probably charmed the girls when he was younger.

'The apple pie is good,' she recommended.

'Sounds good. Do you do it with vanilla ice cream?'

'We can do.'

'Great.'

Peter and I went for lemon meringue and blueberry cheesecake respectively and Beryl took her middle-aged, hard-smoking smile to prepare the food.

Meanwhile, Joey – who was born Carmine Tilelli – started telling me his story about how he lied when he was 15 to get into the army. He borrowed a friend's birth certificate and the name on that was Joey Giardello.

'So that became my name,' he explained.

But life in the 82nd Airborne wasn't settled. He missed his friends at home in Brooklyn and vented his anger on his sergeant who was cracked in the face for pulling rank one too many times.

Joey deserted and turned pro only for his actions to later catch up with him. The FBI traced him to a fight card in Washington DC where he was boxing in a prelim bout.

'I knocked my opponent out in the first round and I could see the FBI agents on the other side of the ring in my opponent's corner,' he excitedly recalled. 'As soon as I knocked the guy out I jumped from the ring. They tried to catch me in the parking lot but I had already gone. I left them my boxing gear to let them know so they didn't waste their time waiting for me. I outsmarted them that night but the next day I handed myself in.'

He was given a dishonourable discharge.

Our food arrived and we continued our conversation as Beryl placed it firmly on the table. Joey winked.

Occasionally we were interrupted by diners who would stop to say, 'Hey, Champ.' People would stare at Joey, hoping to make eye contact with the former middleweight king.

'How you doing?' he would occasionally say, lifting his head to acknowledge fans. We were only a few miles from Philly and Joey was often remembered as one of the city's finest fighters despite being raised in New York.

'Today it's the best neighbourhood in Brooklyn, all beaches,' he said of his old stomping ground. 'But when I was in Brooklyn I was a fighter. I just loved to fight, if a guy said "Boo" I would fight him. I would let it all out but I never used a bat or anything like the kids today. I would just use my hands.'

Joey neither saw himself as a New York fighter nor a Phila-delphian, particularly as he was 'robbed' of decisions in both cities.

You could understand how he felt when he spoke of some of the controversial verdicts that went against him. And he wasn't as bitter about having to wait 12 years for a title shot as one might have expected. There was no resentfulness, just complacency with life today.

Like Rocky, Joey had no amateur experience but he learned fast and hard with 33 fights in his first three years as a pro between 1948 and 1951. Arguably his initial significant contest was against Bayonne's Ernie Durando.

'Ernie and I were friends,' Joey said. His voice was gravelly and when his lips widened at the sides dimples showed in his cheeks. 'When we fought I used to talk to him and tell him, "You can't beat me, you son of a bitch!"'

The three of us laughed, and so did the elderly couple now listening in next to us.

Joey's record stood at 84 wins against 17 losses and five draws when he finally got a crack at the title belonging to a real bruiser in Salt Lake City's Gene Fullmer.

Joey was paraded around the ring on his cornerman's shoulders after their physical and foul-filled brawl, a 15-round draw. They were all certain he had won. It was one of *The Ring* magazine's disputed decisions of 1960 with many thinking Fullmer retained purely because it took place in Montana, much closer to Gene's home state of Utah than Giardello's New York.

'Oh, it was a tough fight,' Joey accepted. 'He really butted me.'

Fullmer was known for his roughhouse tactics.

'He had his own judges there and everything,' Joey went on. 'Sure, he was the champion, but it was called a draw and he wouldn't fight me again because he knew I would beat him.'

It was typical, really, of Joey's career.

He fought in quite possibly the richest era in middleweight history. There was the incomparable Sugar Ray Robinson, brawler Fullmer, the ferocious Dick Tiger, the explosive 'Hurricane' Rubin Carter and any number of fighters who had the ability to be champions on their day.

Joey lost to more people in their hometowns than just about any top champion in history.

After taking part in *The Ring*'s 1962 Fight of the Year with Henry Hank, he suffered another dubious decision, this time to quality stylist George Benton in Philly, where George was from.

'But I don't mind now, too much,' he said, salvaging the light mood.

Peter added that Benton's colour might have played a part in the decision.

'If it was close, you were out of luck. Black fighters in Philadelphia would always get the better of you,' he explained. 'Their crowds were all black and if their guy didn't get a decision they would start a riot so the promoters would give them the decision to avoid having the venue wrecked.'

Joe, as Peter called him, bounced back and won four on the trot to earn another title opportunity.

One of those was a victory over an ageing Sugar Ray Robinson, a faded version of the legend who had won welterweight and middleweight crowns. They squared off in an eliminator to meet champion Dick Tiger nearly ten years after Joey's pal, Castellani, had floored and extended Ray.

Like Rocky, Joey put Robinson down – in round nine – in the Philadelphia Convention Hall, winning on points in front of nearly 9,000 witnesses.

'Sugar Ray Robinson would never fight me,' Joey said, when I asked why he hadn't got a fight for the world championship any sooner. 'None of the champions would fight me except for Dick Tiger. The only reason Robinson fought me in the end was Dick Tiger, because the winner was going to get a title shot against him.'

Giardello said that when they did eventually meet, Sugar Ray was the 'smartest' boxer he faced but that was hardly surprising because it was Robinson's 170th fight and not only did he know every trick in the book, he had written a few of the chapters.

But Joey wasn't exactly a novice at the time. It was his 123rd bout.

Giardello split two fights with Dick Tiger in 1959 and four years on he fought the African in Atlantic City.

Tiger held the title after two wins and a draw against Fullmer.

'The first fight I didn't really know who he was other than some guy from Nigeria,' said Joey, his voice becoming huskier the longer we talked.

'Did you want to box and move or stand and trade punches?' I asked.

'I wouldn't even trade stamps with him,' he quipped.

Joey became the middleweight king on 7 December 1963, and it put him in the position to support his new son, Carmen, a Down's syndrome baby who required constant care.

Now, with the title in his hands, he had the chance to provide a future for his boy and so took part in exhibitions and fund-raisers. The majority of his life after boxing had been spent as a patron for the St John of God charity that helped children like his son.

And in 1999 Norm Jewison's movie *Hurricane* introduced Joey to legions of new admirers. In the build-up to his fight with star man Rubin Carter, played by Denzel Washington, Joey told reporters, 'I would like to fight Carter before he learns how to fight.'

He gave Carter a lesson all right.

Jack McKinney wrote in the *Philadelphia Daily News*, 'Giardello did a better job defending the championship than Carter did challenging for it.'

Afterwards Carter lamented, 'He sure kicked the hell out of me.'

But when Joey went to the Riverfront Theater in Philadelphia to watch the movie, nearly 40 years after he and Carter swapped punches in the same city, he was stunned to see Denzel get 'robbed' of the decision.

Following the fight, and with both boxers waiting for the official verdict, the ring announcer says in the film, 'Joey Giardello is about to lose his crown to Rubin "Hurricane" Carter.'

'I got halfway up in my seat and felt like yelling, "That never happened,"' Joey said, with a display of genuine disbelief.

The producers eventually settled out of court, paying him a six-figure sum. They also agreed to mention the facts in the DVD extras.

Still, Tiger came prowling again two years later and recaptured Joey's hard-earned title.

'Did you regret giving him a rematch, Joey?'

'Nah. Tiger had got my word and I told him that was better than a contract, so I had to give him a rematch.

'Would I have ever celebrated winning the title if Tiger didn't give me the fight? He was a great guy and a great champion and what he did for me I had to do for him.

'Of all the fighters I fought he was the most gentlemanly. I hit him in the balls a couple of times and everything like that and he never complained.'

'What a gentleman,' Peter added.

Joey retired in 1967 at the age of 37 with a win in his final fight against the previously undefeated Jack Rogers. He was stopped just four times in 135 fights but insisted he never touched the canvas with any part of his body other than his feet.

'I had a great chin,' he said, proudly holding his whiskers. 'But if you wanted to box me I would box you. If you wanted to fight me I would fight you and I was boxing when fighting was the best sport in the world.'

He undoubtedly had his share of hard luck, though.

He lost around 30 decisions, many in opponents' backyards.

'I don't know how many losses I got, I know I've got a few. But I know a lot of the places I won the fight but lost a hometown decision. If you look at my record, I fought most of these guys in their hometowns.'

A closer look at his final ledger does nothing to suggest otherwise. He lost to Castellani in Scranton, Bobby Dykes in Miami, Joey Giambra in Buffalo, Billy Graham enormously controversially in New York, Henry Hank in Detroit, Holly Mims in Washington DC, Terry Downes in London, Benton in Philly, Joe DeNucci in Massachusetts and Ralph Dupas in New Orleans for starters.

I asked him whether the Mob had helped or hindered him.

Blinky Palermo and Frankie Carbo just about had a piece of every leading fighter, and Joey was said to be the lynchpin of their stable. For a time, Joey was even kept from fighting in New York because of Mob connections, a real blow considering many of boxing's biggest bills were at Madison Square Garden.

He also served three and a half months in jail for beating up a petrol attendant who had thrown a tyre iron at his vehicle when he drove off after 'forgetting' to pay for petrol.

'If I was with the Mob they didn't do a very good job,' he said, a little snappily but not as harshly as anticipated.

'I was always begging for a title shot. I was the top contender for a long time but no one would fight me. The Mob was meant to be able to help people get title fights, weren't they?'

I got the feeling he was playing dumb now, particularly when a hint of a smile appeared.

'The one thing I will say is that my managers were the bravest guys in the world,' he went on, perhaps thinking I wasn't entirely believing his spiel. 'They didn't give a shit who I fought. They made me fight all of the toughest bastards around.'

'Do you follow boxing now?' I asked, as our empty plates were being cleared.

'In those days the champions could fight. They were all good fighters. These days I don't know many of them and it seems that everybody is a champion.'

Although Joey was still standing, dozens of his opponents had died. Tiger passed in 1971, Mims in 1970, Graham and Durando in 1992, Ralph Tiger Jones in 1994, Sugar Ray in 1989 and Harold Green in 2001.

I mentioned that.

'Jeez, am I the only one left?' he said, with a look of stern contemplation, clearly thinking about the names and his time in their company. Like Rocky, he was in a long marriage, happy with Rosealee after 53 years. He was also proud of their four grown-up boys. Son Carmen, now 50, was OK too, but I wasn't overly surprised.

Both he and his father had fought the odds, and both were still fighting.

Chapter 4

IT was around 5pm when I embraced Joey Giardello and the door of the Diamond Diner swung shut behind me. I still hoped to see Jeff Chandler and had an address but no phone number.

Nothing could be arranged so I had to go there and hope for the best. I took the train from Cherry Hill to Philadelphia before catching the bus to the Germantown district, walking the rest of the way.

No one had heard much about Chandler until he showed up for his induction at the Hall of Fame in 2000.

Fortunately, I met Tom Jess there that year.

He had brought Jeff to Canastota. He mentioned then he could help me meet some of the top trainers and ex-fighters in Philly and I loved the city. There had always been something about the place that enthralled me. Whenever I was in New York or Atlantic City there was a temptation to go to Philadelphia just to soak up some of its rich boxing history. For years it was boxing's capital. Great fighters lived, trained and fought there.

Matthew Saad Muhammad, perhaps the most exciting fighter to watch in the sport's past, was an archetypal Philly warrior. He took punishment to give it. He could end the fight with a flash of either fist and had an abundance of charisma.

There were others in a similar mould, like 'Smokin' Joe Frazier, 'Bad' Bennie Briscoe and Eugene 'Cyclone' Hart, though there were a few exceptions to the stereotype.

Jimmy Young was a box of tricks who gave Muhammad Ali headaches with his unique style before losing a hotly contested decision, and some said Bobby 'Boogaloo' Watts was as gifted as Sugar Ray Robinson, he just couldn't stand up to a good wallop.

Mercurial 'Gypsy' Joe Harris was a stylist and Willie 'The Worm' Monroe could be as slippery as his name suggested.

Chandler, a 1980s bantamweight, was somewhere in between. He was a nifty boxer who wasn't afraid of a tear-up because he could dig with both hands and possessed a dependable chin. His career was cut short because of eye problems, but his best days were behind him by then and perhaps the detached retina had prevented the long and ugly fall from grace several Philly fighters like Saad Muhammad and Young had experienced.

I heard Chandler wasn't well off and after leaving the bus it didn't take long to figure out he lived in a potentially violent and dangerous part of town. It certainly wasn't in the city's tourist brochure. It was still mild but daylight started to go and gangs on street corners eyed me up as a potential target when I walked by. All I could do was not make eye contact, appear to look as though I knew where I was going and not seem intimidated.

But all of these were now standard practices, and it's not as if I had the appearance of a millionaire even if mine was the only white face for miles.

A good 45 minutes had elapsed since I left the bus and I was intently following a map and Tom's instructions. But I was sure he hadn't said it was this far.

I was finding out the Germantown part of Philly wasn't a small district.

It was a sprawling place that went on for miles. I had, by mistake, got off the bus several stops too early, meaning more than four miles of needless walking.

The evening got darker and the accommodation shabbier the further I walked. There were fewer and fewer shops and the residents looked a little meaner and more menacing after each block. Some of the houses had boarded windows, while others had neither windows nor boards. Post offices and newsagents were replaced by stores advertising hard liquor at knockdown prices. They were boarded up, too.

I felt I was in the wrong place at the wrong time.

And although I didn't want to stop to ask for directions I had to. I was lost. Time was passing quickly and the last train back to Atlantic City wasn't as late as I had hoped.

Two big guys wearing Phat Farm gear were perched in the porch of a ramshackle house. It was one that had boarded-up windows, needed a paint job and there was a load of trash and broken glass in the front garden.

'Guys,' I said sharply, 'you know where Germantown Avenue is from here?' while trying to disguise the gentle knocking in my knees.

The bigger of the two shot back, 'Where you from, man?'

Damn, I didn't want a conversation.

'Atlantic City,' I said, avoiding the obvious chatter about my accent.

'What a dump,' the other said back.

'Tell me about it. I'm only there for the boxing.'

'You fight?' said the bigger one, softening slightly.

'A little,' I said.

'Oh, OK,' he replied, his voice raising. 'This address is just two blocks down, make a left, then a right and you'll find it,' he said. 'Good luck.'

With survival achieved, a spring in my step, and still being keen to find a safe haven, I bounded up the street I had been told to and was outside Chandler's house within minutes.

It was bigger than I had expected, a substantial detached house. It was a little scrappy from the outside and in need of some fresh paint and damp treatment but not too bad. There was a problem, however. There was no car outside and the lights weren't on.

In my naivety I had simply hoped he would be in.

I knocked on the door and waited hopelessly, thinking about how I might return to Central Philly before the public services stopped for the night.

I was pleased I had done two interviews, sure, yet disappointed because I could have managed a third. And I had put in so much effort. Who knows, I might have seen Chandler and he wouldn't have wanted to talk anyway.

Exhausted, I collapsed on his doorstep, put my sweaty face in my hands and tried to muster the strength and enthusiasm for the long walk back. I wondered if I would even be able to get a bus around there that late. There was nothing but houses and gangs. No parks, nowhere to sleep. I had come all this way, missed Jeff and now needed to get back to New Jersey.

After five minutes of contemplating how rash I had been, cropping up at former world champions' homes on the off-chance, I rose wearily and left. The adrenaline from the hunt had dissipated, leaving me to be double-teamed in equal measure by hunger and fatigue. I couldn't afford to call a cab and go back to central Philly and stay in a nice hotel. Novice freelancers don't get expenses.

I wheeled away, inhaled deeply, staring vacantly into the dark sky. After a few yards I saw a silhouetted figure darting towards me. The light had gone for the day and the shape I saw wore a beanie hat, had a slight build and walked briskly. His hands sat deeply inside long coat pockets. He was looking down.

The person was either walking quickly away from a robbery or on his way to confront me.

I readied myself, walked with an apparent confidence towards him, looked straight into his face and he sped right past.

'That was a close one,' I sighed.

I just caught a glimpse of a trimmed greying beard, but thought the colours had been caused by a flicker from the streetlight. I stopped, let him go a bit further, and turned around, following him closely with my eyes.

He went into Jeff's house.

I jogged up behind him as he went to close the door.

'Mr Chandler, Mr Chandler,' I said loudly, but not with any certainty.

He had partly closed the door and held it ajar to take a look at me.

'Who are you?' he asked. 'What do you want?'

I could now tell it was him.

'I'm a boxing writer from England. I was wondering if I could interview you for a magazine in the UK.'

He looked at me as if I had just fallen out of the sky.

But his shocked face softened, he grinned and said, 'What, here? Now?' I nodded.

'Sure, come on in,' he said obligingly.

His house was big, perhaps made to seem larger because there was next to no furniture in there. He walked me through a lounge and dining room and into a kitchen at the back of the house.

He offered me a chair from around the dining table, he took another, which didn't match, and we sat and chatted like old friends.

He was bright and bubbly. His happiness seemed to carry him higher than his 5ft 7in frame and he spoke about what he had done in life after boxing. Now 46 years old, and 20 years removed from his title reign as a dominant bantamweight, he was working two jobs. As well as being employed by the council to train kids how to fight, he was also a non-teaching assistant (NTA) at a nearby school.

'Being an NTA is a way of me releasing myself,' he said, obviously having looked for alternative buzzes after the crowds had gone silent. 'It also means I do not have to sit back and think, "Jab, left hook, uppercut."

'I thought maybe I should go out and teach these kids so when I come home I can relax and leave it with them.'

He seemed content until admitting, 'Sure, I miss boxing.'

Throughout the conversation Jeff would stop and ask me how I found his house, how I managed to get there on foot and how I did it without getting attacked – something that seemed to amaze him.

He was clearly grateful for the company. He had a deep voice for a little guy, but it was thick, a bit throaty here and there, and he slurred some of his vowels.

When he was a kid he looked up to Muhammad Ali more so than fellow Philly legend Joe Frazier.

'Joe would have to give a shot to take a shot and I didn't have that mentality,' he explained. 'I was taught to hit and not get hit so that's what I tried to do. No one will tell you I fought like any of those great Philadelphia fighters did. They were bangers and warriors.

'I was a warrior, too. I could fight and run with anybody, but my mindset was to box off the jab. Stick and move.

'When it came to a fight I was fully focused and ready. I had been dedicated in my training, had what it took to win and when the time came to fight I was more ready than any warrior you have ever seen in this lifetime.'

With his excitement growing by the second at unexpectedly reliving fighting memories he jumped to his feet and threw a burst of punches.

'I had the best left hand in the world,' he barked, showing me a hook off the jab. 'It was lovely.'

A right hand flowed through.

'I miss Jeff Chandler boxing,' he said, rolling his shoulders as though he was just warming up.

However, he added it in a way that detached him from his career.

He *was* Jeff Chandler, he was *still* the same man.

But he clearly saw Jeff Chandler the champion as a different person from who he had become. It was like listening to a fan talking about how much he missed his favourite retired fighter.

'No one had a style I couldn't work around,' he continued. 'My hand speed and knowledge of boxing were as good as anybody's that there has ever been and I did all this after just two amateur fights, one win and one loss.'

Jeff had been programmed to be fearless in the harsh Philly gymnasiums where wars broke out on a daily basis. Instead of a substantial amateur career, he learned his craft on the receiving end of punches from bigger and better fighters, such as Tyrone Everett whom Jeff, then a first-year pro rookie, helped prepare for his controversial and heartbreaking loss to Alfredo Escalera for the WBC super-featherweight title in 1976.

'I wasn't afraid in any fight I've ever been in,' Chandler said of sparring and boxing. 'There were certain fighters I respected more than others but I wasn't scared of any of them. I went to win every fight I had.'

I asked Jeff, still excited and energised by my visit, how it felt when he won the title from the unbeaten WBA champion Julian Solis in Miami back in 1980.

It was poignant because here we were, all these years later, and he clearly hadn't reaped the fruits of his labours.

'I remember the night like yesterday,' he recalled. 'I'd always dreamed of fighting for the title. I was a young black bantamweight and most bantamweights came from the West Coast, Mexico or Japan.

'When I won I threw my arms up and thought they were going to stretch forever. I couldn't believe I'd got there.

'Actually, I could believe it,' he beamed, quickly correcting himself. 'But the feeling I had was euphoria. I thought it was the best feeling you could get in the world.

'When I knew they had stopped the fight and I'd won the title, that moment, I felt I could jump straight up and never come down.'

Chandler wanted his career to go from strength to strength but matches against some of the best champions and challengers failed to materialise. While Jeff appreciated the crowds and lived for the buzz, he didn't get the fights he wanted to define his career.

'Lupe Pintor wouldn't fight me for all the gold in Mexico,' he said, shaking his head with the corners of his lips curling towards his chin.

'He knew, like everybody else, that I was the fighter he wanted to stay away from.'

He boxed top contenders but insisted there were few he hadn't beaten left to fight.

'At the time all of the elite championship fighters in the bantamweight division had gone, I'd bumped them all off,' he reasoned.

He defended against quality operators including Johnny 'Dancing Machine' Carter, Gaby Canizales, Jorge Lujan and he beat Solis again. He wanted unification fights and his trainer Willie O'Neil, and manager, the diminutive KO Becky O'Neil, tried for him.

Chandler's mother–son relationship with little Becky was well documented and she attempted to get Jeff the recognition his ability warranted.

'I could have won those fights but I never had the chance to win a second title or be a champion in another weight class,' he added.

'I would have liked to have fought 70 or 80 times and nobody win but me. I always wanted to be the best and knew that to be the best you have to beat the best. But my next defence was against a guy nobody knew called Miguel Iriate and I figured it would take a little time for the rankings to re-organise and get some tough guys back up there.

'I made the same money fighting him as I did the others but as far as the enjoyment went from beating top-ranked guys to go to this then no, I didn't get it.

'I was mad at my team and Willie for a long time because of that. But he said, "Yo, you made good money off the guy. What's the problem? You got another defence of your title. You knocked the guy out and he didn't do nothing to you. What's the matter with you?"

'And I told him, "Willie, you know, I want to be remembered as being the best of all time and you just ain't gonna get that fighting dog meat like Miguel Iriate."'

Iriate had boxed just 12 times as a pro, with ten wins, a loss and a draw, before he was stopped in the ninth in a challenge for Jeff's title.

The Ring shared Jeff's frustration and put him on their front cover along with the headline, 'The best fighter nobody knows'.

He lost the title in his last contest, a 1984 bout with hot up-and-comer Richie Sandoval, who had won each of his 22 fights. Beforehand, Sandoval said Jeff had brought the bantamweights to 'a whole new level' and their record-breaking purses of around $400,000 apiece reflected that.

Sandoval ground Jeff down by the 11th and he was floored for the first time in his life.

Chandler reckons he made around $1.5 million in his 37-fight career, retiring after 33 wins, a brace of losses and two draws. There was no sign that any of that money was left.

Still, there was controversy when he was refused a licence to box because of eye problems and, prior to my visit, he had been dubbed a recluse, still bitter that his career had been cut short.

But that wasn't the man I was talking to.

Now it was as if he was the champion again.

He was talking like an overexcited kid and admitted he still followed the sport, albeit without the help of cable providers HBO and Showtime, which he didn't have.

'I like all of the boxers now, they're fighters and they do what I did,' he said proudly. 'As long as they don't want to fight me they can't go wrong. Now if they're bantamweights that's another story. If they're my weight then I don't like them and I want to fight them because that's my territory. I've still got some animosity towards the little guys.'

A mischievous smile spread up his cheeks.

'But I was a happy-go-lucky kind of guy. My parents tried to make a nice life for me and things like that so I kept myself out of trouble all my life. I've never been to jail and have always been a hard worker. But I was also as ready as any warrior you have seen in this lifetime. And don't get me wrong, I always loved Willie.

'He's passed away now but it don't get no better than Willie. He grew up right down the street from where I grew up. Right now, with me talking to you here, I'm missing him. All the time I'm missing him because ever since he went I missed him. In my life I never met anyone like him. He was good people, and his wife KO Becky, she was good people. They were good to me. I miss them.

'She's been pretty sick lately. I haven't seen her for a while but when I do it hurts. I hate to see ill people going through what they are going through, you know?

'She's had throat cancer or something. Then there was another ailment. Then she was in the hospital for something else but she's been going there for a long time for different things.'

Mist was filling his eyes and a tremor entered his voice.

'And now she doesn't have her husband with her because he passed away in 1994.'

Jeff was getting emotional so I decided to lift his spirits by talking about the glory days again. Within a couple of minutes his eyes were dry and he was bouncing, throwing punches and slipping imaginary blows.

He even asked if I could stay longer.

It was pitch black outside and I wasn't looking forward to facing the streets again.

'Jeff, it's been great to meet you but I've really got to go. It's a long way back to Atlantic City.'

Before I could carry on he interrupted, 'Right now, you here talking to me, you helped me, too. You helped me release myself and there were some things I had back in there that I had held back, and I got them out. I appreciate it, man.'

Time was ticking. Jeff's contagious high meant I hadn't looked at my watch for two hours.

'How are you getting home?' he enquired.

'Well, it looks like I will walk most of the way back to Central Philly. It's OK, I've got time.'

There was less than an hour before the last train.

'You can't do that, man. People here will kill you.'

'I'll be all right,' I insisted. 'I made it here, didn't I?'

'You won't,' he snapped, 'and I can't have that on my conscience.'

It seemed rather melodramatic.

'Follow me,' he insisted.

He frog-marched me through the Philadelphia night and across the street to a neighbour's house.

I saw a rusty taxi in the driveway and Jeff knew the guy who owned it. The off-duty driver had the face of a black angel, which was only lit by a dim flicker from a nearby streetlight and the gold teeth in his mouth. He wore a flat cap and a friendly smile. He owed Jeff a favour and agreed to drive me back to the station.

Jeff hugged me goodbye, welling up again while thanking me for 'coming all the way from England'.

He said I had made him feel like a champion again, the first time since he couldn't remember when.

'Do me a favour,' he said, fixing a more serious stare. 'When you fight again, keep your hands up because everything comes from up there,' and with that, more shadow punches were coming my way.

'Oh I love it,' he smiled, throwing blurring combinations. 'Oh I love it. Oh man.'

We pulled away and when I looked through the rear windscreen Jeff smiled and waved, cutting through the shadows with lefts and rights in the dull, orange glow of the dark Philadelphia night.

The further we drove the more pleased I was not to have to tackle the walk. It was about a 20-minute drive and I could see nocturnal deviants on street corners from the safe side of the glass.

At the station, I gratefully shook the driver's hand.

I was on the last train to Atlantic City with just minutes to spare.

What a day. As hungry as I was, I was perched sleepily on cloud nine. I thought of Rocky, Joey and Jeff as the train crawled out of Philadelphia.

Rocky had danced and flickered in black and white on my TV at home and Joey had brawled and bled all over several tapes I owned but they were in a very different part of their lives now and I had met them, 50 years on from their fight, in the flesh and in colour.

I wondered if the three fighters were thinking about me that night as they sat down to their dinners and got ready for bed.

Perhaps Rocky was up playing cards. Maybe he was raiding the freezer for ice cream as Mary slept.

Joey might have been up late thinking about the ring rivals he could no longer speak to.

Or perhaps he was saying a prayer for Carmen and 50 happy years.

Jeff had made my day but at the same time had me believing I had made his.

I knew the lights would be on in the Chandler home in deepest darkest Philly. I could picture him, the former WBA bantamweight champion of the world, running around the house, throwing punches in bunches screaming to himself, 'I'm the champ, I'm the champ. I'm the king of the world, the baddest bantamweight ever. Yes, thank God, I'm the champ.'

Chapter 5

ATLANTIC City sounds glitzy and glamorous, doesn't it? Subtract the Boardwalk and casinos, however, and you are left with an enormous ghetto.

Former WBC light-heavyweight champion Matthew Saad Muhammad lived among those desolate wastelands. A friend had given him a trailer in a Mays Landing caravan park on the distant fringes of Atlantic City and he used some of his own construction skills and roofing abilities to turn it into quite a place.

But he often stayed in Atlantic City with friends as it made the 4am commute to Pleasantville easier and faster.

As a roofer for the Union he would drive his beaten-up Cadillac, with its bald tyres, a few miles before daybreak to queue for work.

Some days he got it, other days he didn't.

His name still carried some clout but at times the elements conspired and when the weather was too bad, as was often the case through the winter months, the rain poured and the opportunities of work dried up. However, boxing kept throwing up bizarre coincidences and he had been working alongside Mike Rossman, the former WBA light-heavyweight champion who reigned in the same era. Between them they must have made and frittered away somewhere between $5 million and $10 million.

Few people had heard anything about Rossman but Saad told me they were friends, even though there had been bad blood between them and their respective managers 25 years earlier.

Matthew's larger jobs included working on top of the newly-constructed casinos and he had spent months on the gazillion-dollar Borgata on the North Shore. From the rooftop he could see the older casinos fluttering brightly on the south side.

They were the same casinos he sold out as a headline fighter and the same structures he had spilled blood in, lighting them up with his own special brand of boxing miracles. When we met the city was enjoying a slight boxing resurgence thanks to Arturo Gatti, who had adopted Saad Muhammad's spot as the most exciting TV warrior in the sport.

The Boardwalk is a colourful place.

'I lost my ass in Atlantic City,' read a T-shirt in one of the tacky souvenir shops. The slogan was accompanied by a picture of a cartoon donkey. Genius.

Happy couples, families and high rollers weaved around broken gamblers. The wealthy were being pushed on rolling chairs by European students and illegal immigrants.

I ended up wheeling them for up to 20 hours a day through the summer months of 2001.

It was a tough and unrewarding job, pushing around wannabe bigwigs and being treated like a peasant for the odd $5 bill. Sometimes you would accept less just to get the business.

The poor and the homeless lived beneath the wooden boards. So while the casinos made, and kept, the money, the rest of the city seemed to miss out.

Thousands of jobs were created when the casinos arrived but those working in the deceptive goldmines held regular protests against poor working conditions, long hours and low pay.

And just back from the Boardwalk, trouble looms.

Block by block the city deteriorates.

Just one block from the Boardwalk, pawn shops offer gamblers the chance to hock treasured gold and diamond possessions while strip clubs advertise seedy 20 cent peep shows.

Budget supermarkets and clothes stores have been replaced by shops selling porn and liquor, diluting the increasingly shambolic accommodation.

Less than ten blocks back and realistically you are in the ghetto.

No stores, few cars. Not many people venture on to the streets while abandoned buildings with boarded-up doors and windows dominate the landscapes.

Children scream and play in dilapidated parks. Adults shout from the tenements.

You might catch a flashy $90,000 sports car pull up to a street corner, meet someone, stop a while and then speed off.

By the time day gives in to night pedestrians don't want to be there, even if they live there.

This is where I found an anonymous Matthew Saad Muhammad almost 20 years after he had won the world title but rewind about five decades to a hot summer's morning in 1950s Philadelphia.

A boy, just four or five years of age, played in the park with his older brother.

They were on their way to their grandmother's house, laughing and jesting as they ran.

As they played hide-and-seek, the younger boy lost pace with his swifter sibling who vanished from the little one's small horizon.

The youngster looked behind trees, under cars and sprinted aimlessly trying to find him.

Time passed quickly and the child began to weep. The already fragile boy lost his confidence and became scared. He stuttered so much he couldn't even ask anyone for help.

Night time came and the air cooled. He thought he might catch a cold and he prayed, convinced his family was looking for him. Finally, he fell asleep under the cold blanket of stars.

The next morning he darted among the rush-hour traffic on the Franklin Boulevard towards a police officer who was directing the vehicles. She questioned him but couldn't understand his muted, stuttered replies so took him to the station. He hoped it would be a matter of time before his family came to collect him.

Nobody came. Nobody was looking.

He spent the night in the station waiting in hope.

A day later, two nuns took him away to a Catholic city orphanage. They asked him his name for days but never got more than the first two letters.

'Ma...,' he would say with a stutter, unable to let them know who he was. They thought he might have been trying to say Matthew, so that's what they called him.

It was also the name of one of their favourite saints, or at least that's how the legend has it.

Because 'Matthew' found the policeman on the Franklin Boulevard, Franklin – they decided – would be his surname.

Years passed as Matthew Franklin lived in the disciplined environment of the orphanage. He thought about his family often, wondering what lengths they were going to to find him.

As the 1960s swung round he was adopted by Portuguese immigrants John and Bertha Santos. John worked in construction, while Bertha looked after the home and children. They had one biological child and nine adopted kids. Matthew was the last.

The stutter still affected his speech but the family showed him something he hadn't seen before – love.

They weren't rich, but they always found a way to feed and clothe the kids. Matthew never wanted for anything though when his teenage years arrived he had to cross gang territories to get to his new school. Numerous factions were at war throughout those troublesome years. The Ku Klux Klan had a hefty representation in the area, as did the Black Panthers and the 13th and South Street gang had a reputation for being one of the most ferocious in the city.

They regularly whupped Matthew for crossing their patch and so he started boxing, not to fight back, but to run faster – so he could get away.

Still, he had a breaking point and after months of torment and abuse he was one day confronted by the leader. The now lean and well-muscled Franklin snapped, leaving the bloodied and crumpled kingpin with his eyes closed, some teeth missing and flesh hanging loosely from his cheeks.

The gang now followed Matthew, their new leader.

So with an image to maintain, and hiding his gory secret from his stepfamily, he began to look for the vulnerable and weak. He made enemies and a long-running vendetta with a policeman, who had been following the adolescent's endeavours for a while, ended when the cop caught Franklin outside a store with a ten-inch blade.

There had been a spate of knifepoint robberies in the area and Matthew, charged with several of them (though not guilty of them all, he contended), was imprisoned for five years.

Having let down the Santos family, Matthew told himself he wanted to be something more than a lowlife gang member.

He wanted to carry on boxing.

In jail he wrapped his hands in bed sheets and pounded the cell walls. He flipped his mattress on its side and fired quick combinations into the padded surface. He spent hours fighting his own shadow, moving his feet and slipping punches from an imaginary opponent.

Sit-ups and push-ups in their hundreds narrowed his waist and filled out his shoulders, chest and arms. The boy grew into a man.

Another inmate handed him a copy of the Nation of Islam paper *Muhammad Speaks*. While Matthew thought religion might help his myopic quest on his release he also knew it would assist him fitting into a prison where a lot of young black men followed Muhammad Ali and turned to the Nation for inspiration, support and guidance. That was particularly the case if they had been arrested by a white police officer, sent down by a white judge and disciplined by white prison guards.

On his release, Matthew worked in construction and on the docks as a longshoreman. He also went to the gym. He found a bedsit in South Philly and saw the Santos family regularly.

In 1974, and after 29 amateur fights – 25 wins and four losses – he turned pro and seven years later, following umpteen of the most brutal wars in modern-day boxing, his reign as the WBC light-heavyweight champion was over.

During that time he fought in a golden era of that division, battling the best fighters around. More often than not he soaked up vile beatings only to rally late and win big.

He often borrowed against his future well-being, coming back to stop Richie Kates, Billy Douglas, Marvin Johnson, Yaqui Lopez, Jerry Martin, Murray Sutherland and Vonzell Johnson, all in captivating clashes. He was Mr Excitement. His wars became the stuff of legend, along with his incredible life story.

The pressmen said it was his drive to find out who he was that kept allowing him to come back in fights when it appeared all was lost. Others just felt his powers to absorb terrific beatings and recuperate, getting unheard of third and fourth winds, were given to him by God in exchange for the bum deal he had received in life. With fame, commercial endorsements, extravagant expenditure and a significant entourage, he continued the search for his identity.

'My parents raised me and then they erased me,' he remembered.

He offered rewards of $50,000 for information to find out who his parents were and where his brother was. He appealed for help in interviews after his fights. It was after reading about him in *Jet* magazine that an aunt called in to collect the bounty.

Matthew told me his father had left town, his mother had died and his brother was a bum. But even with his life's questions answered and his title lost he fought on. He had nothing else.

What followed was a series of comebacks as disastrous as any attempted in boxing. He won only a handful of his last 20 fights. His ability to take a punch was now a curse, meaning he could stand up to a beating for several rounds before finally crumbling. He ran out of miracles.

His phenomenal recuperative powers were shot, his punch resistance became fragile and his reflexes alarmingly poor. His speech had worsened, his health deteriorated and there was little evidence to say it was caused by anything other than his gruelling career.

He travelled the world attempting to reclaim his former glories fighting in Australia, Aruba, Portugal, the Bahamas, Spain, Serbia, the USA and Germany, winning just four of his last 14 bouts and getting stopped or knocked out four times, often at the end of horribly mismatched fights.

He retired in 1992, aged 38, with his best years more than a decade behind him. He was divorced, had a terrifying tax bill to pay and limited physical motor-skills to help him make a good life after boxing. The friends had gone. The hangers-on had left the building. He was an entourage of one.

When we first met, in June 2000, he was still smiling even though I sensed he wasn't happy.

I asked him a question as we sat on the grass at the Hall of Fame grounds in Canastota. It was one I asked him years later in very different surroundings.

Even though he had some trouble talking and walked awkwardly, he said he wouldn't have done anything differently.

Fellow retired fighters, patrolling the grounds like decommissioned battleships in Ken Norton and Marvin Hagler, slapped him on the back and said hello.

'Nope, I don't have any regrets,' he beamed.

'How do you think you will be remembered?' I asked.

'I was a warrior, man. My fights made me who I am and they will determine how I will be remembered. I never had an identity but I got one for myself. I'm Matthew Saad

Muhammad, who went to war and gave the crowds and the fans what they wanted.'

That is the way he will be remembered. But two men shared the same body. One was the legendary light-heavyweight gladiator Matthew Saad Muhammad and the other was Maxwell Antonio Loach, the little boy who was at first abandoned by the world and then by boxing. He was another soul washed up on the sport's wastelands.

It was Maxwell, he always believed, he had been trying to say to the nuns was his real name.

With my flight back to the UK from John F Kennedy airport booked for the day after my Philly exploits, Matthew was the last guy whose story I had time to listen to. I hadn't had to track him down because he was living in the same Atlantic City apartment as me.

I flew home knowing Micky Ward had wedged a door ajar for me and that Rocky, Jeff, Matthew and Joey might have helped me keep it open. Of course, nothing in the UK could match the thrills of America and I soon knew I had to go back.

The decision was made to make it my business to find those who either couldn't be found, like Rocky Castellani, or didn't realise they wanted to be found, like Jeff Chandler.

I would try to meet every ex-champion or contender in every city in America on a minuscule budget.

My own dreams of fighting were over. I'd suffered with terrible back pains for years, which meant moving my head side-to-side from the waist to avoid punches hurt more than standing still and getting nailed.

Besides, I found it intriguing to see what happened to a fighter when the ropes were no longer there to protect them from the people or the pitfalls outside.

Chapter 6

AFTER a few days back in upstate New York at the International Boxing Hall of Fame in Canastota, I hitched a ride to Philadelphia where I had booked two nights in a hostel.

The Chamounix Mansion was in the middle of Fairmont Park and my bed was in a dormitory of eight bunks. It was one of those places where you pay for the bed but bedding and a locker is a couple of bucks extra.

There was just enough time to drop my stuff off before catching a train to meet Tom Jess, who promised he would drive us somewhere interesting. Tom enjoyed looking up the old-time fighters as a hobby, eventually becoming friendly with several of them.

The boxers loved him. He would pick them up, drive them to functions where they were made to feel like champions again, and they'd even make a little side money from autographs and photos. When organisations tried to give Tom expenses, he would pass the money to the fighters. He knew Philly guys like Jeff Chandler, Bennie Briscoe, Jimmy Young, Saad Muhammad and Boogaloo.

Shortly after collecting me from the station, he began to drive us into the Pennsylvanian wilderness.

His car climbed the Pocono mountain trail and we arrived at heavyweight champion Lennox Lewis's training base. He was just a fortnight from defending his title against Canadian Kirk Johnson.

We spent a couple of hours there watching him train with Emanuel Steward. I conducted a short interview with Lucia Rijker, who had her own contest on the bill with British pioneer Jane Couch, and we also watched Hector Camacho Jnr and Steward's touted prospect Octavio Lara working out.

It was a good day and I just made it on to the last train back to Philly that night and when I finally arrived back at the hostel, at 2am, I used the pay-as-you-go Internet terminal to type the Rijker interview for *Boxing News* and retreated upstairs.

I'd be lying if I said I was looking forward to getting into bed.

Although I was tired, the thought of being in a room where seven strangers were already sleeping didn't overly appeal.

Nor did the fact that, on the train back to Philadelphia, I decided I would spend the following day trying to find some former fighters in this famous old fight city.

I had a few addresses to visit and a couple of numbers to try. I also had one more night at the 'Mansion' and then nowhere to go and fell asleep uneasily trying to think about my first move.

The snoring of nearby strangers brought me round before 6am and I hesitantly persuaded myself to draw up some kind of strategy for my first move.

Recalling the terrific buzz of the day I met Chandler, Giardello and Castellani, I tried to see whose address was closest to where I was staying and former light-heavyweight champion Harold Johnson, who held the title in 1962 after turning professional in 1947, was the man I set my sights on.

Being in the same weight class in the same era as Archie Moore and Ezzard Charles, arguably the two finest in the division's history, was not the best time to weigh 175lb.

He didn't have Moore's flamboyance or power, although he could still hit hard. Nor did he challenge for the heavyweight title as the others did, although he did fight heavier men.

Tom Jess had warned me I might not like what I found should I get to meet the former champion.

'Better hurry,' Tom had emailed. 'He's in good health but his brain is fading fast. Last time I talked to him he told me the same story four times in 15 minutes.'

No one in the wider public had heard from Harold in years and he resided in a rest home in the suburbs.

I managed to get him on the phone. While he couldn't believe I wanted to come and meet him he gradually came to terms with my request. I was on my way.

Showing my naivety, again, I decided I would walk. It was about eight miles and I left early believing it would give me plenty of time.

The weather was perfect. It was dry and sunny but not hot. I wore shorts, a T-shirt and trainers. My dictaphone was in my pocket, my camera was secured by the waistband of my shorts and I had a bank card and a few dollar bills in my socks.

When I set out, I had a tremendous feeling of freedom. There were no ties. I was in one of the biggest cities in the world, on my own, doing what I wanted when I wanted and walking to meet Harold was part of the big adventure.

There was no point going from five-star hotels in chauffeur-driven cars to meet people in the ghetto.

Not only could I not afford it but I could talk to fighters because I had been one and because I didn't have the life of a journalist with a company credit card. Expenses were the things dreams were made of. I was doing things the hard way, the way the fighters had done them, and they appreciated it.

Of course, there were times when I would have liked the weather to be dry when rain was coming down in stair rods, when I wished I could have afforded a decent meal, but it made me appreciate the better times more.

Around an hour after leaving the hostel I began to suspect I had taken more than one wrong turn.

Time was ticking and I had no idea where I was. I was so lost I became quite desperate and with each passing minute I grew more frantic, but I was careful to disguise that.

I thought I knew Philadelphia well. I had spent plenty of time there in the last three years but didn't recognise any street names or landmarks.

I wondered if I was remotely close to any of the areas where I had met Jeff Chandler because Tom told me his place was close to Harold's.

By 10.45am I had walked for miles and a taxi was speeding past. I didn't want to be late so I flagged it down.

I gave the driver the address and he knew where it was. His late grandmother had lived there. It was a warden-assisted nursing home. 'Boy, this is on the other side of town,' he said, shaking his head. He wanted me to check that Harold would be in so I called using the driver's mobile phone.

'Harold, it's Tris, the boxing writer from England. I'm coming over to see you now. What number is the building where you live?'

'You're coming over to see me? Now?' he asked. 'Wow, why do you want to see me?'

He had forgotten our earlier conversation.

I told him, once again, that I hoped to discuss his career and he said, 'Hang on, I'll just go and check the number.'

I heard a door open and close before he lifted the receiver to his mouth again but already I knew what he had done. Instead of giving me the number of the building he had given me the one for his room.

The driver followed my orders to carry on and we arrived just before 11.30am.

I entered the tower-block building and signed in at the front desk where I told the two ladies I was there to see Mr Johnson. They didn't know who he was, who he had been, and seemed curious about what the kid from England was doing there.

I ascended the building in a small, shaky lift and, once on Harold's floor, followed the number signs directing me to his room. I broke into an excited run down the long corridor as I counted down the even numbers on the right-hand side.

His door was about three-quarters of the way down. I paused for a moment, composed myself and knocked.

Within seconds, an even louder series of bangs came rattling back. I knocked again and more banging, probably kicks, jarred the bottom of the door.

'Who's that?' boomed the voice.

'It's Tris, the writer from England,' I said.

'What do you want?' he barked.

I explained.

With that, the door swung open and before me was a wrinkled version of the light-heavyweight veteran.

He gave me a long hard stare, one I might have expected from the intimidating Sonny Liston had I cropped up on his doorstep. I walked, without confidence, towards him and offered my hand.

He met it with his huge and firm paw. His grip could have crumbled bowling balls and it locked my arm. I felt like an eight-year-old boy putting his hand into his father's.

He looked like a hard, grumpy old man. His clothes were ragged and there was next to nothing in his sparse room.

He was wearing what looked like pyjama bottoms and a dirty white T-shirt, which was probably older than me.

Yet, even at 75, he possessed the attributes of a physically fit man. He had a narrow waist, a thick chest, broad shoulders and his biceps and triceps still bulged.

He had a head of untidy grey locks, unsurprisingly thinner than the groomed black hair of his prime in the 1950s and 1960s.

In his day, he was a physical specimen and now, in front of me, he was the most muscular pensioner I had met.

There was a colour picture of some relatives on one of the otherwise bland walls. His single bed cut a forlorn shape in the middle of the room, with no headboard and nothing marking the foot of the bed. It looked more like a hospital stretcher. There was no memorabilia, a television that looked as though it was from the late 1960s with a twisted antenna and a rusty bicycle leaning against one of the walls.

He claimed he cycled around Philly every morning.

I didn't believe him. Yet he must have been doing something to keep fit so I didn't rule it out.

When he fought, between 1947 and 1971, he had a physique ahead of its time.

He was ripped and it looked as though he had spent years weightlifting, and that was how our conversation got started.

I experimented with some good-natured compliments, joking that he still must use weights. Bad move.

The increasingly friendly expression quickly ruffled to a face of thunder. His eyebrows narrowed, his forehead shortened and he growled, 'I never touched any weights. People always said I used them, well I didn't.

'Weights are no good for fighters,' he insisted. 'It makes you slow and muscles you up. They might give you power but your opponent will see your punches coming. What's the point having power if you can't hit anybody? People were sure I lifted weights but I never did.' Still, the atmosphere lightened when we talked about his three sons, all of whom, he said, visited from time to time. He then pointed to some pictures of his grandchildren.

'Were you only married once?'

'Once was enough,' he smiled. 'That was the first time I was defeated. My marriage was like getting knocked down by a hard right to the chin. We got a divorce in the end.'

Harold turned pro almost 50 years before I arrived on his doorstep, when my father was just a boy.

'I didn't want to be a fighter,' he explained. 'I wanted to be a boxer. I hit you, you don't hit me. That's the best way to be.'

He took his career seriously and intently answered my questions with sincerity etched across his lined face. He couldn't even stand the smell of alcohol when he was an active fighter, so that never tempted him out of training camp as it had done many fighters.

Harold was old-school.

When he turned over Joe Louis was the world heavyweight champion and when he retired quarter of a century later, in 1971, Joe Frazier ruled the big men.

But there were signs that time, if not his 87-fight career, had taken an inevitable toll.

Incredibly, he said that beating top-ranked contender Jimmy Bivins and giving Archie Moore hell were the two worst things he did. 'They slowed my career down,' he remembered. 'I just couldn't get no fights after that. I'd have to fight bigger guys. I think I was that good nobody wanted to fight me. I had to keep fighting the same person, Archie Moore, and I kept wondering why I couldn't get fights.'

He faced Moore five times in a rivalry that defined Harold's career if not Moore's. He beat Archie, the man who holds the most stoppage wins in boxing history, on points in 1951. They shared 54 pro rounds. Moore finally managed to stop him in the 14th session of their final encounter when Archie defended his light-heavyweight world title.

'He simply had my number,' old Harold conceded. 'When I say my number I mean he beat me, but I stood there evenly with him.'

'What about Jersey Joe Walcott?' I asked, moving on.

'He beat me and my father,' Harold said, with a strange amount of pride. Both he and his dad, Phil, lost to the one-time heavyweight king. Harold boxed him in 1950 and, in the third round, he mysteriously collapsed without throwing a punch. But an examination from Dr Joseph Levey, the commission doctor, revealed he had suffered an injury to an intervertebral disc in his back.

Boxing took him to the top of the world and a long way from a hard childhood.

Harold grew up in Philadelphia during the Depression. When he started boxing, he would give his winnings to his mother and she couldn't believe it when he brought home such large sums. She assumed he had been out robbing. He was saddened by her presumptions but always tried to reassure her that he was an honest kid, pleading with her to eventually accept the money. Harold also discovered that to get bigger purses he had to fight bigger men.

'I fought a lot of heavyweights,' he said, with me pleasantly surprised by how the interview was shaping up despite Tom's warnings. 'I used to put lead in my shoes for the weigh-in to make myself heavier.

'Sometimes I was actually just a few pounds over middleweight. I used to get a stiff neck looking up at heavyweights all the time but the lead shoes made me their weight.

'I'd go to the weigh-in and the commissioner would say, "OK Mr Johnson, you can come over to the scales."'

Harold leapt from his bed and started shouting, 'Clunk, clunk, clunk,' with each step around the room, walking as though it was an effort to lift his feet.

'The commissioner would look at me suspiciously and say, "You better take those shoes off."'

'Then I'd sneeze.'

With that, Harold faked a sneeze that shook his apartment windows and made me jump from my perch at the foot of the bed.

'I would say that I didn't want to take my shoes off because I might catch a cold before the fight. "I think I'm coming down with something already,"' he would tell officials.

'I'd clunk on to the scales; the commissioner would look at me, look at the scales, look at me and look back at the scales again. He'd scratch his head and say "190lb?" And really I was just over 170lb.

'The commissioner would say, "OK, you can walk away now."'

'Clunk, clunk, clunk,' again filled the room as Harold stepped off the make-believe scales and moved around his room.

'I learned to walk up on my tip-toes so they wouldn't hear me so much,' he continued.

With that, Harold tip-toed carefully, demonstrating, on his way back to sit beside me.

Harold not only fought a lot of larger men but he sparred with them too, with Sonny Liston, Rocky Marciano, Joe Frazier and Muhammad Ali among those he worked with. He comfortably beat Ezzard Charles just three fights before Charles gave Marciano hell on his way to losing a close 15-round decision.

'A lot of the light-heavyweights today wouldn't fight heavyweights – weren't you worried about their strength?' I asked.

'I knew a lot of them could punch hard and would have hurt me if they could have. But, thank God, me being as fast as I was and moving as good as I could, I didn't get hurt that much.'

And even though he had skills, it did not stop him from fending off the clutches of pre-fight fear.

'Of course I got nervous before a fight because going into the ring is like walking in a cemetery at night time,' he reasoned.

Harold fought in a time when the sport was plagued with corruption and boxing's mobsters were known to lurk around Philly bars, restaurants and gyms. He denied knowing Frankie Carbo or Blinky Palermo, then the dons of boxing, when surely he would have had some dealings with them. Stories still do the rounds that he was asked to throw a fight against Julio Mederos but Johnson always maintained his poor performance was the result of him consuming a 'poisoned orange' before the contest.

The controversy saw boxing banned in Pennsylvania for 90 days, later extended to 114, as speculation over whether Johnson had taken a dive ran wild. He was suspended for six months, though it was later determined that he had been drugged when a trace of barbiturate was found in his urinalysis.

'One time I had a guy come up to me and he said, "You know Harold, you could lose this fight tonight and make very good money."

'I didn't understand what he was talking about. I said, "What do you mean? I'm going to try to win."'

'He said, "But you could lose."'

'I said, "Noooo way!" In a roundabout way he was telling me to throw the fight. I was scared. Back then there were some bad guys hanging around boxing. Someone wanted me to throw a fight with Archie Moore but they didn't have to. He beat me fair and square.'

Harold chuckled at that one.

'So when you finally won the title against Doug Jones, how did you feel?'

'I was like a kid who got what he wanted for Christmas,' he enthusiastically answered. 'People would ask, "How does it feel Mr Johnson, now you're champion?" And I was speechless. I was so excited I could hardly reply.'

We managed to keep talking for around 30 minutes without any repetition but then Harold told me the same story about putting weights in his shoes.

Again, he was up and walking around the room doing his 'Clunk, clunk, clunk' routine, and sneezing thunderously again.

It came again about ten minutes later, and five minutes after that. He didn't lose his enthusiasm for it, though, even though it was wearing slightly thin for me.

It got to the stage that whenever I could pre-empt the story, I would turn my tape recorder off and back on once I had managed to ask him another question.

Then he would talk about Ezzard Charles beating him and his father once more, or about how no one would fight him.

A friend had asked me to get Harold to sign a piece of 10x8 photo paper so he could scan a picture over it. I asked Harold to make his mark, adding he was under no obligation to do so. He said he would try but wasn't sure he could do it very well. I instantly regretted asking him as he struggled with the pen and scrawled across the slick paper.

With time moving swiftly and the interview becoming increasingly repetitious I asked if he would pose for some photos. A little reluctant at first, he soon warmed to the task.

'Like this?' he asked, standing with his hands clasped in front of his belly.

'How does this look?' he said, changing position.

'Is this the type of thing?' he went on, as he held his hands up in a traditional boxing pose.

'Yes, Harold. Yes, that's great.'

'One more like that?' I asked.

'How about a jab,' he offered, prodding out his once meticulous left.

'Good,' I said, encouragingly. 'And follow it through with a right hand.'

He was getting into it, smiling, and then he suddenly stopped and looked at me.

'You came all the way from England to see me?'

'Yes, Harold, you were a great champion. Of course.'

'Thank you,' he said. 'I'm sorry I might not be how you wanted me to be. I hope you haven't been disappointed,' he said softly, as we sat back on the bed.

'Don't say that, Harold. I'm privileged to meet you.'

'But look at me,' he said.

'Harold, you're brilliant. I can't believe you're in such good shape.'

'Really?' he said, looking up hopefully.

'Are you sure you have to go?' he asked, as I gathered my things.

'Yes, I must.'

He thanked me again and crushed my hand once more.

I promised we would stay in touch and he watched me walk back down the long, dark corridor towards the lift. I turned and waved, then heard the door close.

The difference between Johnson in his prime and now was staggering. It's one of those things. When you see famous people you remember how they were last time you saw them. Well, the last time I had seen Harold the ring technician, his muscles rippled and he moved lucidly around his opponents.

So much had changed.

I didn't really feel like doing another interview. I felt drained and certainly melancholy. However, it was approaching lunchtime and I couldn't afford to stand still. I was in Philadelphia where dozens of old champions and contenders lived. I asked at the desk for directions to Broad Street, so I could get my bearings and make my way to Joe Frazier's Gym.

I looked back at the building, wondering if Harold was by his window looking down on me.

I wiped away a tear, put my head down and walked briskly away.

Chapter 7

THE sun was beaming. My legs were filled with a wobbly optimism and speedily carried me to Frazier's Gym. Everyone in boxing knew Joe's gym was on North Broad Street and I presumed I would recognise a few of the surroundings from earlier visits in the preceding years.

I remembered it was underneath a nearby bridge and also recalled some of the fronts of surrounding buildings and their colours. Thanks to directions from a scattering of passers-by, and seeing the bridge that rang memory bells, I wound up there within an hour or so.

Although I was excited I couldn't get poor Harold out of my mind. Clearly somebody had to be looking out for him. He just didn't really let on who. I wondered if he even knew.

But I thought he had been doing OK since long before he met me and convinced myself there was no reason why he shouldn't carry on that way once I left.

When I walked into Frazier's this time there was no sign of the main man, who I had seen when I visited with Saad Muhammad a couple of years before. Instead, I saw a physically bigger man. One I instantly recognised and who greeted me warmly.

It was Marvis, Joe's son, a heavyweight contender in the 1980s. Jackpot.

I had always loved his story. He might not have been out of the public eye as long as some of the fighters I wanted to meet but while I was in the area we had to chat.

The gym was just as I remembered. There were proud posters of Joe's career on each of the walls. This after all, was Joe Frazier's Gym.

However, I was surprised at how little I could see of Marvis's decent pro career and spell as a top US amateur.

The majority of pictures, many still in excellent condition, reflected the grudge between Frazier Snr and arch-rival Muhammad Ali. More often than not, the images showed Joe whacking Muhammad.

Marvis was a good, nifty boxer as an amateur but turned to slugging as a pro. It would be to his detriment. He had good wins over James 'Bonecrusher' Smith, Jose Ribalta, James Tillis, James Broad and Joe Bugner, and a close victory over exposed contender Funso Banjo in London, yet he was defined by two things – his pair of professional losses and his father.

Twice he fought against modern legends and both times he was blown away, by Larry Holmes in 1983 and Mike Tyson three years later.

The Holmes fight came too early. Larry, near his prime, was 44–0 and Marvis had had just ten pro fights.

When I walked in, Marvis had just finished working with some youngsters. One was former flyweight amateur standout Michael Brittingham, who, Marvis promised, was one to watch.

Frazier Jnr wore an open-neck shirt with red and white horizontal stripes. He had a patch of grey at the front of his otherwise black hair and beads of sweat rolled down his face.

There was contentment in his eyes. He agreed to an interview there and then, showing me into the back of the gym where his office was.

He said he would be with me shortly after saying goodbye to his fighters and that gave me the opportunity to call another heavyweight contender.

I'd been given a number for Jimmy Young, the 1970s heavyweight title challenger, and he picked up the phone after just one ring. I asked if we could meet in a couple of hours.

'Where are you?' he replied.

'I'm at Joe Frazier's Gym.'

'That's in North Philly,' he exclaimed, as though that made things rather tiresome for him. 'I'm down in South Philly, working, but I can make some time if you have to do it today.'

'I will be out of town tomorrow,' I answered, and he gave me an address where we could meet, a cross-section of two streets I was unfamiliar with.

I told him I would be there without fail and soon after Marvis returned.

He was no longer a puncher but a preacher. Sure, he trained fighters in the gym but his new mission was to spread the gospel. He also reassured me that I was in the right place to find old fighters.

'I believe Philadelphia is the capital of boxing and I believe Joe Frazier's Gym to be the White House,' he started. 'The home,' he listed, 'of Jimmy Young, Bennie Briscoe, "Gypsy" Joe [Harris], Willie "The Worm" Monroe, Tyrone Everett, Tyrone Crawley, James Schuler, "Choo Choo" Charlie Johnson.'

It was not long, however, until Marvis began talking about his real passion. He travelled the length and breadth of America trying to tell boys and girls, men and women, about the love and life of Christ and how he can change your life and transform you, if you allow him to. God, he said, had the same persuasion powers as a .357 Magnum – a strange analogy – before considering the streets outside where Marvis most regularly preached.

'I've been running with the Lord since age 16,' he smiled deeply, hypnotised by his memories. 'I was chasing this very beautiful lady and the Lord was chasing me and I found myself in church, married, with two daughters.'

'How is your wife?' I asked.

'As a matter of fact,' Marvis said, the smile hollowing, 'a year and six months ago I lost my wife. But the Lord giveth and he taketh away and he has a divine plan for all of our lives.'

His plan did not include following in his father's championship footsteps even though he was reasonably successful. As an amateur he scored 56 wins against just two losses, beating a number of top hopefuls including Tim Witherspoon, David Bey, Tony Tubbs, Mitch Green and Bonecrusher Smith. He was a classic boxer, not like his slugger father, and many in the game thought that was down to his trainer, the acclaimed Philadelphia craftsman George Benton, former foe of my old friend Joey Giardello.

He had his fighters work with scalpels rather than sledgehammers. But, when Joe's boy turned pro, Joe got in on the act, became head trainer and consciously or not inspired a change in Marvis's style.

Young Marvis became more aggressive but he was missing three key ingredients. He didn't have his dad's devastating left hook, power or punch resistance.

It was a recipe for disaster.

'Why did you change trainers?' I asked.

'George was a great boxer and he believed that boxing was hitting and not getting hit – and that is the game,' he stated. 'As long as you are in there and not getting hit, that is how you play it. So he was teaching me moving, blocking and slipping.

'After I turned professional my father felt I needed more time with him. George had become a prominent trainer so a whole lot of other athletes were beckoning for his time so my dad thought, "Maybe I need to spend more time with my son and work with him."'

'What did you make of the change?' I pushed.

'Well, to me, my father had been there so I didn't have a problem with switching. George was still there at the time until he decided to leave on his own. I always heard two heads were better than one and to have a guy who was a world champion and another who was a world contender was a good match for me.

'I did miss George but you have to do what you have to do as a fighter. Everything George taught me, I never lost it. All the fights I won in the amateurs George taught me for but for the majority of them, when it was time to fight, George wasn't there. It was either another coach, an Olympic coach, or somebody else from his stable.'

It seemed George jumped from the Frazier ship, that he had not been pushed as had been suggested over the years.

'Everyone says, when they talk about the Frazier family, "Joe pushed Marvis into that. I don't know why he pushed him into that…,"' Marvis went on.

'A lot of people thought I was a light-heavyweight. "Man, he should have stayed light-heavyweight," they said. But so many people don't know the history. They go by hearsay, what somebody else said and it was never that way. If you look at my track record of guys that I fought, even as an amateur, 'Bonecrusher' became world champion, Tony Tubbs became a world champion, so did Tim Witherspoon. I beat some great guys and it was God's will for me to be there but not to be world champion.'

'Did you believe that, with your dad training you, you could win the world title?'

'I *did* believe I was going to be heavyweight champion of the world. I *knew* I was going to be heavyweight champion of the world.

'One of the reasons I got into boxing was when my father lost to Muhammad Ali in 1975, in the Thrilla in Manila, I thought it was my quest to bring the championship back to him and back to the Frazier family. But God had different plans. He said, "No, it's not your job to bring the heavyweight boxing championship of the world back to them. It's to bring the heavyweight gospel and Jesus Christ to everyone." So that's what I believe I'm the champion of. I believe I'm the champion of the gospel.'

'But when you fought Larry Holmes after just ten fights, did you think it was too soon?'

'Maybe I should have waited for the fight with Larry but the money was there,' he reflected. 'I had already torn a retina and my father knew about that and I had a neck injury but he told me it was my opportunity and I really did believe that I could beat Larry.'

'The Holmes fight,' I interjected. 'What do you remember about it?'

Marvis's face lit up as if he had just been given $1 million for nothing. It was seemingly the question he was waiting for.

Excitedly, he began telling the story of the night Frazier fought Holmes.

'I trained to fight Larry for seven whole weeks, getting up at four o'clock every morning and running two and a half or three miles. I was working with guys like Tim Witherspoon, Tony Tubbs and I was having my way with them in the gym and when the fight came I wore the same robe and trunks my father wore when he first fought Ali. The green and gold sequinned attire, even down to my socks and shoes, because I thought it was God's will. Then came the night of the fight.'

Marvis was growing more animated with each sentence. He leaned over his desk, his enthusiasm drawing me to the edge of my seat.

'Mills Lane was the referee,' he went on. 'He came in to the locker room and gave me my instructions. Then he went and gave Larry his instructions and about 25 or 30 minutes later, after I had worked up a good sweat, a guy came in and said, "All right, it's time to go to battle."

'Prior to going out the door, we got round in a small circle and my father led the prayer and he said, "Son, is there anything you would like to say?"

'I said, "No sir, I'm ready to go."

'We started walking out the door and you could hear the crowd, "Crrrsh". I got in the ring and they got up and went, "Crrrsh", and Larry Holmes came down the aisle and they went, "Crrrsh", and the announcer grabbed the mic and said, "Good evening ladies and gentlemen and welcome to Las Vegas, Nevada, the boxing capital of the world. Arrrrre yooooou ready?" And the crowd went, "Crrrsh".

'"This first young man I'm about to introduce to you hails all the way from the City of Brotherly Love, weighing in at an even 200 pounds with ten wins, eight by way of knockout, here he is, in the red corner, the challenger, Marvis Frazier."

'And the crowd went, "Crrrsh".

'"And in the blue corner, weighing in at 219 and a half pounds, with a professional record of 44 wins, 27 by way of knockout, here is the undisputed heavyweight champion of the world, the Easton Assassin, Larry Holmes."

'The crowd went, "Crrrsh".

'We both went in to centre ring and Mills Lane said, "You heard your instructions in the dressing room, touch those gloves, let's have a good, clean fight."

'I looked Larry in the eye and he looked me in the eye and I said, "You're mine."

'I turned back to my corner and my father said, "You know what to do, son?"

'I said, "Yes, sir. I know what to do."

'The bell rings to start the fight for the heavyweight championship of the world and I believe God is willing Marvis Frazier to win and bring the championship back to the Frazier family.

'I come out swinging and feel about four or five of Larry's jabs and about a minute and five seconds into the first round I drop my hands, start showboating and, "Bam", Larry caught me with a straight right hand.'

Marvis went down.

We were back in 1984.

'I caught the attention of Mills Lane at the count of two and when he said "two", I rolled over and got on one knee and when he said "eight", I stood up and he said, "Are you all right to continue?"

77

'I said, "Yes, sir. I'm all right to continue."

'He said again, "Are you all right to continue?" I said, "Yes, sir. I'm all right to continue."

'"All right. Let's get it on."

'And when Larry came back he hit me with 13, 14 unanswered punches. I forgot what punches he hit me with.'

Marvis chuckled softly – his delivery was becoming less intense while he recalled the incoming punishment, as if he was throwing the towel in on what happened after having such high hopes.

It was a short, hard beating.

Joe watched on as his son spent painful moments of the round pinned on the ropes while Larry's laser-like punches kept coming.

To make matters even more emotional for Frazier Snr, Holmes showboated, cocking his right arm at the elbow and rotating his fist.

After spending too long hitting Marvis at will, even Holmes pleaded with the official to intervene.

Downbeat, Marvis continued, 'Mills Lane stepped between us and said, "Son, I apologise, but I have to stop the fight."'

There were three seconds remaining in the first round.

'And when he said that, I dropped my head, tears started running down my cheeks and you know what, that moment in my life I felt like a maggot, or a worm. I felt I had embarrassed my whole family in front of the entire world.

'And I wasn't concerned about what the media had to say and I wasn't concerned about what my friends or my fans thought.

'I wasn't even really concerned about what my wife or my kids or what my mother said. The only thing I was concerned about was what did my father have to say? Joe Frazier. Because I thought I had messed up. I thought there was no way in the world that Joe Frazier could forgive Marvis Frazier for embarrassing him and the Frazier family in front of the world.

'Now I was standing in the middle of the ring with tears streaming down my cheeks and I can see my father coming through the ropes and walking towards me.'

Marvis pretended to well up.

"Paps, I didn't do it. I failed. I feel so bad. Please forgive me"

'And my dad had a big smile on his face as he opened his arms up as wide as the world. Man, and he grabbed me and he hugged me and said, "Don't worry about it. Your daddy loves you. You're my son and I don't care if you got knocked down. I don't care if they call you a bum. You're my son and I love you."'

Marvis went quiet for a few seconds and looked down at the table.

'Just like I tell the inmates that are behind bars, every time you get knocked down, every time the world tells you you're not going to amount to anything and that you're not going to be anything, I'm here to tell you that Jesus Christ is here right now. He's got a big smile on his face, he's got his arms open wide and he's got the door open saying, "Come on in".

'God didn't want me to be the heavyweight champion of the world,' Marvis said, shaking his head.

'He wanted me to be the heavyweight champion of the gospel.'

Religion, family and boxing went hand in hand for Marvis.

His sister, Jacqui, had lost to Laila Ali, Muhammad's daughter, a year or so earlier. Marvis reckoned Jacqui deserved the decision.

But Marvis didn't want his two teenage daughters, Tamyra and Tiara, to fight. He said they weren't interested in it, anyway.

You couldn't really blame them if they had seen footage of their father's shocking knockout loss to the man-child Tyson.

Frazier was on the wrong end of a cruelly swift 30-second destruction.

Everyone at the time was talking about how Joe would have done against Tyson and that might have spurred Marvis to try and slug with 'Iron' Mike as his dad would have.

In the run-up to the fight, more people were saying Tyson was like Frazier Snr than Marvis was.

When Tyson pinned him in a corner, just 20 seconds after the opening bell, he nailed Marvis with a vicious uppercut.

Frazier Jnr wilted like a quickly dying rose. He collapsed on to his knees with his backside on his feet.

But Tyson remained a hurricane at full force, lashing out at stricken Marvis repeatedly as he groaned on the canvas until the referee could come between them.

'I think Mike needs salvation,' Marvis offered. 'Mike needs a whole lot of love and he needs to listen. Nobody's perfect but we have to be willing to listen and he who humbles himself should be exalted and he who exalts himself, God says he will look after you.

'I disagree with Charles Barkley when he said, "I'm not your role model." Well, yes, you are, because athletes to our children are the heroes. And God had given Mike the ability to be exciting.

'I learned a couple of things from fighting Mike Tyson. Number one was, whatever you do, never underestimate an opponent. Number two was whatever you do don't get caught with an uppercut. You've got to move your head, man.

'He was God's great warrior. He had tremendous speed and power and it's the shot you don't see that hurts you. I know he caught me with an uppercut but I don't know how he caught me with it. If I knew he was gonna throw it I would have got out the way.'

Marvis was prepared to laugh at himself now. His competitive career had long since passed; his fighting spirit had been eroded by time.

'Boxing is a great sport and I have no regrets at all in boxing,' he shrugged. 'If I had to do it again I would do it all the same way. It's a warrior's game and not everyone can be a warrior. It takes a special breed. If there's a challenge you have to be there to meet it.'

We took some photos in his office, and then outside with Brittingham, on the same spot I had my picture taken with his father a couple of years earlier during the visit with Saad.

The day was getting longer and I had more walking to do to keep my appointment with Jimmy Young. I hadn't eaten but my stomach was not yet whining for food.

I was on a roll.

All I had to do was track down Jimmy.

We arranged to meet where Broad Street and Columbia Avenue crossed, and although I didn't know where it was, I had given myself a 3.30pm deadline to meet him.

Broad Street, I was to learn, had to be one of the longest roads in the USA. It wasn't just Broad Street, but there was South Broad Street and North Broad Street on their respective sides of the city. Marvis had no idea where the meeting point was, either.

So I aimed myself in the direction of the central skyscrapers, walked briskly through the centre of the city and out the other side. I broke into a jog at times and despite some anxious moments made it to the cross-section on time.

The only remaining problem was that the roads were large and interlocked. There were four corners to meet people on and none of them were particularly close to the other. People were milling around on each corner.

I knew what Jimmy looked like in 1976, when he lost a controversial decision to Muhammad Ali, and I knew what he looked like when he forced big George Foreman into retirement in 1977 after beating him on points. I had also seen pictures of the somewhat different version of Jimmy who slumped to defeats against Tony Tubbs, Tony Tucker and Eddie Richardson in the early- and mid-1980s.

But they were 20 years ago and I hadn't seen or heard anything of him since. I didn't know what to look for.

A lot of ex-heavyweights allow themselves to become overweight in retirement. There were whispers Jimmy had a drug problem and stories circulated that he was living rough and could not hold down a regular job. Still, with a dollop of good luck our eyes met fleetingly from diagonally across the busy junction.

We half held our hands up and nodded shyly towards each other. I ran to him, weaving through traffic.

'Are you the kid from England?' he asked, stretching out his hand to shake mine, warmly holding my shoulder with his left hand.

His palms were like plates but far from fragile. They were clammy, yet I couldn't squeeze my hand out because the grip was so tight.

His hair was grey and he was slender for a former heavyweight, almost wiry. I doubted he was a heavyweight anymore. His sunken face looked drawn, tired and weary.

He wore a white short-sleeved shirt with blue checks. It was undone almost to his sternum, revealing a few chest hairs and some body odour having completed several hours of manual work. The sweat dripped from his forehead yet there was no shifting his smile and as we walked he tried to make sense of how 'the English guy' had cropped up out of nowhere to meet him.

He stopped after we had stepped only several yards, asking me if I was hungry. I said I was, but only after he had made it clear he hadn't eaten.

My last meal was noon the previous day and more than 24 hours had since elapsed. I was too excited to be hungry, really.

Still, I sensed his desperation to find food and we dived into a cheap KFC wannabe chicken place, the closest available dining venue. I picked up the $7-or-so bill and we took our seats, waiting for the grub. I wouldn't exactly call it food.

Despite the air-conditioning, Jimmy was still sweating profusely and said he had been doing 'bits and pieces' of construction work.

Not since the T-Rex devoured the raptors in *Jurassic Park* had meat disappeared from once fleshy legs so quickly. Jimmy sucked the skin off the bones and guzzled a 32-ounce bright pink fruit punch soda as if he was about to dehydrate on the spot. Within three or four minutes he had inhaled his fries, was wiping his mouth with the back of his hand and hoovering up the few remnants off his fingers.

It looked like a starving man had just been fed.

He made jokes, made fun of himself and was devastatingly frank. He began by approaching each subject with humour, even when discussing the issues that came close to destroying his life. And although I'd heard how his over-extended boxing career had damaged his health, I saw no clear-cut signs of it. I had read reports that Jimmy could hardly talk and that what he did say was badly slurred.

Jess had paraphrased Mark Twain when he had said that 'Rumours of Jimmy's demise have been greatly exaggerated.'

Well past his prime, Young lost nine of his last 13 bouts between 1982 and 1988. He had absorbed punishment from some of the heaviest hitters in his star-studded era, including Earnie Shavers, Ken Norton, Ron Lyle, Gerry Cooney and Foreman.

Among 19 losses there were just three by stoppage and he came close to avenging the early Shavers defeat in Philly with a draw in Maryland 18 months later.

Young's voice was a little gravelly but adequately audible.

Like Jeff Chandler, his vowels were a bit drawn, gently slurred at worst, but not once did I think I wouldn't be able to listen back to it on tape.

When Jimmy became overexcited some of his words bumped into one another but I put that down to his enthusiasm to engage, not because of taking too many head shots.

And what astonished me most was his outstanding recollection of intricate details about his career.

He could remember dates of his fights and even what day of the week they happened on. The same went for landmark events in his life. He rarely had to hesitate, turning the interview into a pop quiz.

His professional record was in my hands and he would give me a date he fought someone and information about what happened and where it took place. Then he'd implore me to check whether he'd got it right.

He started boxing in June 1963, he recalled. I was a little taken aback that he named the month but that was just for starters. He said he forgot the exact date, which didn't come as a shock, although I wondered who in their right mind would remember such an inconsequential item? He first went to the gym because he had heard about a young Philly amateur named Joe Frazier.

'Joe was 19 years old and a heavyweight,' Young smiled. 'I was 14 going on 15 because my birthday was in the November.

'I liked Joe and I really wanted him to win the Olympic gold medal in 1964.'

Jimmy commenced training at Frazier's Gym, they sparred, the bond was forged and, after a short amateur career, Jimmy joined Frazier as one of the top heavyweights in a golden era for the division.

Jimmy repeatedly glanced at the cheap KFC imitation counter. I wasn't sure if he was hoping for another meal deal or not.

'So who was your best performance against?' I enquired, clumsily tackling some chicken thighs.

'Ken Norton,' he shot back, keenly. 'We fought 15 rounds in Las Vegas, November 7, 1977 and I looked good,' he smiled, emphasising the 'goooood' by drawing it out.

'They robbed me of the fight and gave it to him so he could fight Muhammad Ali again. That's Don King bullshit.'

Jimmy's mood descended and he hung his head.

'When did you get involved with King?'

'December 1975, the first fight I ever had for Don King was February 7, 1976. I fought ten rounds [against] Joe King Roman in Puerto Rico. Muhammad Ali fought the main attraction.

'Two months later, in April 1976, I fought Ali over 15 rounds for the title.'

'That's good,' I said, trying to keep up with his record. Those sharp, accurate recollections made me find it hard to believe I had heard such pessimistic reports about his health, speech pattern and memory.

'You like that?' he said with a gaping smile, proud of his unique talent.

He had boxed Ali in a couple of exhibitions, making $200 for the privilege, before they finally met in a controversial bout. It is best remembered for Ali getting a favourable decision. Some ringsiders felt The Greatest had been outboxed in a dull fight that left no one, aside from Jimmy and his family, wanting a rematch.

What baffled onlookers most was that Young would often stoop low, through the ropes to avoid Ali's punches. No one had seen it done before, but Jimmy explained it was to avoid Ali's 'dirty' tactics.

'He would hold me at the back of my head and I would duck down to keep the pressure off,' he explained.

Jimmy's loyal wife Barbara, to whom he was still married after tying the knot in 1967, said at the time, 'This is just a setback. Jimmy will win the title one day. You watch.'

He never had another chance.

'You won most of your early fights on points,' I said, urging him to take me back further into his vault.

'I'm not a knockout artist,' he countered, still in the present tense.

'And then you ran into Earnie Shavers and he was a knockout artist.'

'Oh man, Earnie Shavers. I fought him on February 19, 1973 at the Philadelphia Spectrum way down in South Philly and I hadn't fought in a year. The fight I had before that was when I lost to a white boy from New Jersey, Randy Neumann.

'Diana Ross and the Supremes were there that night. They sang the national anthem because one of the girls was related to Ernie Terrell and he was fighting the main attraction.

'Earnie Shavers whooped my ass so bad that after the fight Diana Ross and the band came to see me in the dressing room to make sure I was OK.

'But you know what? When I signed up with Don King I fought Earnie a year later, in November '74, and I beat him down, man. They gave him a draw. Does it say it was a draw there?'

He checked with me as I looked at his record.

'Yes, Jimmy.'

'It was ten rounds. He knocked me down in the third and the crowd went, "Oohh" but I got up and fought seven more rounds.'

CHAPTER 7

'Ron Lyle could hit, too,' I added.

'When I fought him I was just getting into the top ten. I was No.10 in the WBA ratings and No.9 in the WBC. When they offered me a fight with him he was ranked No.3 in the world and only had one loss on his record. The only one who could beat him was Jerry Quarry, remember him? He went undefeated for a long time.

'So I travelled from Philadelphia to Honolulu in Hawaii and I liked that, man. I liked them girls and the way they looked, and for $4,000 I shut him out good.

'I won at least eight rounds. One of the other rounds was maybe a draw and the other maybe they could have given to him as a split.

'Then, later on that year, in December 1975 – we fought in February 1975 – in December I signed with Don King and then, in February 1976...'

He saw me scampering through my notes trying to keep up.

'It's all there,' he smiled, laughing as he shook his head at me doubting him. 'Look at November 1976. And then later 1976,' he carried on, 'I fought Lyle again and it was 12 rounds of the same thing, textbook. We fought 12 rounds and I looked good. Boy, I was hitting him with everything.'

Jimmy thumped his fist into his palm repeatedly. His eyes glazed a little with the memory. He was temporarily lost in the moment of outboxing his feared adversary.

'I shut him out, 12 rounds. I remember, see. I remember,' he said, as I looked up from his record, conceding he was right again.

With that, Jimmy revisited the bones in front of him and went to work on them once more. I gave him some time to finish and we talked about his fights in the UK.

'Billy Aird, I fought him in England at the World Sporting Club in 1973. I forget the month. You might want to see,' he said, in what appeared to be light-hearted mockery with a hint of contempt for me double-checking his answers. I told him that I wouldn't really need the month specifically but he insisted I scoured my sheets.

'We fought to a draw. But there was another guy, Richard Dunn. He weighed 218lb and I weighed 203lb and every American they took over there to fight him he had knocked out. I went over there and stopped him in the eighth.'

Not only was Jimmy now reeling off dates, but he was even giving me the weights.

'How do you remember all these things?'

With that he shrugged his shoulders, screwed up his face and giggled like a toddler who had been given a toy.

'I don't know,' he smiled, embarrassed by the compliment.

'Eat that chicken,' he said, pointing to the last piece on my plate.

'Eat it,' he urged.

'No, I can't,' I said, full on my small meal.

'You have it,' I insisted.

Within seconds it was gone.

'So of all these great fighters you faced,' I said, trying to get back on topic, 'who was the best?'

'I think I would have to say Muhammad Ali because he had a lot of tricks with him, but he can fight dirty when he wants to.

'I'm the kind of guy who thought whoever I got in the ring with I swear I could beat anybody.

'You won't believe this but you will like it. The toughest fight I think I ever had was with a guy back then in, I think, 1972 when I had finished four-round fights.

'Floyd Patterson and Oscar Bonavena fought the main event and I only got $200 or something and I fought a Puerto Rican boy named Jasper Evans. Look at it there, when was it?'

I referred to the stats. My papers were muddled from trying to match his frenetic pace.

'1972,' I replied.

'All right,' he smiled gleefully, pleased he had got another question of the impromptu quiz correct.

'Man, that was a hard fight. Especially because I only got $200!' he added, as though a larger purse would have made it easier. 'He was on my ass like white on rice.'

Despite being thrown in with the superstars and lethal bangers of his day, his career earnings didn't amount to much.

It explained why life after boxing hadn't been quite so smooth.

Jimmy stared longingly at the food counter again, then switched his attention back to me, asking what I was doing in Philadelphia and what I was like as a fighter. He wanted to see me box and even stood up with his plate-like palms open asking me to show off some combinations. I threw a jab at his left hand, a right at his right and as he curved his left hand inwards, finished with a left hook.

He asked if he could take a look at me in a gym and said we could either go to Augie's Gym, where his son Jason was learning the ropes, or Frazier's. I politely declined.

But with my rejection he seemed to become despondent. I had hurt his feelings. He wouldn't look at me. He gave me one-word answers to questions that previously would have evoked lengthy responses. I tried to recover but was sinking quickly. I scrambled, trying to get our conversation back on track.

I asked if he had any regrets about his career.

'I don't know. What's done is done.'

He wasn't in the mood.

'You still hungry?' he asked.

'No Jimmy, are you?'

'Not if you're not hungry. I'm OK.'

'If you want anything else let me know because I will get it for you.'

'Do you want something then?' he tried again.

'No Jimmy, I'm OK thanks.'

'Yeah, no, I'm OK,' he said, refusing to eat on his own.

I pursued the regrets angle. Surely, seeing him now, he would have had some. Perhaps he had wished he had done something differently or retired sooner.

'In the fight game you expect to get hurt sometimes. I didn't get hurt and I enjoyed it,' he said, tailing off at the end as though he hadn't really. 'I enjoyed it,' he added again, almost inaudibly.

A lot of his sadness seemed to come from being mistreated. Like many fighters, people had taken advantage of him, stripping him bare and leaving the shell that sat before me.

He brooded when Don King's name came up. 'We went with him because he could get you a chance to get ahead,' Jimmy explained, looking ashamed.

'What did he do to sign you? Did he bring you a briefcase of money?'

A famed King ploy, the promoter would show fighters wedges of cash and a shiny new car totalling far less than a cheque for a million dollars.

They tended to accept the poorer offer, dazzled by instant riches.

'No, I had to fight for everything,' Jimmy said, exhibiting defiance and pride.

'Did you enjoy being in his company?'

'Yes, because I wanted to get ahead and start making some money.'

'Did you ever hang out with him?'

'No.'

'What about the Ali fight, what did you make for that?'

'Ali made a million and a half dollars. I only made 75,000. My manager took half of that. That left me with 37,000 and half of that I gave to the taxman. It hurt man.

'I made $250,000 in Puerto Rico fighting George Foreman. Out of that $250,000 I took home $62,000. Six-two,' he exclaimed.

'Where did the rest of it go?'

'Managers and taxes.'

'But did you make much money in your career, you fought until 1988?'

'No, I fought until 1990. My last fight was in Biloxi, Mississippi. I turned professional in June 1969 and I fought professional until 1990. I was 42 then.'

'But it says here you fought until 1988,' I said, offering him the paper with his record on.

'Well it's wrong,' he snapped, declining to even look at it.

It didn't tally with his official record. Perhaps they were exhibition fights, maybe even tough-man contests. Although the record stated his last fight was on 13 August 1988, against Frank Lux in Saint Joseph, Mississippi, I questioned its accuracy not only because Jimmy had but because that would mean he went out on a win.

He was actually victorious, stopping journeyman Lux in the tenth. Jimmy didn't seem the type who could quit while he was ahead. Life had not been that kind.

'Do you know who my easiest fight was?' he suddenly volunteered.

I was about to hazard a guess before he went straight in to answer his own question.

'George Foreman.'

He saw disbelief on my face.

'George Foreman,' he repeated so loudly that many people in the restaurant who overheard looked up expecting to see the former heavyweight icon. 'He was the easiest one. I knew I was going to beat Foreman. I knew it.'

'Yeah?' I said, imploring him to go on, encouraged by his mood swinging back to a more positive vibe.

'George was real big, he was a real big guy and you could see his punches coming so you had time to get inside and get out of the way.'

'He retired after that fight,' I said, pushing for more.

'He retired because I beat his behind but I wasn't surprised I won.'

It said it all about his life, really, that his easiest fight was against one of the most ferocious heavyweights to lace up gloves.

If facing Foreman was easy what did that say about the rest of his career? And what did it say about his battles after boxing?

Arguably his last good performance came in 1981, seven – or nine – years before he retired, depending on whether you take Jimmy at his word or opt to go for the official record books version.

The *Philadelphia Inquirer* reported of his fight against prospect Marvin Stinson, 'There were still faint traces of magic in Jimmy Young's gloves. And last night at The Sands Hotel and Casino they traced a trail of memories across Marvin Stinson's face… It was Jimmy's remember me performance.'

But his ensuing decline was alarming. His involvement with drugs was the catalyst for a descent that took him lower and lower. As the 1980s came and slowly dragged on Jimmy was running out of money, running out of friends and losing the respect he had earned. He was defeated by up-and-comers, journeymen and guys he should have beaten had he still been at the top of his game and clean.

He had become a 'name', an opponent who is selected because his name looks good on a young fighter's record.

Jimmy could still teach them a few tricks, too, and provide them with rounds and a valuable ring education, but he wasn't the force he had been when he was off the drugs.

'What do you remember of your fights with Ossie Ocasio?'

A future cruiserweight champion, Ocasio beat Young in successive fights. When they first fought, in June 1978, Jimmy was passing his prime. Ocasio was undefeated after 11 bouts while Jimmy's heart had been broken by Norton seven months earlier in the same venue, Caesars Palace in Vegas. Jimmy lost a close, split decision. The rematch, in January 1979, saw a narrow but unanimous win for Ocasio in Puerto Rico, where Ossie was from.

'I lost them both. I remember that the first fight was 25 years ago Monday.'

Naturally, I was stunned he could put things into such a timed perspective.

'It was June 9, 1978, and the first time I went into a fight with that stuff [drugs] in my body. I didn't know what it would do. I didn't know,' he sighed.

'I was over my fighting weight. My fighting weight is 213lb and I was like 220lb. I was seven pounds overweight and I didn't know what the drugs would do. I didn't know. We fought six months later, on January 27 or 28 1979 and I lost again. I knew when I felt right and when I felt wrong and it was the wrong thing to do.'

'When was the first time you tried cocaine?'

'February 15, 1978, it was on a Friday night in Las Vegas, Nevada, at the Hilton Hotel and I was watching Muhammad Ali lose his title to Leon Spinks. People had been talking about cocaine but I had never seen that stuff before,' he protested innocently. 'I knew a little bit about weed but I didn't know about this stuff and when the friend brought it to me all I saw was white powder and it was $100 or something. They would talk about highs this and highs that but after a while I kept fooling around with it.'

'Did you get addicted?'

'Addicted,' he shouted, raising his voice so a few people looked up again. 'Oh yes I did. I was spending like $1,200, $1,300 a week on that stuff. A week. I would stay up like six days at a time. I got addicted bad. Real bad.'

'When was the last time you did a line?'

'It had to be about four months ago. I was at this party in Jersey in February and someone said "try this". I did it for the hell of it. But afterwards I said to myself, "No, it's not what I want." It was a chapter in my life.'

'How did it affect you in your later fights, like against Greg Page?'

'When I fought him in May 1982 what happened was I had lost a decision but I didn't take the fight seriously. That's not an excuse. I don't make excuses. It's just the way it was. Luckily I was smart enough to keep guys from hurting me.'

'What about Tony Tucker and Tony Tubbs?'

Both future heavyweight title holders beat him over ten rounds but neither could stop him.

'Those guys, I lost to both of them. Back then I was in my addiction… I was in my addiction…'

A gloomy depression resurfaced.

'They won the fights,' he said, quietly. 'I lost on points.'

'If you had been straight could you have beaten them?'

'I think so. I lost five fights in a row. Five fights in a row,' he said, astonished, almost unable to believe it had happened. Then I came back and started winning again and I didn't get knocked out, I didn't get knocked down. I didn't lose no blood, I just got outscored.'

He then switched subjects and again directed me to his record in my hand.

'Look. Look at May 1980. I fought Gerry Cooney and I've still got the scars right there.'

He pointed proudly above his right eye.

'It was the third round when they stopped it.'

'My sheet says it was the fourth on a cut.'

'Maybe it was,' he said, scratching his head in doubt for the first time.

'Do you miss it, boxing?'

'I kind of miss the training side. I think I would make a good trainer.'

And with that he turned his attention back to me. 'How big are you? Are you cruiserweight or heavyweight?'

'Cruiser,' I humoured him.

He probed further still, again asking me to train with him using the dated line that 'white fighters can make big money'.

I reverted to talking about him, even though it was now apparently boring him somewhat.

'Are you religious?' I asked.

'Kind of,' he muttered. 'I'm thinking of getting into it. I think it will be a good thing for me. I think it's the best thing for me.'

He didn't have many options left. I thought Marvis, his old friend's son, might be able to help him.

'Jimmy, before we go can I take a couple of pictures?'

'Sure. You don't want to do them in here, do you?' he said, looking around the increasingly busy chicken house.

'No, let's go outside.'

The afternoon sun was beating a hasty retreat and a yellow glow fell on Jimmy's friendly face.

'How about here in front of this computer?' he offered, as he walked in front of an ATM. He started to pose.

I snapped two pictures and thanked him.

He pulled me close and as we shook hands I could smell his sour body odour escaping from under his arms again.

He said loudly, 'I hope I see you again, Tris.'

'I hope to see you too, Jimmy. I will be back in Philadelphia and I'll look you up.'

It had been quite a day. There had been a cocktail of depression and joy at talking with Harold, the contagious preaching of Marvis and the priceless opportunity of spending rare time with Jimmy Young. I don't claim to be a particularly religious man but when I got back to the hostel I prayed for both Harold and Jimmy.

I felt Jimmy needed every prayer he could get.

With Harold, however, there was something almost instantly telling me to call him and make sure he was OK. It played on my mind throughout the next morning and it got worse as time went on.

In the early afternoon, after the time when most people have lunch but I was going hungry, I called.

The old champion picked up, which was a good start.

'Hi Harold, it's Tris, the boxing writer from England?'

'Who?' he responded.

I didn't want to say I met him yesterday and imply he had forgotten who I was. I didn't want to make him feel bad.

I quickly said I was a fan just calling to say what a wonderful career he had and how much he was admired by people, myself included, for all he accomplished. He thanked me and the call was soon over.

I wasn't sure if I should have been pleased or not. At least he hadn't been thinking about me as much as I had been worrying about him.

But he had changed me, matured me in two hours. It is both a humbling and shocking thing to see legends no longer living in unreachable realms. They were all human; too human for my liking.

They all had once bounced off the colourful pages of magazines and books in my childhood like superheroes. They were strong, muscular and powerful. Now they were simply like great old uncles or grandfathers. Yet after every sorrowful encounter with a faded champion I felt more worldly-wise.

I felt myself hardening with each encounter.

They were helping me grow and mature. I was on the proverbial writer's journey. Harold would never know what a difference he had made to me. Neither would Jimmy.

Chapter 8

AFTER two heartbreaking and failed world title bids, Atlantic City's Leavander Johnson was back in the No.1 spot to challenge for the IBF lightweight title.

Having trained in the Atlantic City Police Athletic League Gym throughout the previous summer I knew where he was at 4pm every day so finding him wouldn't be difficult.

The hour-or-so bus journey from Philly, however, was an eye-opener. I had spent so much time in New Jersey I felt I had done it all before. I was going somewhere I knew to see people I was familiar with and it felt so very safe. Really, it felt as though I was on the road to nowhere. The adventure was not there.

This wasn't what the trip was about. It was about tracking down people that couldn't be found. It was about exploring America and going that extra several hundred miles for rare interviews.

Before I even disembarked the New Jersey transit bus I told myself I would stay in Atlantic City just two nights and that, while I was there, I had to find someone new to interview before leaving or else I had failed.

Importantly I had a place to stay, back in the tenements of New York Avenue, but I knew there were so many other great stories out there and they wouldn't come to me.

Bill Johnson, Leavander's dad, welcomed me back into the gym with his charismatic smile and always firm handshake.

I asked if he was expecting Leavander.

'He's having a rare day off,' he said.

'He deserves it,' I smiled. 'He's a hard worker.'

'Yes he is,' beamed Mr Johnson, who had spent time working with me on the pads during previous visits.

'I was hoping to interview him for a British magazine.'

'He's at home if you want to go there,' Bill offered.

'No, he can get some rest. I know he's got a lot on.'

'He would be happy to see you,' Bill insisted.

I declined.

We shook hands as he took a seat in the gym office by the front door. I savoured the atmosphere in the third-floor gym. At times, it looked more like a prison yard than a boxing gym with all kinds of people pouring in from the ghetto to improve themselves, getting bigger, stronger or harder.

Shamone Alvarez, then a novice pro welterweight but seasoned amateur southpaw, had shown me a thing or two in the PAL ring before and came over to catch up.

He had since turned pro, was 4–0 with three stoppages, two in round one, and doing well.

Within minutes, Bill came bounding over and said, 'Leavander will be here in a minute.'

Almost instantaneously his son strolled through the doors.

'He's here,' Bill announced, proudly.

We shook hands and embraced as people stopped and stared. He was like royalty in the PAL, a hero to people who grew up just like him, poor in Atlantic City. He was an example that if they worked hard they could use boxing to become somebody.

Since I had last seen him he had won the USBA title, beating the capable Julian Wheeler. He'd also drawn with the always dangerous Emmanuel Augustus and comfortably outpointed Jesus Zatarin.

The fight with Wheeler was an eliminator for the IBF world crown, so Leavander was on the verge of getting what would be his third title shot.

Leavander, his dad and I sat on a couple of wooden gym benches that were more often used for being stepped on and off by fighters rather than for interviews. Nonetheless, we spent the best part of an hour chatting.

Leavander had always been quiet and didn't talk smack. The one thing he emphasised, over and over, as he had told me many times previously, was that he wasn't going to rest until he had won a world title.

In fact, he was already talking about the championship as though it was his, discussing it with such a passion that it bordered upon an obsession. He always referred to the elusive crown as 'my title' and everyone in Atlantic City knew him as the 'uncrowned champion'.

As we spoke, I heard a booming voice behind me.

'It's about time this guy was interviewed,' Matthew Saad Muhammad said, pointing at Leavander and taking a seat next to me. 'He's a helluva fighter. A helluva fighter who doesn't get the respect he's due.'

By now a crowd had gathered and they were nodding in agreement.

Leavander said he would know by the end of the month when he was going to get his chance at Paul Spadafora's IBF lightweight crown.

There was talk of Spadafora going up in weight. I'd heard stories from around the gyms that he was pissing blood in his attempts to make the weight, and that was the case after his hard draw with Leonard Dorin.

Leavander didn't care if he fought the awkward southpaw or not.

'As long as he's got the title all I want is that world title fight and to be that world champion. I don't mind who I've got to fight.'

One of Leavander's former ring victims, Sharmba Mitchell, was on the cusp of fighting welterweight champion Kostya Tszyu for the Australia-based Russian's world crown.

'That makes me work a little harder because I know I done beat the best out there and I know I can beat a world champion,' he said of Mitchell, who reigned for a while as the IBF champion. 'So I know I can be one. It makes me work a little harder when I have the opportunity to showcase my talents.'

He challenged rising star Floyd Mayweather and said he would consider a showdown with another Atlantic City favourite, Arturo Gatti, at light-welterweight.

Leavander had won 32 fights, drawn three and lost two. Both defeats were in attempts at 'his' world title and each time he was a long way from his beloved home on the New Jersey shore.

The first title try was in 1994 against WBC champion Miguel Angel Gonzalez, the tasty Mexican who had 33 straight wins on his record.

Leavander went to Mexico to fight him in a bullring, only to be stopped in the eighth round of an intense battle.

'I don't think they should have stopped it because I was beating him up,' he said. 'If that was the case they should have stopped the fight when I had him hurt so many times during the whole fight. That one little hit he got off was nothing and they stopped the fight like that when they knew I was going to knock him out.'

Two years later, following another four victories, he was pitched in deep against Orzubek Nazarov, a tough battler from Kyrgyzstan who was unbeaten in 23 and had defended his WBA belt five times.

Johnson was halted in the early stages of round seven and said it was his toughest fight especially, Bill added, if you consider it came on the back of a 12-month lay-off while Team Johnson tried to settle legal differences with his former promoter. Bill said it was the only fight he had seen Leavander lose legitimately.

'It was so early in my career I was just knocking boys out,' Leavander said of his short, sharp title shock. 'Going through the ranks I was treating everybody the same way and I didn't respect him. I went out of my game plan.'

Leavander's televised draw with Augustus, then fighting as Emmanuel Burton, had renewed his confidence.

In previous bouts, Augustus had narrowly lost a Fight of the Year contest with Micky Ward and had given Floyd Mayweather one of his most difficult nights.

'I don't care about what anyone's done before they fight me,' he said. 'Once I get in that ring that's my territory, they're stepping into my ring.'

It was the sort of response I was accustomed to hearing from Leavander. He oozed modest self-confidence.

Saad then took over as the interviewer.

'Who in your weight class, if you're true to yourself, do you think would give you problems?'

'If I'm true to myself, the stuff I'm seeing out there, I could adapt to so quickly that a fight could go either way but if anybody gets touched,' he said, cocking his right fist and staring longingly at it, 'they could go.'

Saad went on, 'So what you're saying is you'll be victorious whatever?'

'No doubt. I feel that way. In the lightweight division I haven't really seen nobody with spectacular overwhelming skill and the talent that I've got.'

Leavander had been fighting a long time and looked up to artful warriors like Wilfred Benitez, Aaron Pryor and Roberto Duran as a youngster.

'Benitez was my man,' he enthused.

As an eight-year-old, Leavander's older brothers and father encouraged him in the gym and he was a good amateur, racking up a record that included around a century of victories with just 'six or seven' defeats.

'He had an excellent amateur career,' Saad interrupted. 'He was coming up as I was going down.'

'So was your decision to turn pro financial?' I asked Leavander.

'Uh huh.'

'How are you doing?'

'I'm coming along good,' he smiled.

'But you're 34 now. You've had more than 35 pro fights and a long amateur career. How much longer do you see yourself fighting for?'

'I ain't trying to fight too long, I just think I deserve recognition that I haven't got yet. I deserve to be a champion. That's what it's all about.'

'They love him here, they love him,' Saad cut in again.

'I've been in the game a long time but I haven't been beaten up.'

'His time is now,' Bill stepped in, boldly professing his son's future.

'My time is now,' Leavander repeated.

'Right now,' Saad chipped in.

Bill looked at his boy. 'You haven't been worn out and beaten down and abused. You haven't been in those sort of fights.'

He fixed his stare at me.

'A lot of his fights have been round two, round four, round five and out. He had a 17-fight winning streak going into a San Antonio bout against Bobby Brewer, a tough guy. Leavander hit him with rocks and he came back to his corner shaking his head and I told him, "Leavander, you're not going to knock everybody out. Some of these guys you're going to have to wear them down, beat them up, take their will, make them quit."'

'Right,' Saad nodded.

'He stopped him in the tenth round,' Bill smiled. 'But he made him quit. He beat him down until he said, "I don't want no more."'

I thanked Bill and Leavander for their time while Saad got up to leave with me.

The Johnsons posed with Matthew for a picture. They wore enormous smiles. Matthew was shouting "This is the next champ" and hugging Leavander. Proud Bill couldn't stop grinning.

'Anything you would like to add?' I asked Leavander as we shook hands. He thought about it and shook his head. 'No, I'll save it for next time.'

Chapter 9

IMAGINE being a world champion, fighting George Foreman, being involved in the last truly great 15-round fight against Evander Holyfield and then being lost to society having left so many memories. Dwight Qawi's name was in the history books and it was gathering dust but there were whispers that the former light-heavyweight and cruiserweight world champion was working in a centre nearby, helping drug addicts and alcoholics overcome problems.

The place where he worked was called the Lighthouse and when I called they said they couldn't give out Dwight's details.

Instead, they took my information and said he'd call me back. I believed they would give him the message, I doubted he would ring. The only way to reach him would be to go out there.

I hadn't slept well in Philly, though, having packed five interviews into three days and walked many miles.

The tread on my nearly new trainers was already starting to show signs of wear and tear.

An early night was in order and I would renew my attempts to find the 'Camden Buzzsaw' the next day.

I was staying back in my friend's apartment with Saad Muhammad, ironically the man Qawi had defeated for the title more than two decades earlier. Matthew had heard his great rival was around but that he was no longer on the boxing scene.

Qawi served time in Rahway Prison for armed robbery before carving out an excellent if overly-long pro career. When he got out, he was a stocky, 5ft 7in powder keg of determination, power, venom and mistrust. And he was ready to blow.

He retired way too late and way too heavy in the 1990s, when he was also an alcoholic. In between he battled legends from light-heavyweight to heavy in his long, violent career.

GRANTON K   3/5

ROUTING SLIP 14/04/22 09:34

Item 9027856702
Road to nowhere: a journey through
boxin
g's wast

Reservation for G005464021
Mr Karl Granton

At DRI/Driffield Centre

  East Riding
Web Reservation

As I put the world to rights with Matthew, I thought, I should at least try the phonebook to find Qawi.

Switching on a rusty table lamp, I scoured the pages, first checking under Braxton, Dwight's name before he changed it. It wasn't there but when I searched the Qawis there was just one, and his first names were Dwight Muhammad. There it was, proudly on its own with his full address and phone number.

He was living nearby at Somers Point, a short bus ride away. Saad couldn't believe it and I scribbled the details down.

It was too late to call but I would phone the ex-convict in the morning and see if I could visit.

That night, Saad took the sofa and slept on the single spare bed in the same room in deepest, darkest Atlantic City.

It was around 9am, long after Saad had left to work on the roofs, when I eagerly called, certain I had got my man. The phone was answered within two rings.

'Is that Mr Qawi?' I asked.

'Who's calling?' came the gruff, guarded and moody reply.

I knew it was him.

I gave him the rundown.

'What time shall I come over?' I asked.

'No, hang on a minute,' he interjected. 'Where are you?'

'I'm in Atlantic City, staying with a friend.'

'Where in Atlantic City? What is the address?' he asked.

I gave it to him and he said he was familiar with the area and even the tower block we were in.

'I'll drop by on my way to work but it will only be for around an hour,' he signed off, as the phone clicked.

I would like to have seen his house and how he was living, but if this was his preference, and from his abrupt tone it clearly was, so be it. And he was coming to meet me in a place where his former ring rival Saad, who he beat in this very city – less than a mile from where we were staying – had crashed out many a night.

Dwight actually arrived a few minutes early. I was waiting on the porch in anticipation. He waved at me from his middle-sized, mid-range car window as he pulled up on the other side of the street before running over.

I couldn't believe how big he was.

A friend who saw him shortly after said he was 'as big as a house', and he wasn't far off. That was the first thing I noticed.

Although Qawi was only 5ft 7in tall, he was almost as wide. The second impression was how small he was. It seemed like 5ft 7in flattered him. His shiny bald dome could do serious damage and he had a steely glint in his eye, a fighter's stare.

He asked where I would like to talk and declined the seats to the front of the building, overlooked by some of the ghetto tenements. Instead he said we should go to the room I had been calling home. In the compact lift, a bit cramped with the two of us in it, we made small talk and he asked what I wanted to discuss with him.

'Just about everything, from childhood until now,' I said.

'We aren't going to do my life story, I'm not going to do a book today,' he fired back, laying down some ground rules. 'I've only got about 45 minutes so we have to make it quick, but we can talk boxing.'

'OK, whatever you like,' I smiled passively.

We walked into the room and the logical place to sit was the unappetising sofa.

It was tough to comprehend how life works in such mysterious ways.

The night before Saad was sleeping on the same couch that his once bitter rival, the man who took his hard-earned crown, was now perched gleefully upon, reflecting on how he sent Saad stumbling into the boxing wilderness after taking his WBC title. It felt like I was seeing Qawi behind Matthew's back; like I was cheating on him while he was out at work. There was a nagging feeling of guilt.

Though I found the extraordinary coincidence quite startling Qawi, strictly business, didn't seem fazed. Perhaps after a traumatic life and career of ups and downs, what was another minor insignificance?

He didn't look 50 and there was no sign of any physical damage from his brutal wars with Saad, Holyfield and countless others without focusing on the stick he had taken from up-and-comers and alcohol as he slid down the pecking order and into obscurity and obesity.

I told him about my efforts to track him to the Lighthouse.

'I work with kids and help them overcome drugs and alcohol now because I conquered it,' he began.

'I went to the Lighthouse rehabilitation centre in New Jersey and worked for them. The one thing I love is recovery and helping people. I do something I really have a passion for. I don't fix anybody and I don't claim to. But I am helping them and I think I have a knack for it. I'm a mentor to those kids and I'm loving it. It's rewarding and gratifying.'

No longer was he playing the bad guy, a role he almost automatically assumed when he whipped fan-favourite Saad.

He now wanted to be an example to his sons, Thomas and Dwight Jnr, having been dealt a poor hand to start life with.

'I got in trouble when I was younger and I did some time,' he continued. 'As a matter of fact, I did five and a half years for armed robbery and while I was in there I changed my mind and made a decision right then. I was 19 when I got into serious trouble and knew I was going to have to change my ways.

'I had an ABC plan. I had just come out of prison and being in there, it changed my heart and my mind and I said I would not come back. I took advantage of what little opportunity I had in there. I went to school in there, got my GD [General Diploma]. That was plan A. I learned a trade and that was plan B. Plan C was boxing.

'By the time I was released in March 1978 I was in a social programme, you know, where you help people, and I was waiting on a job. While I was waiting for what I wanted to pursue to come up an old friend of mine, Ike Hammonds, came along. I had done a little street fighting at the time and he jumped out the car all excited and he said "Man, what you doin'? What you doin'?"

'I told him what I was doing and he said, "You got to get in the ring, man. You can fight."

'He brought me sneakers and shorts and took me to Joe Frazier's Gym and told everybody, bragging, "This guy can fight."'

Sparring with veterans like Willie Monroe, Boogaloo Watts and Bennie Briscoe proved to be the only education he needed.

He didn't box as an amateur but relished the challenge of facing the top local fighters daily, saying he frequently had his way with future light-heavyweight champ Marvin Johnson in the gym.

'They put me in the ring with those guys and I did good,' he said, puffing out his barrel chest. 'They were seasoned professionals and I had no amateur career, no nothing. Philly was where I started.

'I used to get up at 4am or 5am and catch the train from Camden, go to work, do a day, go to Joe Frazier's Gym, catch the train and be home by ten o'clock and do it again the next day.'

Following a mixed bag of results, including a draw on his debut, a victory on points and a loss in his first three fights, he considered jacking it in.

'I had a pro fight in a month after getting out, in April, and I beat the guy but they gave the guy a hometown decision and called it a draw. His name was Leonard Langley and I came back to knock him out in a later fight [in two rounds in 1980 in Atlantic City].

'Then I fought on the Sugar Ray Leonard–Rafael Rodriguez card at the Baltimore Civic Center in June and I beat the guy, Lou Benson Jnr. He was 11–1.

'Then I fought Johnny Davis, he was a four-time Golden Gloves champion in New York and they robbed me, really.'

A glance at *The Ring*'s report of the fight says as much.

'Braxton bullied and pummelled Davis in the corners all night only to lose a split decision in six,' it read.

'So I was 1–1–1 and coming back on the train after my third fight. It had been a tough fight. Davis kept running and I kept coming after him. I had made a little bit of money and I said to myself, "Man, I don't know if I want to do this or not."

'I had fought my heart out and I said to my trainer, "Can you teach me better defence? There's got to be a better way of getting at these guys when they're running."

'He said, "Sure, are you willing to learn?"

'I said, "I am." And I went to school.'

He passed many tests over the next four years, winning all 18 fights.

'My trainer taught me to cross and block, to keep moving my head and I did a lot of floorwork. We got the right opponents and I moved up and I learned. I learned my skills well and knew boxing wasn't all about blood and guts. You need determination and a killer instinct but it's a sweet science. For every action there's an opposite, an equal reaction. There's a counter for everything.'

Dwight's eighth contest was in South Africa, during apartheid, against Angelo Dundee-trained Theunis Kok and Qawi struggled until a hard right kept Kok down for several minutes.

'It was a step up and I needed exposure,' he explained of why he travelled during a controversial time. 'He was a southpaw, 6ft 3in and tough. I had trained well but it was a dog fight. I've got it at home on tape. I come out in the tenth round and I was beating him up but it was one of those fights that I can't tell you nothing about, it was that intense. I couldn't tell you nothing about no rounds except the last one and I hit him with a right hand and he went down. I wasn't going all the way out there and coming back empty-handed. It was determination like that that won it for me.'

It was a hard-earned $2,000 and victory announced him as a major player.

'I came back and Angelo Dundee was saying to people, "Dwight's had more fights than he's saying. He's going under pseudonyms. Who is he really?"'

The next stage of his development was sparring Michael Spinks for an ESPN tournament. Hard training, Dwight believed, fast-tracked his career.

'Before you knew it, I was on TV. They had heard about me from Philadelphia and they were using me for getting Michael into shape just before I fought Rick Jester. I knocked Jester out in the third round in the ESPN tournament. Spinks was training to fight David Conteh and we were in Baton Rouge going eight five-minute rounds a day. Do you hear me? We were going at it, it was even better than the fight we had.

'But it was like that. I was dedicated, working hard and knew I had to learn with each fight. By the time I fought Mike Rossman here in Atlantic City I had learned my trade well.'

He stepped up in class when he accepted a fight with the 'Jewish Bomber', pitting his 16-fight record against experienced operator with more than 50 of his own.

'To be honest, though,' Dwight remembered, 'I didn't think he could beat me. I was confident I could just look at a guy and stop him. I knew he would be catching punches because he boxed straight up. I knew he could dance and he could move but he didn't have real good lateral movement.'

Dwight steamrollered Rossman, stopping him in seven, but in his next fight there was a man just as fearsome and ferocious staring back.

James Scott was serving time in Rahway Prison on suspicion of murder after what cops believed was a bungled armed robbery.

HBO had begun to televise Scott's fights while he was behind bars as the State built its case against him.

Qawi, already acquainted with many in the crowd in the prison gym that day, sneered back at Scott as if to say, 'I'm out now, and I'm not coming back.'

Qawi cackled disdainfully when asked about an atmosphere that had caused other fighters to freeze. If anyone could meet Scott on an equal footing it was the former inmate.

'I'd been in there several years earlier,' he went on. 'They'd moved a lot of prisoners out and there were just a few people in the audience who were right there.

'So, you know, I was familiar with it. It wasn't hostile or nothing. I can punch and he took a helluva punch. He was in great shape and even in the tenth he was trying to come back at me.'

Because of a shoulder injury, Dwight boxed predominantly with his left, putting pressure on with the jab and winning a unanimous decision, 5–4 and 6–3 on the cards.

'Qawi always seemed ready to slug it out, bearing his gumshield and a wide grin as he came forward,' *Boxing News* said. The writer believed Scott allowed himself to be bullied.

He was later convicted of crimes around the robbery and never fought again. As far as Dwight knew, Scott was still in Rahway. After ten hard rounds together their situations couldn't have been more different.

Qawi was in line for a world title shot in front of scantily-clad girls in the Playboy Casino whereas Scott was condemned to a minimum of 30 years of dodging men in the showers and avoiding gang attacks.

Poor James.

Although Qawi's past contained moments of ferocity the man before me spoke gently. He recalled sparring as many as 30 rounds per day in long training sessions to fight Saad Muhammad, the man with an inexhaustible engine and unheard-of recuperative powers.

'In training I told myself, "This guy keeps coming back," Qawi said. 'I told myself, "If he can't get knocked out then I've got to beat him for 15 rounds so I'm going to train to fight 30 rounds."

'They put me in the gym, turned the heat all the way up, put two sweat suits on me and then set all the sparring partners on me.

'I felt like a demon. I knew I could go 30 rounds, that I had it in me.'

He took everything out of Saad and viciously battered him in ten rounds to take my friend's title in 1981.

'When I faced Saad, I knew he was made for me,' Dwight said. 'I knew it. I knew what was going to happen in the fight.'

I pictured Matthew next to him on the sofa, sat where he would be watching TV with me later.

It was a shame they couldn't come face-to-face again.

'I don't know if he took me lightly but he took some shots, that's for sure. He was tough.

'I can punch and let me tell you he took a hell of a shot and even in that tenth round he was trying to come back. He was in great shape. He was a champion, he fought regularly and I don't know how he was mentally but physically he was all there.'

As Matthew had done, Dwight changed his name after winning the title, proclaiming his Muslim faith.

He felt obligated to give Matthew a rematch because of the opportunity Saad had afforded him earlier in the year.

'I'm going to knock the "a" out of him so he will be Sad Muhammad,' Qawi bragged, rather unkindly if prophetically at the time. Unfortunately for Saad's legion of loyal thrill-seekers, Dwight extricated any resistance 'Miracle' Matthew had left. It was beaten from him in the sixth as Qawi retained.

'The second fight was a blowout,' Dwight said, playing it down. 'I was right at the top of my game.'

There was speculation Saad would meet WBA champion Michael Spinks in a unification megafight but Dwight crashed that party and, in turn, captured the lucrative Spinks assignment.

Against former sparmate Spinks, Qawi remembered a close fight in which 'Some people thought I won, I thought I won, but he ran and looked good.'

Spinks, who took the decision by narrow scores of 144–141 (twice) and 144–140 in March, 1983, nabbed Qawi's WBC light-heavyweight title while ending his two-year title reign and 22-fight unbeaten streak.

Dwight wanted an immediate rematch.

'They wanted to make it a ten-rounder and I said no. I was angry with the way everything went. HBO told him "don't take another fight", and he fought Eddie Davis and HBO said "that's it" and they dropped me [by] $500,000.

'They were going to pay me $750,000 but they came back with 250,000 so they basically just told me to kiss their behind. I was pissed off anyway because my father had been killed and all of that came up on me and it was too much. I was going through a divorce at the time, things just happened all at once. I had pressures. I had weight problems and there were other things, too. I was supposed to fight Eddie Mustafa Muhammad and that fell through and I was put on the shelf a lot.

'So then, right around that time, the cruiserweight division came out and I started campaigning there and I went and I won the title and I thought Spinks would fight me again. But by that time he was after the heavyweight title and there was no more me and Spinks because Larry Holmes was asking me or him to fight.'

Dwight returned to South Africa, won again, and became a two-weight world champ by stopping Piet Crous in 11 for the WBA cruiser belt in July 1985 at the Superbowl in Sun City.

He made his first defence against Michael Spinks's brother, Leon, who was famous for his toothless smile, his 1976 Olympic gold medal, beating Muhammad Ali in just his eighth pro fight, losing the rematch and being Michael's brother.

'Did you want to fight Leon because you had lost to Michael?' I wondered.

'Yeah, I wanted to get him to fight me but Michael dogged himself. I figured that if I whipped his brother good then he might fight me again.'

One of the two things Dwight hoped would happen happened. He did whip Leon but couldn't tempt Michael into another fight.

'I beat Leon good but Mike didn't care about his brother, watching his brother taking a beating like that, you know what I mean?'

And by then there was another Olympic star coming through the ranks, one from the class of 1984.

Many said a fighter as young and green as Evander Holyfield shouldn't have been in the ring with Qawi when they clashed in 1986.

Evander was 11–0 while Qawi had been involved in 30 pro fights and had been world class for five years.

It was a crossroads contest, similar to when Qawi had fought the vastly more experienced Rossman. Holyfield gave Dwight everything he could handle and more, winning a tight and thrilling cruiserweight championship fight, often heralded as the last great 15-round bout.

'I was big for cruiserweight, I was muscled,' Dwight insisted. 'People said, "He ate himself out of light-heavyweight," but it was genes or something and I got big and at that weight I did the best in my career. I didn't kill myself at the weight and I could have moved to heavyweight.

'But the Holyfield thing was tough. It shouldn't have went to Atlanta and it went to Atlanta [Evander's hometown].'

'They gave me six weeks' training, gave me a few dollars, but they had it in for me. All he had to do was stand up at the end.

'The thing that bothered me about that was I watched him against Terry Mimms six weeks before and he couldn't even go six rounds [he hadn't needed to, he stopped Mimms, who had a 12–11 record, in the fifth].

'With me he went not just 15 rounds but 15 rounds in one of the most gruelling fights ever. The punches that we threw, the pressure that was there… He fell down in the dressing room after that fight and was in hospital for two days. He was so damn aggressive.

'I remember my trainer Wesley Mouzon, we watched that fight recently, and he said, "Everyone gets a second wind but in the ninth round you don't come back and get a second wind and look better than you did in the first."

'You don't do that. Not with the kind of pressure I had on him. He kept bouncing, bouncing, bouncing…

'He had too much energy.'

Implying foul play, something Holyfield has always stringently denied, Qawi was getting angry talking about his younger nemesis.

'The reporter, Alex Wallau, called me a few weeks after the fight and said he thought that after watching it again I won because I made the fight.'

The split decision victory for Holyfield wasn't good enough for the fans who demanded a rematch and a year later it was set.

I tried to change tack, sensing his irritation at Holyfield.

'Who was the biggest puncher you faced?'

'I don't know,' he said, almost snubbing the question. 'The second fight with Holyfield,' he went on, reverting to what I figured to be his least favourite subject, 'I wasn't even in it. I found out his manager, Lou Duva, gave Holyfield $1 million. They gave me 75,000 and when I took the fight I thought, "I'm going to knock him out."

'In the third round, boom, I stopped him right in his tracks but then he came back, caught me and there were two flash knockdowns and I remember I wasn't there that night. I waved it off and I didn't care. I said, "If you're only going to give me $75,000 then I'm not going to be here all night."

'They treated me like a piece of meat, like they all did, and that was my way of saying, "Here's one back at you. Stick it."

'I gave the fans my all but I waved that one off. I was down but I wasn't out. I knew I wasn't out. There was a count but I knew it wasn't me in there. I didn't go down when I was in shape. But he was stronger than the last time, not that it worried me, even though he was getting more bulky.'

Dwight was secretly fighting depression at the time, too.

He had problems with his son's mother – 'a lot on my mind', he recalled.

Whenever he won, he would down a few beers to celebrate and when he lost he would have harder stuff to console himself. Regardless, there was always drink.

It became an addiction. His biggest fight had begun.

He piled on the pounds and was soon swapping punches with heavyweights. He was getting ready to fight the big-hitting Bert Cooper for $25,000 when a real opportunity to get back on track came his way.

His manager offered him the chance to fight George Foreman. Qawi admitted that he did not even know that Big George was still boxing, but in exchange for taking the match in two and a half weeks, he would be paid $50,000.

'I had a week and a half at camp and a few days in Vegas to promote the fight. He came into the ring weighing 250lb and I had never fought anybody that big. He looked like a giant.

'I looked at his legs and thought, "How the hell am I going to fight this guy?"'

But he reckoned he had Foreman struggling in the first round only to feel himself getting tired in the opening three minutes.

'His arms were bigger than my legs. My legs were getting tired and, if I'm being honest, I wasn't really into it.'

By then Dwight was almost 50lb above the light-heavyweight limit but was still a stone shy of Big George, who, of course, towered over him.

Afterwards, Dwight managed to lose around 40lb and fought at cruiserweight again but he still battled depression.

Alcohol and cocaine were tough opponents.

'Then I decided I wanted another run at the title but I got in with the wrong people, bad people.'

He shook his head and looked down.

'I went to France, fought Robert Daniels and I beat him. Anyone who knows anything knows I beat him,' he said, gritting his teeth and firmly emphasising 'beat'.

'I hit him, his mouthpiece came out and they stopped the fight and after that they took his mouthpiece and brushed it off, gave him some time and then he ran like a thief. I couldn't catch him and they gave it to him. That was a big rob job.'

The crowd booed the verdict.

'But then again, at the time I was drinking and I was doing other things,' he said softly, as he dipped his head and put his chin on his chest.

He had done things he wasn't proud of.

'By the time I got back on track a lot of stuff had happened and my weight was mounting again.

'I even used cocaine during that period. I wasn't training, I was cutting people off and I was really badly messed up in my head. I got to the point where I was just real depressed. I had a big ego but no self-esteem and I didn't know what recovery was.'

This no longer seemed like an interview. I was counselling the counsellor. I didn't feel like a 20-something amateur fighter who was so wet behind the ears Qawi could probably have seen the water dripping when he looked at me through his damp eyes.

After falling back into his deep and dark world of drink and drugs he eventually decided he needed treatment.

'Right after that I came back and as soon as I did I went to a place called the Lighthouse, where I'm working now. I came out and around 1990 I fought "The Bounty Hunter", Mike Hunter. I lost. That stuff affects your body. It was starting to take an effect on me. It takes hold of you. I didn't care, I was cocky. I wasn't focused and it took a big edge off me. I think I would have knocked him out if it hadn't been for that.

'Then I picked up again but this time I went to Florida. I tried to make a comeback at heavyweight and I was beating guys and that's when I was having big problems with my weight, when I was about 240lb, 250lb. I hit a wall. One of my old trainers said, "If you keep training hard one day your body is not going to respond," and that happened in the Nate Miller fight. I went to do things and it just wasn't clicking. I just couldn't do it. I was just standing there. People knew he couldn't carry my gym bag and that's why I retired. I could feel it.'

Dwight was 39. He boxed Miller in Philadelphia, back in the city of some of his finest triumphs, and was widely outscored on all three cards after ten rounds.

And like them all, almost, he came back.

Five years after calling it quits, he optimistically thought he could have another run.

It was 1997 and he was 44. He boasted an addictive personality and was hooked on boxing as well as booze. He cut a forlorn, sad figure of a short, podgy heavyweight. His hair had receded and he looked little like the brutal warrior who traded dazzling bombs with the very best. He weighed so much that he couldn't run in training because it made his ankles sore.

'I always wondered how I would do as a heavyweight,' he explained. 'I was older now and I thought I should have done it way back. I should have won the light-heavyweight title, the cruiserweight title and then the heavyweight title, but there were a lot of missed opportunities and a lot of years passed. I was winning but then they took me to Chicago and they robbed me against Tony LaRosa and when that happened and they gave him the decision, normally I know that I'd knock a guy like that out, but I let him run and get away. He was a young 'un and I said to myself, "I'm not going to come back and be a name for nobody. This stuff is not going to happen to me. They're not going to rob and steal from me." So I walked away and said "That's it." I was 45 years old. It's not like I was a young man and I could try again.

'As far as the sport goes it's over now. I'm 50 years old, back then I was 45, it was my last fight so I want to get into the International Boxing Hall of Fame and move on. I walked away, got sober, sorted my head out and I'm in good shape today.'

I looked at him, waiting for him to perhaps make a joke about his rotund physique, but I did so in earnest. I knew what he meant.

Qawi, so different to the moody street guy that buzzed around before and after prison, hoped that a fund and pension plan for boxers could be set up and believed the governing bodies should be accountable for retired fighters.

'If they stop looking at us like pieces of meat there's enough money out there to do that and have some left over. So why shouldn't they?' he said. 'They make money off us but their attitude is that we owe them.'

I admired his enthusiasm for the cause but we weren't optimistic it would happen.

As we bundled awkwardly back into the lift and descended to the ground floor and back into the ghetto he said, 'It's funny how I got into working at the Lighthouse. What happened was I had to do community service and I got to working with the kids, talking about drugs and alcohol. I worked with a school and I realised it when I was with them that it was the thing I loved. I love recovery. So I went back.

'I learned in boxing that if you do something you love you get rewarded and I do something I really have a passion for. I love the people. I don't fix nobody, as I said. I'm here to help. You provide them with opportunities and I go beyond that. I mentor the kids and I love it. It's rewarding and gratifying.'

When Saad returned from work he couldn't believe Qawi had been in the apartment. He shook his head, flashing that charismatic smile. 'He was here? Today? Really?'

He shook his head again. 'Man, that's crazy. Where did he sit?'

'Right there,' I said, pointing at the couch.

Matthew sat beside the indent Qawi had left, staring at the sofa.

I'm glad it wasn't lost on him.

He wanted to know what Dwight looked like, what he was doing and what he had remembered about their fights. He smiled when I told him Qawi had said he had his number in the ring.

We laughed for a while and then I said I was leaving the next day, having bagged two interviews.

Matthew repeatedly exclaimed that what I was doing was madness, as he always did, and hugged me the way a father embraces a son he is proud of and wished me well.

Saad waited with me at the bus station. He gave me another paternal hug as my Greyhound pulled up.

As always, when I looked back on a city as it disappeared into the horizon from the bus window, I thought about the fighters I had met.

I smiled thinking that lightweight Leavander was taller than the heavyweight Qawi and thought they could both still get the closure they needed.

Dwight could be inducted into the Hall of Fame and put boxing behind him. Leavander could win the title, too, and fulfil his life's ambition. I still worried about Saad.

But I needed to kick-start my travels. The East Coast was all very familiar by now and I headed back to New York City with some decisions to make.

Chapter 10

THE familiar road back to Lowell ended with Micky Ward again greeting me at the station. His BMW had been replaced by a sleek, black Corvette and, eight days removed from his third and last battle with Arturo Gatti – the last of his crashing, bashing career – he was unmarked, though still complained of double vision.

After 30 tumultuous rounds with Gatti, a few hospital visits, more than 4,000 punches and three of the most definitive crowd-pleasing slugfests the sport had seen, Micky Ward was taking his money and running.

Between them, he and Gatti had split in the region of six million dollars.

There had been no grudges, no animosity and with memories of their last clash still fresh Ward, wearing baggy black shorts, a pale grey tank-top and a baseball cap, attempted to surmise how their rivalry generated such great business and good feeling in the sport.

'Probably because we weren't trash-talkers,' he said, surveying any possible damage to his hands as we sat back in his front room. 'We like each other. We just go in there and try to win. Basically, we were just two good people trying to win, me trying to end my career with a win and him trying to further his career with one.'

Gatti had earned the second fight.

I watched from the cheap seats in Atlantic City's Boardwalk Hall as Gatti rattled him early in the fight with a shot that burst his eardrum. Off balance for the remaining eight rounds, Micky did well to survive, let alone make it as competitive as it was.

The third fight, typically, swung one way and then the next. Gatti, a superior boxer and mover, used his skills to pull away on the scorecards but Ward lashed away in another scorching battle.

When Gatti cracked his right hand on Ward's hip midway through, and was then clubbed to the deck for a knockdown later on, the possibility of it swinging back in Micky's favour increased. One-handed Gatti, unflinchingly heroic, fought on using that brutalised paw to snatch the decider.

Ward continued light-heartedly, 'He was like Jason from the *Friday the 13th* movies – you can't keep him down. It was like the movie *Weekend at Bernie's*. He just kept popping back up.'

Their friendly rivalry had captured boxing's imagination. They were everything good about the game; honest, respectful and courageous. They had since been on the cover of video games, had their fights plugged on billboards in Times Square and on yellow taxis around New York.

'It's like I wasn't even there,' Micky smiled in reflection. 'I think it's pretty amazing. It's probably going to be part of history and it's been great to be a part of. Those Gatti fights were the high points of my career. Even the ones I lost were great fights.'

At the time, particularly in the second bout when Ward was caught off balance, popped in the ear and sent, dazed, spearing head-first into the turnbuckle, it hadn't always felt as good for him as the relief of retirement clearly did.

When that happened the New Jersey crowd erupted, partly to praise their hero Gatti but also in shock that the fight they hoped would be just as good as the first might end inside just a couple of rounds. They should have known better.

'That was when everything started moving,' Micky recalled. 'When I was being hit I was fine!'

Warriors don't have regrets, they have only successes or failures.

Ward had skipped the chance of a major shot at a world championship to give Gatti a rematch and then attempt to get the upper hand in their series. He didn't mind.

The fights, though, told him he'd more than served his time in boxing after a career that had been split in two. As a young prospect he'd been fed to more than one veteran lion which resulted in him retiring for a while in the 1990s.

He decided to give it one more shot, not knowing he had nearly another ten years left in the tank.

'I didn't want to have that burden on my shoulders,' he said, of the time he walked away but found himself drawn back to the sport. 'That can make you a cranky person, bitter and grouchy. I had to give it a shot while I was still young enough. It's been a long, hilly, windy road. A lot of peaks and a lot of valleys, and a lot of twists and turns. It's been a very bumpy ride.

'I'm never fighting again, I don't care what anyone comes up with. There isn't enough money in the world that would make me fight again.

'I could see myself getting old when I looked back at that third fight. I slowed down a lot. I could see my body slowing down. I couldn't feel it in there doing it, but looking at the tape he slowed me right down a lot. I could see it. I felt great in training camp but I was a step behind him the whole time.'

I told Micky I was going to try to see Gatti in Jersey City the following day and asked if he had any words for his conqueror who was looking towards big fights with the likes of Floyd Mayweather and Canada's Leonard Dorin.

'I'd maybe tell him to take an easier fight now,' he smiled.

Then he thought about this bloody business for a moment longer and concluded, 'Unless he gets big money for a tougher fight.'

We again went to the diner before Ward dropped me back at the station, wishing me well and sending his best wishes to his buddy.

It is around 200 miles from Lowell to Jersey City. In Greyhound terms that might be 300 or so. There were long layovers in Boston and New York before I arrived in Gatti's hometown early the next morning.

His manager, Pat Lynch, had given me Arturo's number and the man known in boxing as 'Thunder' agreed to meet me briefly in a nearby coffee shop. He could not stay long because he had an appointment to have his hand checked out after an operation to correct it following the third Ward brawl.

I'd met Gatti a few times over the years and his content smile radiated warmly as he perched on a bar stool next to me. Unlike Ward, though, ambition still burned in his eyes.

There was some minor discolouration beneath his optics and his hand was in a cast. He'd had bone grafted from his hip and placed into his mitt while torn tendons and ligaments in his fist were likely to hinder the healing process. I sent him Ward's regards and he asked after Micky, saying he would call him later in the day. Aware that time was of the essence, we talked about the three fights and how fondly the pair were now thought of by the fans. Gatti and Ward had always had their supporters but by bringing the best out of one another the audience was magnified.

'It was just the type of guys that we are, the way that we were,' he sighed. 'We went in there and fought, we gave it everything we could, 150 per cent, and we showed you don't have to hate someone to give it your best. I think we inspired a lot of people who watched us fight.'

Remembering the cauldrons they fought in front of – when the fans punched the air as they punched one another – and as they cheered for blood to be spilled, not by either one but by both, Arturo said, 'All the fans, they were jumping up and down because they were great fights. People were just cheering us for the way we fought – not cheering either one of us but both of us.

'I'd always said, "The day I fight somebody who has the same mentality that I have I'm going to have problems." Then Micky Ward came along with that mentality.'

While Ward had to deal with the agony of a perforated eardrum in fight two, Gatti had that dreadful hand break in fight three.

'I would have punched until I passed out from the pain,' he insisted, somewhat proudly.

We spoke briefly about his career up to that point. He had been expected to beat Ward in their first meeting but after he lost many saw him as an also-ran.

Two fights and victories over 'Irish' Micky later and he might have been back on top but the mileage on the clock was substantially higher and it was not an uncommon view that there was not enough left in him to wear a world title once more.

He disputed that.

'I was counted out in boxing,' he responded. 'I was counted out a few years ago. People don't understand I've come back and am one of the top boxers. I've won a world title before and I can do it again. I want to win it and keep it and show I became a world champion again when I was counted out.'

It wasn't long, though, before we were discussing the trilogy again.

After their final encounter, when they were both battered, bruised and broken, the fighters were taken to the hospital in

Atlantic City straight afterwards as a precaution. While Gatti was getting checked out he heard a commotion on the other side of the curtain, drew it back and saw Micky there.

'It was like in *Rocky*, they had everything ready for us,' he smiled.

The two laughed like the oldest and best of friends, having put each other into a medical care facility.

As we finished our bottled waters, Gatti said he was running low on time. He planned to play golf with Micky once they were well enough and, putting his shades on his forehead before walking out, concluded, 'I'm glad I was the one that Micky made some dollars with before he retires. It's a tough business to make money in. I was fortunate to fight Micky and it was an honour to fight him. He was a gentleman.'

It typified what they were as individuals and, more to the point, what they were collectively. They were gentlemen who beat the living heck out of one another for 30 rounds and made history together. They were now also soul-mates.

Chapter 11

THE bowels of the Port Authority bus terminal in Manhattan were not particularly attractive but they were at least shelter. The possibilities were endless, too, with departure gates signposted to just about every major city in North America. Nowhere was out of reach. There would be no revisiting any of my old haunts and no more familiar faces. The only thing I could think was to dip my toes into mainland America and pick one of the buses, any of them, stopping in a city where I knew an older fighter lived.

There were no excuses, ties or commitments. I had no deadlines and no one had commissioned any work because no one knew what I was doing. Aside from a slender rucksack, all I had was the 30-day open bus ticket. Armed with that travel pass, I could sleep on the buses to save spending on accommodation, travelling overnight to arrive in a village, town or city and then trying to find an old champion or contender.

The Greyhound bus pass guaranteed me a roof, whether it was on one of their buses or in one of their stations.

When the homeless and the drunks were kicked out of Greyhound stations after midnight ticket holders could stay provided they could say where they were going. That meant I could sleep in stations, too. It was a win-win scenario.

I eventually decided on a route that would take me through Pittsburgh.

It was another fight city with a proud tradition, the hometown of legendary light-heavyweight Billy Conn, who had given Joe Louis all he could handle. Harry Greb was another of the city's finest and uncrowned middleweight champion Charley Burley spent much of his life there.

The only active boxer of note when I passed through was lightweight Paul Spadafora. The IBF champion was coming off a hugely entertaining draw against light-punching Canadian warhorse Leonard Dorin and he had a mandatory defence against Leavander Johnson to make.

I called his manager, Mike Acri, to set up the interview. Acri assured me the champ would come and get me from the bus station the following morning and I rode through the night on the Greyhound to be there.

I was tired and hungry, though not irritable, when I arrived at around 7am.

We fixed a time of 9.30am for me to phone a friend of the fighter, who I understood was helping him move house. I waited patiently, perched on my rucksack, the same way a dog would sit for a bone.

Spadafora declined to come and see me, instead granting me a rather pointless phone interview.

I remonstrated that I had travelled several hundred miles to meet him and that I could do with taking pictures to accompany any potential feature. I was fighting a losing battle. He wasn't interested.

I was still saying goodbye and thanking him for his brief time when I heard the line go dead. More than 400 miles on the bus and an overnight journey, with a layover, for that?

After a short walk around the city to take in some sights, I grabbed my map of North America and looked for another destination in anger.

I had started crossing the continent, so I figured I may as well continue. I wanted to find a place far enough away so I could spend a night on the bus without paying for accommodation and arrive at a decent time the next morning.

Detroit was too close. Chicago would see me miss too many places in between.

I had been given a number for a friend of former heavyweight champion Buster Douglas, the most famous underdog in history who sensationally downed unbeaten Mike Tyson when he was a 42–1 long shot in 1990.

Until then, critics steadfastly believed he had no heart after throwing away a title fight with Tony Tucker, which triggered him to part company with his long-time trainer, his father.

Some said Billy 'Dynamite' Douglas had just had enough of his son. He knew Buster had the tools but just couldn't get the best out of him. Others said that when Douglas Jnr won his next six fights after losing to IBF champ Tucker, Buster was victorious because he didn't carry with him the pressure of having to please his dad.

Buster, who wasn't without natural gifts, wanted to prove he could fight to himself as well as his old man.

And going into the contest with Tyson, he had been hurt by something far greater than anything 'The Baddest Man on the Planet' could inflict upon him. His mother, Lula Pearl, suffered a massive stroke and died 23 days before the fight.

Buster's trainer, JD McCauley, later reflected, 'All he ever talked about was what he was going to do for his mom. That's all he ever said. She was his world.'

In the run-up to the Tokyo showdown, the guy who people said never really wanted to fight now had a great excuse to call off the biggest night of his life.

'She meant everything to me,' Buster said later. 'I always wanted to please her so I just continued on.'

On the night, Tyson was confused by the underdog's bewildering determination. He was shocked by his incessant stamina and most of all, one of boxing's most notorious intimidators looked sorry for himself because after landing heavy shots on his possessed opponent, Douglas kept looking down on him and firing his own meaty blows in return. The whole thing smacked of the schoolboy standing up to the playground bully.

After each punch Buster threw it was almost as if he was telling Tyson, 'Fuck you, I'm still standing. I can't be hurt any more than I already have been.'

He not only showed character but he showed balls to get off the floor after getting chinned by a bone-crunching right uppercut in the eighth.

Buster was so good that February morning in 1990 it was all Tyson could do to throw around 25 punches per round and most of those were single shots, looking for the one-punch knockout that had served him so well.

As his former trainer Teddy Atlas later said, 'We found out Godzilla didn't have green skin after all. It was paint.'

Throughout Douglas's 18-year career there had been the inevitable highs and lows, and no one seemed to know much about the person behind the Tyson win and the subsequent mauling at the hands of Evander Holyfield.

I decided to go to Columbus, in Ohio, and track down the real Buster Douglas.

He had been out of the spotlight for several years. His last fight, in 1999 against Andre Crowder, was so far beyond the media glare it became a genuine collectors' item for boxing tape and DVD buffs.

Even though he wasn't what I would call an old-timer, he was a significant part of boxing's rich tapestry.

On the bus, I penned the feeble Spadafora interview before resting my head on a jumper against the bus window and getting some sleep until we reached Ohio, around 200 miles and a few hours later.

At the station I checked my e-mails and looked on some of the boxing websites. The headline story was from a press release by Acri Promotions revealing that Spadafora had agreed to vacate the IBF lightweight title because he could no longer make the weight. Most of the interview I'd done had been about him continuing at 135lb.

I binned it. It was garbage, anyway. The whole thing had been a waste of time.

Still, there was no sense looking back when there was so much to look forward to. I just hoped other fighters would be more helpful.

The one good thing to come out of it all was that Leavander was now going to fight for the vacant title. Also, I felt encouraged in Columbus as my momentum seemed to be picking up in spite of the Spadafora debacle.

My tidy, compact network of contacts sent me details for fighters on a regular basis. Some, they said, were still in date, others they weren't so sure about. I wasn't bothered. I didn't mind going to any city and knocking on a door. What was the worst that could happen? That they wouldn't be in? That they didn't live there anymore? There was no real point thinking 'what if'.

I waited for a decent hour and then called Buster from a payphone.

I think I woke him although with Buster's somewhat drowsy voice I couldn't really tell. It was soft and quiet, a touch hoarse. He said he was busy until lunch but he would be happy to meet in the early afternoon. He told me to find a place to stay and we'd take things from there.

There was always a feeling, when this happened, that one promise would lead to another and I would end up spending money on a motel and having nothing to show for it. But I never really doubted Buster.

He seemed sincere.

Several days had passed since I last slept in a bed, in the Atlantic City apartment. Sometimes, on the longer journeys, there would be layovers in far-flung stations that split the night in two. I generally used those stops to shave and wash.

Motels in Columbus were nothing like as expensive as New York, Boston or anywhere like that. At $35, the Days Inn was the cheapest option and I booked the room from the bus station and took down directions. It was about a mile away and outside it was hot and humid once I escaped the chill of the station's air conditioning.

The motel allowed me to check in early and I prepared for the interview.

I also called Buster, told him where I was staying and we arranged to meet in the afternoon.

He described an open grassy space, a plot of land, and gave me the cross-street location where he would be waiting. He asked if I was driving and when I told him I wasn't he enquired how I would make the trip. I told him I had plenty of time and proposed to walk, and initially he went quiet.

'You're joking, right.'

'No, I'll be fine, Buster,' I assured him.

'OK,' he said. 'If you're sure. Have you got a map?'

There was one in the motel room and it had both the starting point and destination on it. It didn't look so far. I felt more certain of seeing him there than he seemed of seeing me.

At around 11.30am I set off, knowing I would rather be an hour early than five minutes late. I tucked my tape recorder into the waistband of my shorts and let a T-shirt hang over the top. My room key card was in one shoe, a bank card in another and my camera also tightly gripped by the drawstring on my shorts.

The heat by now was extraordinary. It was well over 90 degrees and my brown T-shirt seemed to be blurring into a hazy red under the powerful sun.

After half an hour, the size of the task at hand struck me.

The map wasn't to scale.

Columbus was a huge place that seemed to go on forever.

I tried to walk quickly while respecting the heat at the same time. I felt I was travelling without moving. The blocks between road junctions were abnormally long. The skyscrapers of the city didn't seem to get closer, and the interview was on the other side.

I was hungry but again didn't eat. Firstly, I knew it would save me money and secondly I was fearful I might not be able to make it to the meeting point on time if I stopped.

The sweat was pouring from me.

My T-shirt was clinging.

My thighs were getting sore from rubbing together.

I could feel blisters forming on the soles of my feet.

I walked and walked.

I hiked alongside the city centre and carried on in the direction of the destination.

As I looked over my shoulder, it seemed to take ages for the skyscrapers to shrink in size to let me know I had walked a decent distance.

I had been going for a couple of hours and became genuinely concerned about not being in time for Buster.

But, with about ten minutes to spare, I started to recognise landmarks he had mentioned. At bang on 3pm I was there.

I stood patiently on an open, grassy rectangle, perhaps a couple of acres in size, with roads all around, and houses and a few stores on one side of the street. There was a makeshift car park made from gravel in the centre.

I was wide open for the sun's powerful glare but didn't dare move for cover in case Buster came and went without seeing me. I worried he had already been and gone before I had arrived.

I lay down on the grass and looked up. I was excited but apprehensive. I waited, hoping that my Columbus efforts hadn't been in vain and within a minute or two of touching down on a thick bed of parched grass I heard tyres skidding through the gravel. I sat up and saw a huge black pick-up truck with an equally enormous black Harley-Davidson trailer in tow.

It looked like Megadeth were lost on tour.

The windows were blacked out and it drove right beyond me. It braked sharply about 50 feet ahead of where I was, parking on the gravel but close to the border with the grass.

I walked slowly over. The vehicle and its respective trailer didn't look particularly inviting in midnight black with biker logos all over them.

The driver's side window dropped down and Douglas, wearing a bandana, peered out.

'Buster, I'm Tris, the boxing writer.'

'Shit man, you made it,' he said with a disbelieving smile and a shake of the head.

The man monster got out of the vehicle to greet me.

He was huge. We shook hands and his palm stretched all the way up my forearm, engulfing the skin and giving it temporary reprieve from the sunlight.

He was larger than life. Everything about him was big. His arms looked like thick branches, his legs like tree trunks and there was nothing twig-like about his fingers. They looked like Germany's biggest bratwursts.

His tummy was big, too, and his chest flopped uncouthly over it. You could see all that underneath his baggy black Harley T-shirt.

But the red and black Harley-Davidson braces that were attached to his dark jeans and wrapped over his huge shoulders kept it mildly in check.

He was every bit 6ft 4in and every ounce 300lb.

He had chunky, heavy-set cheeks and wide eyes that were trying to figure me out. His two boys burst out of the back doors of the pick-up.

'This is Artie and this is BJ,' Buster said, as I smiled at them, not quite sure how the youngsters would amuse themselves while daddy told the strange Englishman his old stories.

But Buster wasn't just here for the chat. He opened up the trailer and drove out on an expensive-looking sit-down mower. He briefed the kids about the work he expected of them and said the grown-ups would sit in the truck where we could benefit from air-conditioning as they tackled some landscaping.

We looked out on to the grassland and Buster began to reveal what was happening. He spoke of his plans for the

Douglas Center and was going to pick up architect's drawings later in the week.

His vision was a $20 million project to provide shops, apartments and town houses in an area that required regeneration.

'I knew this was going to be my cash cow,' he said optimistically, looking out over the grounds.

Buster had driven from his place on the outskirts of Columbus but he also had another pad in Florida.

He would sometimes go there on his custom-made Harley, leaving his boys, Artie, 12, and 10-year-old BJ with their mother, the same woman Buster was at odds with prior to the Tyson fight. The boys tended to the land to make sure it didn't become shabby as their dad waited for the developers to move in.

The former heavyweight champion of the world used to employ a firm to look after the area, but after their rates increased and his sons had grown to an age where they were not only available to help but wanted to, Artie and BJ had become very useful. Their reward was McDonald's for dinner and a couple of games at the bowling alley.

As we talked, Buster said he was beginning to feel 'the buzz' of boxing again. He had been helping his younger brother Billy, a novice heavyweight pro, in the gym and loved it.

Billy was 4–0 as a pro, 'coming along really well' Buster said, excitedly.

'I'm going to the gym from time to time and helping work with him. His trainer is Vonzell Johnson.'

'Vonzell?' I asked, completely taken aback. 'Vonzell Johnson, the former light-heavyweight?'

'Yeah, Vonzell Johnson, "The Eiffel Tower" himself,' Buster joked, referring to the former light-heavyweight title challenger's height.

'Does he live around here?' I asked, hoping he might be able to point me in Vonzell's direction.

'Yeah, they are training at the Lula Pearl Recreation Center that was named after my mom at Cleveland and 18th Avenue. Today is Thursday. They'll be there tonight at about 5.30pm.'

'So maybe I can speak to him while I'm over here?'

'Definitely,' Buster assured me. 'Definitely.'

Young Billy, a late starter at 33, had pressure on him that Buster could identify with. Not only did he have a famous brother to emulate but their father, Billy Snr, was a boxing cult hero. He had been hugely respected in the trade, winning 40 of 57 pro fights. He boxed a who's who of superb fighters through the 1970s, including Saad Muhammad, Victor Galindez, Willie Monroe, Don Fullmer, Bennie Briscoe and Marvin Johnson, but he never captured a world title.

He died in 1999, a huge loss for the Douglas boys who idolised him.

'I just got into the game from him,' said Buster.

'I think I was about eight years old when I really wanted to start fighting but he kept me out until I was about ten. Then he took me into the gym, which is across the street from here at Blackburn's.'

'Did you feel you had big shoes to fill?' I probed.

'It wasn't even about that. It wasn't about trying to fill his shoes because he was always an individual. He always talked about how things worked for me, do what I have to do. It wasn't "be like me" or stuff like that. In a sense, the only thing my dad did was fight. He really wasn't a strategic guy. He was just war.

'Guys would tell me when he fought Bennie Briscoe down there in Philadelphia at the Spectrum for the NABF title, and they would say to dad, "Give it five or six rounds, work him but just get some rounds under your legs and try and get into it later in the fight."

'My dad was like, "whatever", and from round one until when they stopped it, it was all bang, bang, bang. He was a big puncher as a middleweight. He carried that up to light-heavyweight because that's how he dropped Matthew Saad Muhammad.

'I was rooting for my dad, of course, but Saad was a sharp dresser and ever since then I've always been a fan. He was a class act. He would go to war. He was a gorilla in the mist, a monster. Saad was sweet. I went to that fight when he fought my dad in Philly and Saad was a real classy guy. I was really impressed with him.'

'Your dad put him down,' I said, encouraging him to go into more detail.

'My dad knocked his ass out but they stopped the fight on a cut [in Saad's favour] like a round later.'

Saad, then fighting as Matthew Franklin, cut up 'Dynamite' in the sixth after the Philadelphian was dropped in the fifth.

'That light-heavyweight division was a nightmare,' Buster reflected of his dad's era. 'Marvin Johnson was no joke, man.'

I kept hearing Marvin's name and the more I heard it the more it fuelled me to find Indianapolis's three-time world light-heavyweight champion.

'I remember Marvin fought Vonzell Johnson at my high school in the amateurs,' Buster went on. 'They were both top-notch amateurs. That was a very strong division. Usually most divisions have like five really top guys and that's it. But if they had the exposure then that there is now with TV and all the different outlets they would have been really off the hook.'

As an amateur, Buster looked up to Jose Napoles, Muhammad Ali and his father was alongside them.

He fought in the Junior Olympics and was 'very active' from 10 to 15 and was even ready to go on to the national team.

But he became interested in basketball, football and baseball and later returned to boxing after his junior year in college, going straight into the pros.

'Basically, it was me and my father starting out in his basement training and stuff and then we would go to the recreation centre and after that we started getting fights and so on.

'When I turned pro I felt I had the ability to be heavyweight champion, you know what I mean, if I could get the opportunity.'

Not having had such talent I didn't have the faintest idea what he was talking about. 'Sure,' I said.

'If I got the right fights, you know,' he went on, unconvinced by my response.

He felt he had a 'decent' career and retired with 'a good record', 38 wins against six losses and a draw.

'There were a lot of highs, a lot of lows,' he said, as many fighters seemed to.

He paused.

'Well, a few highs, a lot of lows, really. Especially early in my career which I endured because I knew I could do it.'

He classed wins over future WBC champion Oliver McCall and former WBA ruler Greg Page as two highlights, along with the Tyson victory, naturally.

'I fought some pretty decent guys. I fought about four or five champions.'

'You didn't get your shot at Tyson for nothing, did you?' I said, despite people over the years thinking Buster had been plucked from obscurity to box for the title.

He was on a seven-fight winning streak that included McCall, former WBC champion Trevor Berbick and Mike Williams as victims.

'Exactly,' Buster agreed. 'Hell, it wasn't like, "OK you fight him", it wasn't that. I earned that shot to fight Mike, it's just I wasn't one of the guys that was a TV darling or a media darling so to speak. But I was there in the thick of it with all of them. When Tyson and Michael Spinks fought, I fought on that card and beat this dude Mike Williams and he was a prima donna. He was supposed to be the one who was going to take Tyson out.

'So Don King fed him to me. It was like, "I'll give you a shot at Buster Douglas and after you beat him you'll get a shot at Tyson" and I destroyed him so, you know, I had my moments.'

He smiled to himself.

After about half an hour, the boys got the mower stuck in a damp patch of grass. It was in the shadows of the tall surrounding buildings and clearly hadn't seen the sun. Mud was churning out the back as the wheels plunged deeper into the mire.

'We might have to go and help those guys out, they got it stuck,' Buster said.

'Shall we go?' I offered.

After a couple of minutes of trying to push the mower, with my lone pair of trainers getting soaked, stained and thick with mud, Buster took matters into his own hands. He lifted the back end and swung it around, playfully telling Artie to try and avoid the wet areas next time. Buster was still strong; that was one immensely heavy piece of kit.

After talking about McCall, Page and Tyson – who combined had knocked out almost 150 fighters in three long pro careers – I was surprised when Buster said the heaviest puncher he faced was a former sparring partner.

'This guy I used to work out with here in town, a light-heavyweight called Darnell Hayes, he was a real good natural puncher,' he said.

Hayes was a journeyman who dipped his toes into the cruiserweight division and retired in 1984 with a spotty record of 11 wins, 24 losses and just eight knockouts.

Surely Buster had faced harder punchers?

'Were you impressed with anyone's power in particular?' I asked, suggesting McCall and Tyson as obvious candidates.

'They were all punchers, but there isn't one that jumped out.

'I thought Page was good, he was a good boxer and pretty nifty with his hands. He came at you a few different ways.'

Buster was concentrating on Artie and BJ, making sure they weren't struggling. I could see by the way they were with each other that they were close. He was like a lion with its cubs.

'As the champ, what kind of life were you living?' I asked, expecting him to analyse the difference between life now and then.

'It was all right,' he said calmly, but with a nod and a wink. 'You know that movie *I Spy* with Eddie Murphy?'

'Yes,' I lied.

'That's pretty close to what it was. It wasn't my private plane, it was someone else's but I could have seen myself doing that, winning the title, defending it a few times, buying a plane.

That was pretty impressive. And that's pretty much how it is with the money they are making nowadays. If things had worked out I could have been like that, too.

'But I lived the high life. It was OK.

'As soon as I signed for the fight with Tyson life changed just like that,' he said, clicking his thumb and second finger. 'We were going first class and that was as soon as I signed.'

The boys were bogged down again. Artie ran over for advice and Buster wound down his window.

'Just tell him to go back and forth, back and forth to get out of that,' he offered.

The message relayed, BJ manoeuvred to drier patches.

'Yeah, that's pretty much how it has been, man.

'If I had got past Holyfield I would have fought Tyson again and that would probably have been it. But that's just me.

'But doing the things that Lennox Lewis has done and the champions before him like Holyfield and Tyson, to continue and sustain, it's an awesome thing. It's truly an awesome thing.'

Buster could not do it.

In 1987 he had lost in his first try for a world title, a ten-round stoppage defeat to Tucker. It was a setback but Buster believed the crown would one day be his.

'I knew the desire was still strong and I was going to be champion; that I could still come back. And the funny thing about it is I was really looked at to beat Tucker, I was given a chance.

'Then, coming back to fight for the title again when I was really ready, I said, "I've got to do what I've got to do. Nobody is going to stop me against this great." People had said, "Forget it, you blew your chance."

'I was more determined against Tyson than I was the first time. I had been there and done that. I enjoyed being the underdog.'

He wound down his window again and warned the boys, 'That's a wet spot.'

'I see it,' yelled Artie, who was navigating his little brother around and reporting updates to his dad.

'We were going to fight Razor Ruddock but then that got cancelled and it was like, "Oh, so we're going to get the shot at Mike." Then we didn't know where and we found out it was going to be in Japan and I thought that was cool. I had never been overseas before.'

Tyson was then a terror. He was undefeated, an apparently unbeatable beast who had thrashed almost everyone in his path, leaving a string of crumpled former champions in his wake.

If Douglas couldn't beat Tucker, surely he didn't have a prayer against Tyson.

The odds-makers didn't believe so. Many didn't even open books for a Douglas win.

'I wasn't even worried about everybody writing me off because I was totally pissed off, man. I had just lost my mom. Then my wife and I were at odds so really it was a blessing for me to get the fight. There was a lot of hostility I had to let out because I was pissed. You know, I had been through so much in my life at that point that it seemed like more and more things were happening to where I would just say, "To hell with this. Fuck this."

'But then I knew, deep down, that was just the devil trying to stop me from succeeding.

'Why was all this coming down on me at one time? Why, when I'm finally trying to do something with my life, do I get all this other stuff that is basically trying to distract me from the main goal? Because if I hadn't gone through with that then we wouldn't be sitting here today. I wouldn't be sat out here with my kids talking about developing a $20 million project. So we came through it and we have seen the light at the end of the tunnel.

'And then before the Tyson fight I was left alone. I didn't have nobody bothering me because nobody gave me a fuckin' chance and I did what I had to do to prepare for the fight.

'We had a press conference in Japan and it was a big old room and there were like four people there and you know when Tyson had one it was packed.

'But the guys there with me were scratching their heads trying to think of questions like "So what colour trunks are you going to wear?" just to find an angle.

'I had been on about five undercards of Mike and to me I was looking at the guy… Like I said about Saad, when he was at the weigh-in to fight my dad and he had on a blazer, a nice silk shirt with a collar, low-cut shoes. He was real class in a nice little ensemble. And then there was this fucking Tyson. He was walking around in this tight-ass leather suit and he was goofy as fuck. He's a monster, he's a beast but that's it. He can't be normal. He's short to me. He's one-dimensional. He had no fucking coolness about him, he was just a monster in a suit all bulked up. I never thought nothin' of that fucker, man. I'm telling you. I never thought he was shit, man.

'My biggest thing going into that fight was that it wasn't going to happen. That he might pull out. That was my biggest concern.

'My tactics were just box him and throw out that right hand, keep my hands up and keep my eyes on that psycho because he likes to hit on the break and all that. My dad was like, "Look, what he does to you do back to him" because no one would do that with Tyson. People would stand and look at the referee for help. Fuck the referee, the referee isn't doing nothing. They can't see round the back.'

'What about when you hit the deck in the eighth?'

'I was getting ready to get up real quick but I used my experience and thought I'd go ahead and pick up the count, relax, and then get up. In the next round I almost knocked his ass out and then I did the following round.'

Buster acknowledged Tyson hadn't got to where he was by luck. He agreed the New Yorker had been misrepresented when media outlets said he got $20 million plus for blitzing Michael Spinks in 91 seconds back in 1988.

'People forget he would have done a seven- or eight-week training camp and years of training,' Buster explained.

'It's not like he just went out there and hit the lottery. It had taken him a long time. All that time out on the road. It's cold, it's 5.30am and you're running and some days you just don't feel like it.

'My dad would cuss me out. "Come on, Buster, damn it, run. You ain't gonna get shit if you don't run." I had to run.

'"If a dog was coming you'd run," dad said.

'"No I wouldn't, I would fight it," but that was my dad. We would go on and on like that. The public and the press don't see none of that. All they see is the end result. Being a fighter is hard. You can't just hang out and be normal. If people invited me to a party I would say, "I can't do that, man. I've got to be in shape and get up in the morning."'

'Was it worth it?'

'It has been. I've always been my own man. I've always paid my own way. I look at my kids and see how they're living. It's like all the hard work I put in, the lives they have, it's a beautiful thing.'

'Who wins, a prime Tyson or prime Holyfield?' I asked, knowing Buster was the one fighter who faced them close to their best years.

'I think it would be a toss-up because that's all they did from day one to the world championship. It's got to be a toss-up. Before I beat Tyson I would have said Tyson but I opened the door for Holyfield to beat Tyson. I gave all of them the blueprint; Lennox too.

'That [invincible] aura stuff I wiped away.

'I thought Larry Holmes was going to beat him. Holmes was no joke. He did very well in the first two rounds then he started bullshitting and he was looking at him like, "Yeah motherfucker, what" and he got caught. And if Tyson hits you hard you're gonna go. It doesn't matter if you're a bad dude like Larry Holmes. He was a bad motherfucker. He was a bad, bad dude. I've got nothing but love for Larry.'

There were similarities between Buster and Holmes in life after boxing. Both had invested money in property and were milking more than one cash cow.

Holmes just about owned Easton, Pennsylvania, and it seemed the Douglas mark was over much of Columbus. The kids were bogged down again and this time Buster and I combined couldn't budge the mower.

We left the boys to look after the equipment and got back in to the truck to go to a DIY store to get some wooden planks to place under the wheels for the mower to drive out, and some woodchips for the flower beds.

As we turned out of the car park with R&B tunes playing loudly, a car hooted and a group of men yelled, 'How's it going, Buster?'

'All right, now, how you doing?' he responded, with a cheery wave.

And just like that, we were talking Tyson again and on our way to the store at speed.

'When you saw him groping around for his mouthpiece, what did you think…?'

When he floored Tyson it provoked an image that lasted long in the memory. It was one of the defining moments of Tyson's career, and of heavyweight history.

'I knew it was over although I thought he was going to get up,' Buster recalled. 'But when I saw him reaching for his mouthpiece I thought, "It's over. It's over, baby."

'He was tough, I knew he was. He fought Frank Bruno and Bruno hit hard. He fought Bonecrusher and he hit hard so he fought some guys who got some shots in.

'It's always hard to stop a guy with one shot. You need combinations because as my dad always said, "You've just got to keep on rockin' 'em because everybody's strong at the beginning."

'The same shots I knocked him out with in the tenth were the same he had taken in the first, second and third rounds. It's like knocking down a tree with an axe. Eventually you will cut it down.'

Buster conceded he had been one of Don King's 'puppets' in a way that made me think of poor Jimmy Young, who had said a similar thing.

Jimmy and Buster were massive outsiders against two bona fide heavyweight destroyers, Tyson and Foreman. But they had convincingly won the fights and even put the bullies on their backsides.

But with the battle won, life for Buster would never be the same.

'We were ready for the war, but we weren't ready for the aftermath because we just got caught up. We had every Tom, Dick and Harry saying, "Do this. You should do this."

He sparked a promotional bidding war, which resulted in Las Vegas casino magnate Steve Wynn winning the race for his signature and reportedly giving him more than $25 million to make his first defence against Holyfield in Vegas.

Unusually, King fell at the first hurdle because, after the Tyson fight, he tried to get the verdict overturned to keep Tyson's perfect record intact by claiming Douglas had been on the deck for more than ten seconds in the eighth when Douglas had responded to the referee's count to stand at 'nine'.

Everyone thought Buster hadn't trained for Holyfield. They said his desire was gone, that he had grown lazy and spent his training sessions in fast-food joints and ice-cream parlours.

'People knew you had problems before the Tyson fight but they seemed to think that as soon as you won they would go away,' I prodded.

'Right, absolutely,' he said, almost relieved that someone saw it from his perspective. 'It didn't bring my mom back and a lot of things I had left on the shelf I still had to deal with. But now people close to me said I wasn't me.

'I couldn't talk like I would normally talk because now I'm the world champion it was like they thought I was looking down at them. I hadn't changed at all but people's perception of me changed.'

It made his life difficult, particularly with his mother's side of the family.

'Being heavyweight champion of the world is like being the President. As an individual you're on top of the whole world. You've got football and the NBA and all that but as boxing heavyweight champion you're the MVP in sport.'

'Do you think you should have taken on someone with less ability than Evander Holyfield first?'

'No, no, because it had to be someone I was going to train for. I needed to be well prepared. It wouldn't have mattered if I fought Joe Schmoe.'

After the three-round Holyfield blowout, Buster quit boxing.

He piled on the pounds and ate himself into a depression-induced diabetic coma.

He fought again six years later, in 1996, because of health problems. His doctor warned him that if he didn't get in shape he could die. While back in the gym, he fell back in love with the sport.

'I was depressed until I started fighting again and I kept it all to myself. I was bottling it up. I didn't care. Everybody I had loved had gone, and I had a lot of personal problems.'

It was ironic that Tony LaRosa, the man who would end Dwight Qawi's pro career two years later, was the comeback opponent for Buster after his hiatus.

This boxing world was getting smaller and smaller.

Buster knocked out LaRosa in four, in Atlantic City, and won five more before stepping up his comeback against Lou Savarese, only to be floored three times and wiped out in a round.

He made good money in the comeback – not that he was short – and claimed he had taken some medication before the Savarese fight that had made him 'drowsy', causing him to fight out of character.

That was in 1999 and Buster reckoned the current crop of heavyweights wasn't much cop.

He was right, of course.

'What do you think when you see…?'

'John Ruiz and them guys winning the title,' he continued for me. 'I can't fuckin' believe it.'

'What about when you see all those guys like Oliver McCall and Tyson still fighting?'

'If things had been different, I would still be fighting. I take my hat off to them. I heard about Greg Page getting paralysed in the ring, that was a shock but he had taken some shots. That's one thing about this game, you need to be careful. It's a young man's game, really.'

'So no more comebacks?'

'There's always a comeback,' he said, a cunning smile spreading from the sides of his mouth as we pulled up back on his land.

'Going to the gym with my brother and working with him, I'm getting the buzz back. It feels good. I keep telling him I'm glad he's fighting because he's got me motivated and back doing things.

'It's part of my life, man. There's no denying it. I grew up in it. The fight game will always be a part of my life.

'That's my life right there now.' He smiled proudly as he pointed at the kids.

They waved back, pleased to see their old man. Buster grinned.

The four of us combined to have the mower out in minutes. I helped them with some light landscaping and weeding in the flower beds and Buster let the boys do the finishing touches.

'It's all done, Dad,' they shouted happily.

'Beautiful,' Buster smiled proudly. 'Beautiful.'

My shoes were ruined.

But what I watched between Buster and his boys was exactly what they all said. It was beautiful.

Chapter 12

H E WAS affectionately called 'The Eiffel Tower' and he loomed large over me. A baseball cap and large pair of shades disguised the ageing process although one could clearly see that Vonzell Johnson, light-heavyweight contender of the early 1980s, had moved north of that weight class.

It didn't take Buster long to take me to the Lula Pearl Recreation Center, which was named after his mother, and Vonzell was there getting ready to work with Billy. Johnson also trained amateurs and boasted several winning programmes in the city. Vonzell and I moved into his no-frills office at the side of the darkened gym and as we sat down Johnson remained hidden behind his cap and glasses.

Originally from Richlands, Virginia, he moved to Columbus when he was 13 and his solid amateur career included around 80 wins against around ten defeats.

'I did good,' he smiled.

Picking up from what Buster had told me, I asked him how he fared with Marvin Johnson in the amateurs.

'I fought him right here in Columbus,' he smiled, raising his eyebrows. 'I beat him up. I tore his butt up. We fought in one of the high schools. He was 17 and had just won the national championships and my coach called me up and said, "Do you want to fight Marvin Johnson, the 17-year-old kid out of Indiana?" I said, "Hell yes."

'We fought three hard rounds but I boxed too good for him. He boxed left-handed and he couldn't catch up with me. He came after me but I just boxed him and actually I hurt him a couple of times. But he did hit me with a left-right and woah. They called it a hometown decision but I beat him fairly.'

By his own admission, Vonzell was a standout amateur and his lone disappointment was his decision to leave the unpaid ranks too soon.

'I should have waited,' he mused, lifting his hand to his chin and stroking his stubble.

'I turned professional in 1974 and that year I won the National Golden Gloves in Denver, Colorado. Then I won the National AAU in Knoxville, Kentucky, toured Russia and I became the only American to ever win all my matches in Russia. So I made a little history there.'

Johnson had won the 1974 Golden Gloves as a middleweight, the same title Buster's dad had won in 1963, here in Columbus.

'I should have waited two years for the Olympics but because I had done all those things people said, "You should go ahead and turn pro," so I said, "OK." But I should have waited two years.

'If I had waited I would have got on the Olympic team, and if I had waited I would have been in that class with Sugar Ray Leonard and Michael and Leon Spinks and all them.

'Michael Spinks, that year in 1974, was supposed to fight at 156lb so I'm sure if I'd waited until '76 I would have made the Olympic team. Michael would have went down to 156lb, I would have fought at 165lb, Leon would have fought at 178lb and so on. With hindsight, if I had made that team and got a gold medal, that's the gravy train.'

Instead, he went to fight out of the Motor City, making Detroit his home.

The late Del Williams and Robert Mitchell trained him.

'Del was one heck of a trainer,' Johnson recalled. 'A lot of guys were trained by him in Detroit, like Emanuel Steward and different guys.

'You go to different gyms in that city and sparring's a fight. I remember some of these guys who never made it, there was a guy there called "The Sandman"...'

Vonzell scratched around in his memory for the name.

'Willie Edwards,' I suggested.

'Willie Edwards,' he repeated, nodding his head. 'I fought him on a regular basis. He was hard-hitting, he couldn't beat me because I had too much experience for him, but that guy could punch.

'And that's how it was in Detroit. You go to the Kronk Gym, it's a war. You go to Powerhouse, it's a war. You go to King Soloman's, it's a war. You go to Brewster's, it's a war. Everywhere they had fighters there was a war.'

He wasn't protected like Olympic gold medallists are early on, he was pitched in tough. All hungry fighters want a shot at an Olympian but few want to fight one who didn't make the team but could have made a big splash. Anyone who boxed Vonzell early on would be taking a high risk for little reward, hardly the stuff of managers' dreams.

So Johnson's education was hard.

'You always remember the fights where you learn stuff,' he said. 'There's a certain style, you might have seen Tommy Hearns doing it,' he offered, tucking his chin into his shoulder, lifting his right hand to his chin and holding his left low. 'It was a Detroit style. You would roll, get behind your shoulder real good and we had that style. That was Detroit all the way back to Joe Louis.

'I remember back to my early career I travelled to Maryland and I fought a guy named Wayne McGee and McGee was tough. He had a funny overhand right and I remember the first round well.

'I was OK but he nailed me and I said, "Damn, how did this guy hit me with his right hand?" So Del says, "When you get in there roll and then hit him with a shot."

'So in the next round, he threw the overhand right, I rolled and I could see he was wide open and I nailed him. So I learned the roll works. Then I fought a guy named "Smokey" Joe Middleton from that area, and they called him "Smokey" for a reason, he fought like Frazier. This guy comes. He would take a beating. He was somewhat like Saad Muhammad, he would take a licking and keep on ticking. He came, came, came, so I had two hard fights with him,' he said, adding emphasis on 'hard'.

'You remember things like that.'

Buster poked his head around the corner and we both looked up.

'I will be outside,' he said quietly, not wanting to interrupt.

'Are you going to take off?' I asked, preparing to say my goodbyes.

'No, I'm waiting for you. Is that all right?'

'If you don't mind, yeah, no problem.'

'All right,' he said, disappearing from sight.

'What a nice guy,' I told Vonzell.

'He's a great guy,' Johnson smiled, sensing my gratitude.

I told Vonzell I had met his former opponent Saad Muhammad and that I had interviewed Qawi less than a week earlier.

'It was a great era,' he reflected. 'That's when you had so many great fighters that could beat anyone today. You're talking about Yaqui Lopez, Saad Muhammad, Richie Kates, Marvin Johnson, Eddie Mustafa, Eddie Davis, Jerry Martin, James Scott, there were loads of them. Even in that era we wouldn't have stood a chance with guys like Archie Moore and Ezzard Charles. Every era has its own tough guys.'

Though there were many in Vonzell's time, he maintains few were interested in going up against him.

'They all ducked me,' he said. 'I was someone to be reckoned with. I was one of those guys they call sleepers, they sometimes compared me to the great light-heavyweight Bob Foster.

'In the prime of my life I was ducked. A lot of guys wouldn't fight me and I missed some primetime years of getting an opportunity. If I had won a gold medal I would have been there, so I should have waited.

'But that's the past.'

Spinks and Saad Muhammad were the two exceptions.

If a little regretfully, he had fond memories of going toe-to-toe with Saad. 'He's the guy you could beat on for ten rounds, which I did, and he would still come out victorious,' he stated. 'He just had inhuman stamina. Here's a guy who didn't get to his strongest until the 11th, 12th, 13th and 14th rounds. I beat him for ten rounds and he stopped me in the 11th and I was just numb.

'I knew I could beat him. What a lot of people didn't know was Angelo Dundee called me and said I could have a fight with Saad. I only had three weeks to train. The reason I got the fight was the fight with him and Eddie Mustafa, a rematch in 1980, fell through. That's how I got in the picture and I said I would because you've got to take a chance. So I said, "Yeah, come on."

'If we were fighting 12 rounds back then I think I would have beat him because I would have gutted out the last two rounds.

'I went to the corner and my trainer Angelo told me it was the ninth round and I said, "What? I've got six more rounds? I can't go six more rounds."

'If he hadn't told me that I could have gone maybe 13, but 15?'

'What were you thinking when Saad kept coming back?' I asked.

'He had his trainer, Sam Soloman, in the corner and I could hear him yelling across at Saad, "He's fadin', he's gettin' tired," and I was like, "Shut up man, don't tell him."

'But I was. If I could have mustered up enough to go 12 rounds I don't think he would have believed in it anymore.

'Finally, in the 11th round he made it and I didn't have nothin' left.'

Having fought Spinks and Saad in their primes, there were few better placed to ask about who would have won the mouth-watering showdown fans never saw.

'I would have to say a primetime Saad because Michael wouldn't have had enough to take him out. Michael had a good pop but it wouldn't have been good enough and Saad would have walked through it. Not many people would have beaten Saad Muhammad, I can tell you that.'

I asked for a little more on Spinks, who dropped him with a hard right hand and stopped him in round seven.

'Michael hit me on the break, everybody saw that. It was a cheap shot but it was my fault, I dropped my hands so I blame nobody for it. Dundee couldn't negotiate another fight but I wanted to fight Spinks again and Michael would not. He flat out said "No, that's never going to happen," which was a smart move on his part.

'So I just got frustrated at that point.

'I was scheduled to fight here in Columbus. They wanted to bring me home and I told myself that if I get to the point where I wake up in the morning and I just don't want to run then I'm done. And that day came. I got up one morning and I said, "To hell with this."

'I officially retired in 1984, three years after I had fought Spinks. They still had me on active rosters and they would call me from time to time and if they had offered me something really meaningful I might have taken it.'

Nothing appealing came up and Vonzell edged into a barren wilderness. He no longer watched boxing and even switched off when he saw it on TV. Yet in 1985 he got the itch again.

'I went to one of the recreation centres in town and asked if they wanted some help with the kids so I started training fighters,' he said, his tone lifting. Organisers bit his long arm off and he not only began a programme, he created a winning system.

'Everywhere I have been I have had a winning programme and then they gave me this one at the Lula Pearl Rec. This is the best one in the state and one of the best facilities. It used to be called Windsor but after Buster won the title he changed it to his mom's name so everybody knows this place. We've got a pretty good gym.'

Vonzell had also coached former world champion Tom Johnson but was equally happy working with pros and amateurs.

I asked if he'd considered moving up in weight as several of his colleagues had done. Qawi, Mustafa Muhammad and Spinks had all fought at heavyweight with varying degrees of success.

But despite being a big man now, Vonzell said he could never put on enough pounds.

'We talked about it but I just could not make the weight. I just could not make it past about 185lb. We tried protein shakes and everything until I felt sick and I just couldn't get past 185lb.

'Now I can't get down to 185lb. I can't get down to 250lb, you know.'

We laughed.

'I guess it's age.' He shook his head.

Boxing had seduced him back into its addictive arms but he was happy to feel its embrace.

'What about Saad? When did you last see him?' I asked.

'I saw him a few years ago,' Vonzell replied.

'I was kind of sad because after I talked to him for a long time he didn't know who I was and I finally told him and I feel kind of bad for him. But that's time and boxing for you. Time and boxing.'

We will never know what Vonzell could have achieved had he kept on fighting. Not every champion was a Spinks or Saad Muhammad and Vonzell had plenty of miles left on the clock.

Now 51, he was just 29 at the time of his last fight and had a 25-fight career that included 22 wins and three losses.

Boxing had not set him up for life financially.

'For 1981 I made good money, for now it would be pittance,' he accepted. 'They make all this money now but that was the era of real fighters.'

It was a familiar line I had heard on my travels.

'So do they send you everywhere?' Vonzell asked as we walked out of the office and towards Buster, who sat patiently in the pick-up with the boys.

'No, I had to sell my car to come over here.'

'You do this on your own? Is that right?' he said, approvingly. 'How did you get started?'

'People like to know what happened to you guys,' I explained.

Johnson went on, 'Yeah, in a couple of months, they will say "There's Vonzell Johnson, what's he doing now?" I'm paying my dues, that's all.

'So you're getting the Greyhound bus all over the country?' Vonzell said, as I got into Buster's truck. 'Jesus. My hat's off to you pal,' he added, with one last handshake.

He said his farewells and within a few minutes, we were back at the Days Inn.

As we pulled up on West Broad Street I was hungry but shattered.

It had been another day without food and Buster said I could join him and the kids in McDonald's. It was right outside my hotel room.

I told him he had done more than enough.

'But you haven't eaten,' he insisted. The boys said they didn't mind.

'I'll be OK,' I smiled gratefully and waved goodbye.

I was just relieved I hadn't had to walk back from Buster's plot of land.

From my window I could see Buster, Artie and BJ laughing and joking and playing around in McDonald's. It was a family's time together and I had no business there.

I was asleep in minutes anyway.

An early start saw me back on the Greyhounds. I was heading west to Indianapolis in search of Matthew Saad Muhammad's old rival Marvin Johnson, the man Vonzell had enjoyed that amateur tear-up with.

Marvin had been a three-time light-heavyweight champion, a southpaw warhorse.

You could tell you were in for a particularly long search if you googled a name and no recent stories came up. That only served to enhance the challenge, however.

I wanted to talk to the fighters time had forgotten.

There was something appealing about being able to dust off a lost warrior's legacy. I had heard on the boxing grapevine that Marvin was in some form of law enforcement but did not know where to start. It was only around three hours from Columbus and that time hurried by.

My need for food also dissipated with the arrival of a fresh challenge. I was approaching the 48-hour mark, a new record, and knew that the more I buried my head in my efforts the less I thought about feeling hungry.

I leafed through the phone directory at the Greyhound terminal and unsurprisingly there was more than one M Johnson.

There were about half a dozen and I tried them all. They unanimously said people had called looking for Marvin over the years and so I tried a fresh approach to the old trail.

I took to the city centre.

Using a scattergun approach, I asked people on the street if they knew where I could find the ex-fighter. Some did not know who he was while others knew but had no idea how to find him. There were, of course, plenty of blank expressions. I had tried around a dozen people in the first half-hour when I got a lead.

'Excuse me, sir,' I said, running after a guy wearing a baggy FUBU sweater and Sean John trousers. 'Do you know where I can find Marvin Johnson?'

'The fighter?' he asked.

'Yeah, the old fighter.'

'No, sorry man, last time I saw him he was doing a commercial for Chrysler on the TV.'

'The car company?' I said curiously.

'Yeah.'

That sounded odd. I had been certain he was involved in law enforcement in some way. Anyway, back at the bus station I got the number for the local Chrysler dealership and called.

A man named Larry picked up and I enquired if Marvin was there.

The reply was negative and he asked what my motives were. Within a minute or so, Larry – Marvin's cousin it turned out – had pointed me in the right direction.

He gave me the former champion's work number and explained that Johnson had promoted the cars in the city on local TV.

I quickly dialled and after several rings the handset clicked.
'This is Sergeant Marvin Johnson.'

Pause. Breathe. Speak.

'Marvin, it's Tris Dixon from…'

'If you'd like to leave a message, do so after the beep.'

OK, so he was not there. But I had his number and left a message.

His voice sounded gravelly and aggressive and there was a hint of a slur to his words.

A few more attempts throughout the day and Marvin was still not in. Or he wasn't picking up. Late afternoon came and went and I kept calling. Finally a colleague answered and gave me an out-of-work number.

I tried that, too, but to no avail.

Everyone I had spoken to said they would pass my messages on and I didn't doubt them. I'd understood Marvin was a churlish character and assumed he did not want to talk. I just would have rather heard it from him.

I scampered around the city trying to locate a cheap place to stay as the night closed in but was unable to find anywhere reasonably priced. Having stayed in a hotel the evening before I could not justify paying for accommodation for successive nights, particularly if I was going to be leaving empty-handed.

I conceded the interview with Marvin wouldn't happen.

I might have had some numbers for him but by now he would have had mine, having left it everywhere, and if he had wanted to contact me he would have.

It was close, a good effort. It had been worth a try but I got the feeling that reclusive Marvin Johnson just did not want to speak to anybody. Not just me.

Chapter 13

THE bus zigzagged through the Midwest and a time zone or two, travelling in and out of towns not even Americans knew existed and with little but vast expanses of nothingness on view.

I was always surprised, and a little horrified, to see some of the McDonald's locations. Sometimes they would be in the middle of nowhere with nothing else around for miles. So much for freedom of choice.

Sometimes there was choice but it was all crap; Taco Bell, Burger King, Wendy's. Boycotting fast food was the only option until there was a reasonable selection of alternatives available.

Fifteen hours on the bus drifted into 25 and the journey dragged on.

We spluttered more than 1,500 miles west as I considered making my new temporary home in Las Vegas or Los Angeles.

I had been through St Louis and seen the Arch. I had been through Kansas City and was turfed out for three-hour layovers in the middle of the night, something I loathed but was learning to endure and tolerate.

Just when I finally seemed to be in a deep sleep the bus would grind to a halt and we were told it was going to be serviced, or we had to change vehicles.

Cue some light, uncomfortable sleep on the floor of the station using my rucksack as a pillow, or no sleep at all.

One leg of the journey took me to Cheyenne in Wyoming and onwards to Utah. The 30-hour mark came and went as the bus driver announced we were approaching Salt Lake City.

Stir-craziness had started to kick in and I began thinking that the fighting Fullmer brothers, middleweights from the 1950s, lived around here.

Two nights had passed since I left Indianapolis having eaten a superb salad in a traditional diner. I was weary and famished once more.

I needed to wash and shave and as the bus pulled in during the early hours, I decided the West Coast could wait and I'd try to find the Fullmers, Gene, Don and Jay.

At 5am, there was plenty of time to search for an affordable place to stay. It was off-season as far as tourists were concerned, too; there was not a snowflake to be seen in the mountainous city. Still, I would only book a room if I could first find the brothers. Otherwise I would be back on the bus and Vegas or LA-bound.

Again I reached for the phone book.

Upon finding the Fs there was a large advert promoting a landscape business, run by the 'Fullmer Brothers'.

How many sets of Fullmer brothers could there be?

I'd hit the jackpot but was a little sad they were still working. They would have been 72, 66 and 64 respectively. Between them they had a combined boxing record of 129 wins, 31 losses and ten draws. Gene, an incredibly rough, uncompromising middleweight, was the only one who had won a world title but Don had challenged for the crown.

I waited for a respectable hour to call, using the time to explore the picturesque city and reflect on quite a week.

Less than seven days ago I had been in Philly with Harold, Jimmy and Marvis but it felt like a lifetime had passed.

I dialled the business number at 9am only to get voicemail but a further effort reaped rewards. The man who answered owned the firm, proudly telling me he and his brothers were nephews of the fighters. He happily gave me Gene's number, too, instructing me to ring later in the morning. Certain of success, I took a short walk to find a cheap motel and ducked into a reasonable Travelodge.

If I could interview more than one of the brothers I would deserve a two-night stay and I began hand-washing my clothes in the sink as soon as I checked in.

The deal included a free continental breakfast of a muffin and a coffee. It was comparative luxury.

Eventually I spoke to Gene's wife, Karen, and arranged the interview at their home in West Jordan, about a 20-minute local bus ride from the city centre.

Salt Lake City was sleeping. There was hardly anyone around and I was the only passenger on the bus. Maybe it was a Sunday thing. Karen had given me directions and, with a free map from the hotel, I followed them closely and found their home without problems.

I stepped off the bus about half a mile from where Gene lived in the Salt Lake suburb. Together, Gene and Karen opened the door and greeted me warmly. Karen looked much younger than Gene but they had been married 19 years and Gene, like his old rival Joey Giardello, was convalescing after major surgery.

As we took our seats in their front room, me on the sofa, Gene in an armchair facing me, and Karen in a chair to my right, Karen opened proceedings.

'He has a tremor from open heart surgery and after the surgery he had tiny cluster strokes. It's not Parkinson's or anything like that,' she said.

'So I wave at you a lot!' Gene smiled from across the room, his left hand shaking in my direction.

They had watched Lennox Lewis fight Vitali Klitschko the night before and asked if I had. I was on the bus but had seen the result on the Internet.

'Oh, he was so out of shape,' Karen said of Lennox.

Gene reckoned Lewis had found the six rounds so hard he wouldn't have managed another six had Klitschko – stopped due to gruesome cuts – been allowed to continue.

'It was entertaining but it was not a good fight,' said Gene, who knew a thing or two about crowd-pleasing brawls.

'I started boxing when I was 12,' Gene began. 'My dad was nicknamed "Tuff" because that's what he was, tough.'

'He had been in a number of boxing matches and fights. My mother named me Gene after Gene Tunney, so I didn't have much choice with a dad named Tuff and being named after Gene Tunney. I had to be a fighter.'

Gene, like a lot of American kids who grew up post-Depression and pre-World War II, was inspired by listening to Joe Louis's fights on the wireless.

He ran every morning, worked in a copper factory, Kennycotts, as a welder all day and went to the gym in the evening.

He fought around 80 times as an amateur but switched to the professional ranks, aged 20, once he 'got tired of fighting for nothing' and 'as soon as I figured I could make a little money'.

Gene was a warrior. Nearly half a century had passed since he upset the great Sugar Ray Robinson and now he talked slowly and did not recall his fights in the same detail he once could.

His road to the top was never going to be straightforward, being stuck out in Utah when much of the action of the day took place in New York and Philadelphia. His first purse, of five bucks, was another reminder of how long the road ahead was. But living in comparative isolation was, to a degree, in his favour.

He was a big draw in Utah.

His power pulled in the fans and he won his opening 11 fights early, stopping six of his first eight foes inside three minutes.

'I didn't have to get hit,' Gene explained. 'I didn't have to get hurt and the judges didn't have to get involved.'

All of that would come later. But as a novice pro his innocence was unblemished by the muddy game.

'Whenever you do something you want to be the best and I wanted to be the best boxer,' he said.

Nervous for all of his amateur fights, as soon as he and his brothers punched for wages the only contests he was scared before were those that involved Don and Jay. Following 17 consecutive wins, and a few heftier paydays, he was drafted into the US military while the Korean War raged.

He became a decorated sergeant, fighting for nearly two years in Korea and Japan. Gene returned a war hero but the humble country boy went straight back to boxing and working long shifts in the copper factory.

Good wins over Germany's Peter Mueller and future middleweight champion Paul Pender followed. Gene said Pender 'wasn't too tough to fight'. Pender later claimed he fought much of the bout with two broken hands.

In 1955, after Gene had amassed 29 wins, experienced Philadelphian Gil Turner captured his undefeated record in New York only for Fullmer to reverse the verdict in a return in West Jordan, Utah, two months later.

'Turner was tough but I wasn't feeling very good. I had flu or something,' Gene reasoned. 'I tried to fight him, it just turned out I couldn't do it that night. After I got better I fought him again and beat him twice.'

Victories over Del Flanagan and Al Andrews were followed by losses to Bobby Boyd and Eduardo Lasse. Rugged Fullmer was dropped in both, too.

'Against Bobby Boyd, Tony Zale was refereeing and he called a slip a knockdown but it was only a slip,' Gene contended.

After tight split decision wins over my old friend Castellani and Turner again, he stepped in with the first of two Tigers.

Ralph 'Tiger' Jones was a Brooklyn hardnut but Gene cracked him, too.

'You didn't have to worry about where he was in the ring,' Fullmer smiled, 'because he would be right after you.'

'What did you think of Castellani?'

'I can't hardly remember him,' Gene shrugged, apologetically.

Two wins later, and boasting a haul of 27 wins and three losses, he had earned a shot at Sugar Ray's middleweight title.

Fullmer's record was good, there's no doubting that, but his opponent in January 1957 had won 139 fights, lost just four and drawn two. There was no shortage of stars on his daunting ledger, either.

Even though he was an underdog, Gene just wanted a shot. 'I'd have fought him for nothing,' he said, with some devil in his eye.

Gene raised his shaky arm and pointed to a framed picture of a Mormon priest hanging on the wall near where he sat. 'We had a word of prayer before the fight. I fought Robinson for 15 rounds for the championship of the world and didn't get any cuts or bruises.

'After that, my manager wanted to keep the priest on to say a prayer every time.'

He won in front of nearly 20,000 fans in New York's Madison Square Garden, unanimously on all three cards 8–5, 9–6 and 10–5.

During the fight, Gene was even heard asking his manager Marv Jensen, 'Can I open up now?'

Jensen simply yelled, 'Keep doing what you're doin'.'

It was a winning formula.

According to *Boxing News*, he shook Robinson in the sixth, eighth and 14th and received the ultimate accolade after the fight when even Sugar conceded, 'I guess the better man won.'

'I put more pressure on him than anyone else did and I didn't let him get at me as much as everyone else had done,' Gene reflected. 'If you don't keep after him he's going to be getting to you.'

Later in the year Ray did get to him.

There was a rematch clause and poor Gene was nailed by what has since been described as 'The Perfect Punch'.

'I guess you thought he had a pretty good left hook?' I smiled.

'No fooling,' he winked back. 'That left hook, *The Ring* did a story a few years ago for the best of this and the best of that and they said the best left hook ever thrown was by Robinson, and I caught it!

'They were going to give Robinson the award but he had passed on so they gave it to me.'

'How did it feel?'

'I don't know. I didn't feel it. When I came to I said to my manager, "How come Robinson is doing exercises in between rounds?"

'He said, "What do you mean?"

'I said, "He's jumping up and down in his corner."

'He said, "He's celebrating. They counted ten over you."

'I said, "Boy, I never heard any of it."'

We laughed.

Time and a good life had relaxed Gene.

Keeping it light-hearted, he joked, 'I wish I had never fought Robinson the second time.'

'You do, too,' Karen argued playfully.

'No I wouldn't,' Gene protested. 'Not if I'd known he was going to knock me out.'

'He's asking serious questions,' Karen said, telling him off. 'You never turned anyone down,' she went on, having the last word.

Gene ducked as many fighters as he did punches. Not many.

He fought everyone the same way, head on, and had a bruising, combative style that brought pain and suffering to everyone across the ring from him. Fighters told of finishing bouts with him with welts all over their arms, on their shoulders, around their ribs and stomachs, not to mention their faces. He was Henry Armstrong reincarnated only more crude, a violent windmill that would swing until there was nothing left to hit in front of him.

After losing to Robinson, he returned to winning ways against 'Tiger' Jones again, Chico Vejar, Joe Miceli and Wilf Greaves.

In 1959 he was matched with Carmen Basilio in San Francisco at Cow Palace, the Madison Square Garden of the West Coast, in what would turn out to be the Fight of the Year.

He had left Kennycotts because unbelievably they would not allow him time off work to prepare for a fight between two of the game's hardest brawlers, even though it was for the NBA world title.

A wild fight was forecast and they did not disappoint.

Fullmer halted the upstate New York onion farmer in the 14th of a vicious slugfest. He was ahead on all the cards at the time of the stoppage and the smaller Basilio, a former welterweight, was getting battered.

'Carmen wasn't all that I thought he was going to be,' Gene offered softly.

'He was not that awesome. He was a good level at his weight and I was a good level at my weight, middleweight. There was only a couple of pounds difference when we weighed in but I'd have to go down in weight and he had to build up so he was not nearly as strong as I thought he might be. The first time we fought I decided not to pressure him but let him come after me and counter.'

I had talked to Basilio several times at the Hall of Fame in Canastota and I always remembered him saying, 'Everything Fullmer did was wrong but it was right.'

He was also aggrieved that he was stopped in the final round with two and a half minutes remaining. 'They let me take a beating for 14 rounds and then they don't let me hear the final bell. I don't know what was wrong with them!'

Gene then defeated the wonderfully named and incredibly tough Spider Webb.

'He was a good boxer and tough. As a matter of fact, in the fight I said to my manager, "I think I'm sick. I think I'm getting the flu."

'He said, "You're sick because he's beating the hell out of you."

'I said, "Well, I never thought about it like that."

'So I beat him for the last six rounds and I never had the flu.'

Still, Gene's good run was broken by a controversial draw with another of my old chums, Joey Giardello.

Just a few months ago I'd snacked on cake and coffee with Joey in suburban New Jersey. Now, after travelling several thousand miles I was on the other side of the United States in mountainous Utah with his rival.

I remembered how Joey fumed, 'He butted me,' when I asked about the Fullmer fight.

It was only right to ask Gene the same question.

'He butted me,' Fullmer barked back just as vociferously.

And Gene was angry.

He stood boldly, walked forcefully over to me and grabbed me stiffly by the arm, pulling me out of my chair.

'He deliberately butted heads with me,' Gene went on.

He yanked me close by my forearms so his nose was almost touching mine, his eyes narrowed with a cold glint.

'Boom,' he shouted as he got on to his toes and motioned a headbutt towards my forehead.

'He ripped my head up,' Gene said, without a trace of humour. 'I started bleeding, yet the referee got on to me and said if I didn't stop butting heads he was going to stop the fight. I didn't headbutt him.'

He turned round calmly enough and shuffled back to his armchair. 'I've got a film of it showing exactly what happened. I did not butt him. He butted me,' he muttered.

'I asked him afterwards, "How come you butted heads with me?" He said he wanted to win.

'I said to him, "No fooling. Everybody wants to win."'

Despite the controversy there was no rematch and the feud simmered more than 40 years on.

Their fight was in Bozeman, Montana. Giardello maintained he was robbed because it was in Gene's territory.

You can see as much on the grainy black and white images on film when Joey's cornermen hoist him on their shoulders in celebration only for them to hear the verdict and realise Gene had retained the crown. Their angry disappointment was not well disguised.

Fullmer defended against Basilio again and this time needed 12 rounds to dispose of the violent upstate New Yorker.

He was sure the naturally smaller man could hurt him, 'So I figured I would put a little more pressure on him,' he said.

The *New York Times* wrote, 'When the referee intervened Basilio screamed, "What do you mean? What are you talking about?" Then, cocking his fist, he said to the referee, "I'll give you one." Two policemen entered the ring and led Basilio to his corner still protesting.'

Modest Gene, who was always slow to self-praise but quick to point out the positives in others, Giardello aside, insisted he had never been asked to take a dive because he was always the underdog for his big fights.

He had a score to settle with Robinson going into their third contest nearly four years after they had fought for the first time.

It ended a draw in a contest that was difficult to score. Ray won on one card 11–4, Gene took it on another 9–5 and a third judge had them level with 8–8. There had to be a fourth meeting and it happened in Vegas in March 1961.

'That one was the easiest of them all,' Gene reminisced.

'I wouldn't necessarily call Sugar Ray the best ever, but then again, no one else knocked me out.'

His next fight was against another tremendous puncher, Florentino Fernandez. Fullmer said the Cuban émigré, who made his home in Florida, broke his right elbow with a left hook, thus forcing him to box the final rounds with a broken arm.

The world then saw Gene at his most destructive. He walked through the best punches of the normally spiteful Benny 'Kid' Paret and clobbered the Cuban with brutal barrages in a gruelling, incessant attack that saw Paret floored three times and ultimately bludgeoned to defeat in the tenth.

It still saddened Gene today that Paret was not withdrawn earlier.

'I beat him worse than I ever beat anybody in my life,' he said, sadness filtering into the room for the first time. 'It was terrible. It was so crazy why they let him fight Emile Griffith so shortly after I beat him because I beat him so bad. I knocked him down three times and he should never, ever, have been allowed back so soon.'

'I can't watch it,' Karen said, her eyes watering.

Three months later, 25-year-old Paret was hammered into a premature grave by Griffith. Many believed the Fullmer beating contributed to his demise.

Paret was dead the next time Gene stepped through the ropes and whether he hit a natural decline after so many hard fights or his role in Paret's death scarred him was something he couldn't answer.

He dropped a wide decision to Nigerian Dick Tiger at the end of 1962. Gene started 1963 by drawing a rematch and then lost a third fight to the African, in Nigeria, in his last outing as a pro.

Manager Jensen asked officials to stop the bout after the seventh.

'We took the fight in Nigeria as they offered more money than anywhere else. Like today, everything was money, money, money,' Gene sighed.

'Tiger was a tough fighter, I had a bad eye and the referee said he was going to stop the fight. I told Marv, "I can't whup him with two eyes, let alone one."'

Around 15 months after the Paret tragedy, Gene pulled the plug on his own career and started helping on Marv's mink farm. He worked there happily until he retired.

Karen was called away from the house, leaving Gene and I to talk.

He was now the president of the Rocky Mountain Golden Gloves Club and had been training fighters at a newly renovated gym by the fire station.

'It's a good gym. We don't charge. Anyone that wants to come can.

'We can look downstairs if you want?' Gene smiled, pointing to the wooden staircase.

'Sure,' I agreed, curiously.

It was an Aladdin's cave.

There were framed pictures, gloves from his fights, championship belts, fight robes and newspaper cuttings.

The sparkly cabinets were filled with memorabilia and decorations for his service in the Korean War.

'This is unbelievable,' I said, in awe.

Gene talked more as we delved through his possessions.

He showed me a picture of his first wife, Delores, who died of a heart attack more than 20 years before. They had two boys, two girls and 11 grandchildren.

'How do you keep track of them all?'

'My wife keeps track of them,' he smiled.

'Is Marv still around?'

'Yeah, he lives just down the lane. He is 86 but his mind is fine.'

'How about Jay?'

'He lives two doors from me.'

'And Don?'

'He's next door.'

'What, now?' I asked, angling for another interview.

'He's out today but he will be back tomorrow.'

'Do you think he will talk to me?'

'Sure he will. I will put in a good word for you,' he grinned pleasantly, holding my right arm.

His fascinating collection kept me mesmerised for a while. It was a tender moment; like a grandfather modestly showing a grandchild his accomplishments.

The centrepiece was his championship belt.

He earned it, it was etched on the gold, by beating the great Sugar Ray Robinson.

It didn't get any better than that.

How surreal that this boy from the New Forest was now in Salt Lake City with a middleweight hero.

What a weird and wonderful world I was living in.

Gene had owned this house for more than 40 years and it said a lot about him. He was not flashy and he was not a braggart. He was still a down-to-earth country boy.

'So what do you do now?' I asked of his spare time.

'Chase the wife,' he laughed.

'Do you come down here and reminisce?'

'Not very often.'

'What do you think when you look at all of this?' I said, searching around the room.

'That I've been pretty lucky in my life.'

When Karen returned she insisted Gene took us out for dinner and we went to an Italian restaurant near the bus stop. We spoke about their family and when I called Don later that evening he sounded sprightlier than Gene had. He was eager to chat and early the following morning I demolished the complimentary continental breakfast, filling my boots and my bag with muffins and pastries.

I took the same bus ride as the previous day. Again, I was the only person on the bus with the exception of the driver. It was the same guy as before, too, and he knew where I was heading.

I strolled beyond Gene's house and knocked on the door before Don and his wife, Nedra, welcomed me inside.

Don was in better shape than his older brother. He looked well and his handshake was firmer, but Gene did have eight years on him.

And Gene had more hair. Don was bald up top with white tufts around the back and sides.

Nedra went out to shop, leaving us to talk.

'My memory's not what it was so you might have to excuse me,' he began.

'No problem, that's fine.'

'How's Terry Downes?' he asked, enquiring of his former rival from London as we took our seats in his lounge.

I told him Terry had been in poor health but was OK last time I heard.

'He was a tough guy,' said Don. 'I thought maybe I should have had him but that's the way it goes when you go over there and fight someone in their hometown. Terry was a tough kid. What's he doing now?'

Don carried on before I could answer.

'I had a great time in London and met some great people. Some Mormons who were on a Mission from here in Salt Lake were working my corner over there.'

Then, Don immediately changed tack.

'I was probably only about six when I started fighting. It was so long ago I don't remember.'

He, like Gene, told me about his father's reputation.

'We were from a rough, tough mining town and he was a pretty rough and tough kid and he battled all the time,' Don added.

'First Gene got started, then it was my brother Jay who was a few years older than me. Then I started.'

Knowing Gene had been named after Tunney, I asked who Don had picked up his name from.

'My middle name is Rulon, after one of my parents' buddies,' he laughed, with red appearing in his cheeks, 'but I never use it. I will only say Don R.'

After winning all of his 60-or-so amateur fights and following regular sparring sessions with Gene and Jay in which they 'banged on each other pretty good', he turned pro hoping to win the middleweight title.

'Of course, that was my goal,' he explained. 'I fell short just a little bit but I won the American middleweight title and I actually fought more world champions than Gene did. I think I fought eight world champions and beat four of them.'

Some of the best he faced included Jimmy Ellis, Emile Griffith, Joey Archer and Billy Douglas.

One man Don particularly wanted to beat was Dick Tiger, not least because he boxed the African shortly after he had sent his big brother into retirement.

'I should have beaten Tiger,' lamented Don. 'I think I had too much respect for Dick. He was a tough kid but I think I could have beaten him. I should have gone in there and banged a little more. I'd love to have beaten him for my brother. Yeah, Gene would have liked that.'

As it was, Don did well to complete the full ten rounds with Tiger despite only coming in at a week's notice for Rocky Rivero.

The biggest night of his boxing life was against suave Italian maestro Nino Benvenuti, travelling to Italy for his only shot at world title glory.

In 1966 Don lost to Benvenuti for the first time in a 12-round tussle. The Italian needed 26 stitches to close wounds caused, for the most part, by Don's head.

Fullmer was certain he could exact revenge when they met two years later, becoming a champ like his big brother.

'Going over there was the only way to get him because he wouldn't have done it over here, I guess,' Don contemplated.

'The first time, I thought I beat him in Rome and when I fought him for the title the day I left to go to Italy I caught Hong Kong flu. Are you too young to remember Hong Kong flu? You probably are.

'Well, there was a strain of the Hong Kong flu and I got it and my kids got it. I had been in the best shape I had been in my whole life and at midnight, the night before we were ready to leave, I started getting stomach cramps and had to get up and go to an all-night drugstore.

'We were going to go to San Remo the next morning. When I woke up, I was supposed to meet my manager and I was drained.

'I had 12 days to get ready over there and I thought I'd be all right, because I hadn't been throwing up. If I had been sick I would have postponed it but we went over there and I was in bed for the first two or three days. Everyone was going crazy, saying, "What's the matter with Fullmer?"

'My manager would say, "Well, you know the jet lag and the time change…"'

'I should have known the first day I went in the gym and sparred with some kid that I really didn't have it. But I had waited 11 years for a shot and I didn't want it to pass me by.

'I somehow managed to go 15 rounds but after the first round I just knew. I've lived that fight 35 years ago over in my head a thousand times, over and over again. I remember it punch for punch and it drives me crazy. I remember when I came back to my corner after the first I said, "We're in for a long night."

'I thought, "Oh man, 14 more." It felt like I had done 15 rounds already. I was just counting them down, "I've got 12 more, I've got ten more rounds."

'In the seventh I hit him with a right hand and knocked him down and should have finished him. He was hurt but I didn't realise and he got up. I was so tired I don't think I realised how tired he really was. I let him off the hook. If I'd went in there and tried to bang with him I'm sure I could have knocked him out. I've got the film and I look at it every once in a while and it makes me sick,' Don smiled regretfully.

'There's no doubt in my mind I could have knocked him out. He was a tough kid but he never hurt me.

'In my career I definitely see a few things I would have liked to have done differently and beating Benvenuti would have been one of them. I go to bed now and every night when I run that fight through my head it still drives me crazy.

'But really,' he paused, closing his eyes and momentarily leaving the room to recall his boxing pomp, 'I've got no regrets. I would have liked to be the champion, like Gene, but I had a good career and a good life. I've got a great family now. I'm not the richest man in the world but I feel like I am because of what I have that counts. I've got a wife I love and a great family. I've been married for 47 years.

'You don't get good women like this all the time,' and he pointed to a picture of him with Nedra.

'So I hope I've got another 47 years with her. I'm doing good for an old so and so. I used to run at 5am, worked as a bricklayer by day and was in the gym every night.'

We walked out to his front garden to enjoy the warmth.

'I used to run down this road. It wasn't like it is now. It used to be gravel. Some of my first pro fights were in a gym that is no longer still standing right around the corner from this house. My first TV fight was in there.'

Eventually Fullmer's breaking body told him it was time to stop fighting.

'I had a floating rib back here,' he said, pointing above his stomach. 'Every once in a while someone would tap it and it felt like I had a broken rib. Oh man. If I took a deep breath it would feel like someone was stabbing me with a knife. I also had a bad hand. I'd broken that a couple of times and just thought, "It's time to get out of here." I had too many things going haywire.'

He'd had 79 fights spanning 13 years, retiring with 54 wins, 20 defeats and five draws.

Behind his home, Don's land included wonderfully manicured gardens and mown-to-perfection lawns, tended to by the Fullmer Brothers Inc.

There was an outbuilding in the back garden where the Fullmer family lived all those years ago and behind that were fields, where Gene kept racehorses in retirement.

We went back inside and Don offered to show me his memorabilia. His was the same style house as Gene's, a bungalow with a basement, and we walked downstairs. His collection was not quite as sparkly as Gene's but equally detailed. He showed me the gloves that had retired Carl 'Bobo' Olson and we carefully leafed through his scrapbook.

I saw the big names of all his opponents in headlines. Some he had beaten, some he had not.

'Of all these guys,' I asked, 'who was the toughest?'

He thought back and paused momentarily.

'You'll be surprised by this,' he said, edging closer to me.

'The toughest one was Eugene "Honey Bear" Bryant and I fought him twice. I beat the hell out of him every round, or at least I thought I beat him up every round, but he was one of those kids that was just so tough. His style and mine made for a tough fight. I don't think he was rated or anything like that. He was just so tough.'

In Don's basement there were plaques and pictures paying tribute to his active life after boxing, working for the Salt Lake City Fire Department.

He had recently retired.

'I loved it,' he smiled, lifting a comparatively-recently framed picture of him wearing a smart suit with medals and commendations on his chest.

'I put 26 years in and it was a whole lot different from fighting in the ring but it was still a great job. You'd get an adrenaline rush every time the bell went off. It's about the same thing as the bell going off in the ring, you get the same rush. You really do.'

When Nedra returned Don volunteered to take me to the bus stop. I declined and started walking, eventually waiting where I'd said goodbye to Gene and Karen 24 hours earlier.

As I waited I heard a loud horn beeping and looked up.

'We forgot to give you these,' Don shouted, pulling up in a shiny new pick-up truck and waving a carrier bag.

'Thanks,' I said, accepting it.

He drove past quickly, turned round in the road and headed for home.

It was an enormous bag of freshly picked cherries from the Fullmer garden.

Chapter 14

THE moon lit the desert road and the bright stars guided us to Las Vegas. There is not a lot to see on the road between the mountains of Salt Lake City and its sinful counterpart. I'd left Utah after saying farewell to Don, embarking on another overnight journey which was made easier by a cherry consumption that alleviated the commonplace hunger. It meant I could at least nap on a full stomach.

I slept quite well, too. It wasn't particularly busy and it always helped when I had a seat to myself. I was at home with this sleeping-on-a-bus lark and, in an odd sort of way, was even starting to get a kick out of it. The same went with hunger.

Whenever I ate, and filled up, I missed the hunger pangs.

I was becoming some sort of travelling junkie, getting weird highs from sleep and food deprivation. Not only could I handle them, I looked forward to them.

I was getting addicted.

It even felt a bit of a let-down that the 500-mile journey from Salt Lake City to Las Vegas lasted only one night.

By 4.30am I was wide awake, though, wondering how I would figure out who was where on my first visit to modern boxing's mecca. The casino neons sparkled in the long distance, projecting light into an increasingly pale blue sky.

Salt Lake City had been warm but by no means hot. Although it was so early, the Vegas heat bit as soon as I stepped off the bus.

I trekked from the Greyhound terminal in downtown Las Vegas to the Stardust hotel and casino on the Strip, a humid and heavy 45 minutes, and went to check-in.

'Are you here for tonight or tomorrow?' the robust-looking receptionist asked. She stared at the clock that still told me it was before 7am. She didn't say it nicely either. She snapped.

'I have two nights booked from today,' I meekly replied.

She pulled my name up on the system and said I had probably arrived earlier than anyone in the history of the hotel for their 2pm check-in.

I could not wait to get rid of my bag to explore and I did not want to take it everywhere with me.

After compassionately pleading with the beast from behind the marble-topped counter she relented and said I could check in as soon as the current occupants of my future room had checked out, providing it had been cleaned.

I offered to clean it to hurry things up and her look of disgust somehow made her even angrier than before.

While some aspects, particularly the free fountain show at the Bellagio – that kept me entranced for at least three songs – were impressive, I was not there for a holiday. The best Vegas had to offer may have looked nice, shiny and enticing, with the exception of the low-rent hookers and immigrants distributing leaflets and calling cards on every street corner, but I was here to work.

I was more than 3,000 miles from where I started and had the same distance to cover by bus to get back for my return flight to the UK in a few days.

Leafing through a business directory, I looked up boxing gyms and the most famous I caught sight of was Johnny Tocco's, promptly aiming north in its direction.

Murals featuring Salvador Sanchez, Muhammad Ali and Rocky Marciano were painted on the bright white walls outside.

Fighters were already training and sparring and I watched closely and quietly.

The first trainer I saw appeared to have seen a few wars. He nodded and walked over. He had brown, leathery skin, white hair, scar tissue around his eyes, a flat nose and thick ears. I could tell by the way he walked he had been a fighter.

I did not know who he was and did not wish to cause either of us any embarrassment by asking him. He asked where I had come from.

'I have just been to see Gene and Don Fullmer in Salt Lake City.'

'Don Fullmer,' he keenly exclaimed, eyes lighting up. 'I fought him,' he smiled, 'but you wouldn't have heard of me.'

'Try me,' I encouraged him, thinking I was familiar with the present subject.

'My name's Eugene Bryant, but folks called me the "Honey Bear".'

'Holy shit,' I slipped, instantly apologising.

'I was just talking about you last night. Don told me you were the toughest guy he fought.'

'Is that right?'

'That's what he said,' I reiterated.

'We had two tough, tough fights,' he smiled, basking in proud recognition.

'Well, when you next see him tell him I said hello,' Honey Bear smiled, signing off and returning to supervise sparring.

After chatting with one of the top female fighters around, Layla McCarter, I headed back to the Stardust, checked my e-mails and Tom had come through for me again. He sent me the Las Vegas mailing address of 1950s middleweight contender Joey Giambra.

He was one of those superb fighters from the crop that had spawned Gene Fullmer, Giardello and Castellani, Sugar Ray Robinson and many more.

The only problem was he was not in the phonebook and there was no number to call him on.

He lived on West Flamingo Avenue, which was easy enough to find in itself as it was one of the main roads that branched off the Strip. All I had to do was keep going until I reached the number of Joey's house.

With little else to do, I started walking.

A few blocks in the heat in the desert pressure cooker was cranked up. It dawned on me that I could be spending as much as an hour walking. The scale of everything was enormous.

The odd bus drove by but I was keen to save every dime I could because I was spending money on accommodation. Besides, I had not been working out and these long walks provided my only real exercise.

There was long, however, and there was just plain stupid.

An hour turned into two and then some. It felt further than the Buster Douglas marathon. The rotating digital thermometers outside several stores told me the temperature was 110 and after each one I passed that number increased by a digit or two.

I was completely exposed. My forehead was burning. The line where there was some kind of parting in my hair was acting as a smouldering pink magnet for the rays. The bright blue sky offered no resistance and there was not even an excuse for a breeze.

As chunks of time ticked by, I became slightly crazed and thoughts of hunger, fatigue and tiredness started to hit me like an out-of-control steam train.

It seemed like the further I walked the further away I was going from the destination. Was I even going the right way anymore?

The numbers were going in the order they should have been. Surely it was merely a matter of persistence.

I started to speed walk the blocks, counting the time it took to pass them. I would try to beat the time from the previous one, counting under my breath.

But the novelty started to wear thin and the heat was sapping my concentration. Halfway through a block I would think of other things and lose my rhythm and the number. Speedy steps sometimes turned into a drunken stagger. Occasionally I veered off the pavement and into the road. I was soaked through with sweat. Breathing was difficult and when I looked behind me I no longer saw the recognisable buildings of Las Vegas Boulevard.

The wide carriageways of Flamingo Avenue shimmered brightly as though they were underwater.

I was in suburban Vegas, not that I knew such a place existed. I was closer to the desert than the casinos.

Traffic was sparse. The blocks were getting longer and the day hotter. I was hours into the mission and blisters bulged every which way in my shoes. They were so sore I did not even want to stop to look at them.

There was that horrible, nagging thought that I might have walked all this way for nothing and still have the return leg to endure as the day continued to get hotter. I resorted to something I didn't want to do, but an air-conditioned cab came crawling by and offered me the chance to ease my pain.

Mahan Washington was the driver and he asked what I was doing in Vegas. I told him I was looking for boxers.

'I used to fight professionally,' he said, proudly smiling in his rear-view mirror.

'Is everyone here a fighter?' I asked.

'This is the fight capital, baby. You're in the fight capital now.'

He was not much older than I but a retired 33-fight welterweight veteran. Roger Mayweather, uncle and trainer of Floyd Mayweather Jnr, was his coach.

After less than five minutes we pulled up alongside an expansive complex of modern condominiums. There must have been a hundred units in there.

Mahan let me out, saying he would stay on and wait to see if I had any luck finding Joey's place. Stupidly I told him not to bother and his car was quickly out of sight, leaving me with an intimidating set of gates to face and buzzers to press.

Giambra's address, however, was the block. It was not any one apartment in particular. There were dozens of doors. Perhaps hundreds.

I tried a few random buzzers by the secure gates but got no reply. It was the middle of the day and I suspected the residents were either bathing in a pool or taking lunch in an air-conditioned restaurant.

With little option, I approached the solid, pale yellow eight-foot high walls, tossed my bag to the other side and vaulted over the top.

I was expecting a security alarm to sound or, worse still, a pair of blood-thirsty Dobermans who fancied a healthy portion of roasted English writer. Looking like an awkward burglar, I tip-toed around, convinced CCTV cameras were tracking my every movement.

An elderly resident was loading up her car so I asked if she knew where Giambra lived. She asked how I had got into the compound so I explained my motives – without explaining how – and she pointed me in the right direction.

My stride adopted a fresh impetus knowing I was walking to Joey's apartment. It was purposeful, even forceful.

Now I just prayed he was in.

A couple of seconds after I knocked on the door it opened ajar and a man who appeared to be in his fifties peered through.

'Can I help you?' came a firm, husky voice.

The man had silky white hair but youth in his tone and his face.

'I'm looking for Joey Giambra,' I said.

'Senior or Junior?' he asked.

'Senior, I guess,' I mumbled, blankly.

'In that case you've found him,' he said.

'You're Mr Giambra, the fighter?'

'Yes,' he replied, smiling broadly. 'That's me. What did you think I would look like?'

As he opened the door further it became clear he was wearing nothing but a white towel around his waist.

His eyes carried an enthusiastic spark, his body was lean and he was in good shape for his vintage. The towel left little to the imagination but I looked as though I'd just finished a marathon so couldn't judge.

Time had been kinder to the 72-year-old than it had to his old rivals Fullmer, Castellani and Giardello.

'How did you get in here, into the complex?' he asked.

'I hurdled the fence.'

'Oh,' he said, nodding while looking at me closely. 'That's good. That's a high fence,' he continued, clearly approving.

He had been a rascal in his youth, too, he said.

I sat on his couch and he faced me from a comfortable-looking armchair. Having baked in the desert I was now in the firing line of America's coolest air-conditioning units. They were blasting so loudly we had to raise our voices to hear one another.

Goosebumps replaced sweat in moments and I was a little uneasy that he did not put on at least a T-shirt as he sat in a relaxed manner draped in just the towel. Still, I was given moral support by his flatmate, KO, a white English bull terrier who wanted to play with the guest.

Joey was keen for his life story to be turned into a motion picture, one that would be based on his autobiography *The Uncrowned Champion*, a title that reinforced the gist of his professional career.

When I told him I collected boxing books he quickly asked whether I had his.

'It's 20 bucks if you want a copy.'

'OK,' I agreed, thinking he would take my address and mail me one.

Instead he jumped to his feet, raced down the corridor and returned with the book, ready to pass it on to me after the transaction had been made. I coughed up and he signed it for me.

'Read it, I promise you you'll enjoy it,' he implored, as though there was not a minute to waste. 'We're negotiating a movie on it. Vegas, as you know because you are here, is the mecca of boxing. The screenplay is all finished and we're trying to get Jack Nicholson to play my manager, Mike Scanlon. Jack loves boxing but he's never done a boxing movie. I'm going to hopefully get him to direct because he wants to direct.

'I'll tell ya, the kid I'd like to play me is Colin Farrell, he can box. Did you see him hit the bag in *The Recruit*? He knows some moves and he's a good actor. *Phone Booth* showed his range.'

Joey's story started in Buffalo in upstate New York, near where my own American adventures had begun several years earlier. He was a good-looking lad when he turned pro, attracting the nickname 'The Buffalo Adonis'.

But his childhood was not as glamorous as his name suggested. He was beaten up by gangs and, aged 12, injured his neck trying to get away from them.

He collected Batman comics and one day, inspired by Bruce Wayne's alter ego, made a cape out of an old umbrella, stashing it in his pocket in the hope it might help him make good his escape.

He went to the second-hand shop, too, buying a pair of sneakers for 50 cents.

He ran from the boys in his 'new' old shoes, scaling a telegraph pole by its metal rungs. At the top, he reached for the makeshift cape, yelling heroically, 'Come and get me, villains.'

He sprung towards a nearby tree. He plummeted like a stone.

He landed in front of the boys, temple-first and motionless.

'A little Italian man who used to run a candy shop called my mother and the reason he wanted to help me was I was the only kid who never stole from his shop,' recalled Joey.

'My mother thought he was kidding. When she came she grabbed me by the hair and started dragging me. My brother was saying to her that I was hurt but my mother wasn't convinced. My sister finally said, "He's hurt, ma."

'They got me home, sat me at the table and my ma brought me food and when she came back into the room I said, "Who are you, lady?"

'I didn't know who she was. She still thought I was acting but my sister saw my eyes were dilated and called an ambulance.

'I was in hospital for 48 hours until I went back to normal.

'The doctor came back and said, "The good news is you're going to live. The bad news is you're going to have a bad back for the rest of your life."'

Joey pleaded with him to do something because the youngster was fanatical about sport. Sensing his heartbreak, the doctor advised him to try some boxing exercises to strengthen the damaged areas.

At the gym, he met boxers with a bully mentality who said, 'So you wanna be a fighter, kid?'

But he did not want to box, he just wanted his health back.

'I was scared and I certainly didn't want to fight,' he protested. 'I wanted to protect my face and didn't want to get hit because I was a pretty handsome kid.'

Eventually, he was made to spar with a bigger and better opponent who was jabbing young 'Billy', his birth name, at will.

'I got angry because I was being beaten up. It was like a trigger inside me so I went to the ropes, came back off them with a slingshot right hand that hit him on the jaw and knocked him out.'

He apologised to the guy as he gradually came round but something had fundamentally changed within Giambra.

He began asking people to call him Joey.

'It sounded more like a fighter's name,' he said. 'I know there was Billy Conn, he was a great fighter, but Joey was more of a fighter's name.'

Within a year he was travelling up to Toronto to fight as an amateur. Eight youngsters jammed into two cars and crossed the border.

'My first opponent was really ugly,' he recalled. 'He had cauliflower ears, scratches down his face, a broken nose and when I went to shake his hand he said, "I'm going to knock you out, punk."'

Joey, wearing those same 50 cent sneakers and just bathing trunks, was told by his trainer to throw a punch as soon as the snarling kid dropped his hands.

Just after the bell rang, Joey saw a chance and his opponent was on his back. The referee ordered Giambra to a neutral corner.

'Where's neutral?' Joey asked.

Regardless of where it was, he won and instead of getting the loser's purse of $5 he hit the big time with $35 and the choice of one of three gifts – a watch, a trophy or a coat with a hood.

'I wanted the trophy but it was cold so I chose the coat. It was a big thick Canadian coat, real warm.'

His mother thought he had robbed the money at first, but when she was able to buy a month's worth of groceries she encouraged him to get back in the ring.

He began making the bigger money upon turning pro in 1949, aged 18. He won 16 of his first 17 fights, drawing the other, while establishing himself as a firm favourite with the New York crowds.

The legendary Cus D'Amato helped train him along with Scanlon, the brains behind Team Giambra.

Unsurprisingly, Giambra got involved with Mob characters. If you were a good fighter on the East Coast at that time it was hard to avoid them.

He knocked about with known fighters who had underworld links, such as Willie Pep and Rocky Graziano, and he remembered Pep buying Rocky some hookers for the night after Rocky won a big fight at the Garden.

But Joey refused to have the Mob control his contract, no doubt influenced in part by D'Amato, the defiant and fiercely principled manager and trainer who wouldn't let his heavyweight champion Floyd Patterson fight contenders 'owned' by gangsters.

In October 1952, Giambra was manoeuvred into a bout with Giardello, the first of three encounters, and it left a bitter taste.

'It was my first ten-round fight and we were two of the first guys to use eight-ounce gloves because they used to use six ounces.

'He was 5–1 on to beat me and even money to knock me out but I didn't care because I could adapt to fight anyone. He was a good counter-puncher but I was faster and I was always in better shape than he was because he didn't like to train.

'After the fight, there was a lot of screaming because it was going to be a big upset and as my manager grabbed me to raise my hand the first judge scored the fight for Giardello. Then the second judge called it for him and the third judge called it for me.

'The two judges were Mob judges. Everyone was booing and screaming, "It's a fix. It's a fix."'

Giambra claimed the commission later found the scorecards had been tampered with. The crowd sympathised and the loser left to a standing ovation. A rematch was granted four weeks later, a foul-tempered affair in Buffalo.

Giambra was determined not to let the judges get involved and fought through the pain of an ugly gash to his mouth to win unanimously.

Joey was savouring the victory again now, in his Vegas apartment.

'The crowd went wild,' he chimed.

He should have had a shot at title holder Gene Fullmer as a reward but it never happened.

However, Giambra returned to beat Sugar Ray Robinson's stablemate and protégé Danny Womber on points before stopping the dangerous Bernard Docusen. Before long, Joey hit the top ten.

One of the bouts he liked to remember was his derby dust-up with Jimmy Herring, a good-looking and popular New Yorker who had fought all but five of his 70 fights in his home state and drew as many female fans to the fights as he did men.

'The old Garden held 14,000 but when I fought him there was standing room only and a crowd of 15,500. And it was all women.

'Frank Sinatra was there and the fight had been billed as the "Battle of the Beauties" because I was the "Buffalo Adonis" and he was a "Blonde Bombshell".'

Giambra knocked Herring out.

But as he closed on the title, Giambra's career stalled when he was called up to fight in the Korean War.

'I did my job for my country when my country called for me,' he said, puffing out his chest. 'When I was 17 I had joined the Naval Reserves and I did drills with them every week. In the summer we would do a two-week cruise but they drafted me into the Marines, which was illegal because I was already in the Navy.

'The Korean War was on and I was number one in the world and had bought a home for my mother and everything.'

While serving, he was picked on because of his good looks and celebrity status. It came to a bitter conclusion when a senior officer spat on a window Joey had just cleaned, ordering him to clean it again.

The officer was battered, Joey was severely reprimanded.

After three court martials to determine what had actually happened, the Marines decided to give him control of their boxing programme – apparently on request from some of

Giambra's powerful New York acquaintances – and things became easier.

The Marines would also allow him to fight on as a pro.

He went to San Francisco to box world champ Carl 'Bobo' Olson in a non-title affair, losing a close decision.

According to *Boxing News*, Giambra gave Bobo 'a tough time' and Olson said he would allow Giambra a rematch if he beat Ray Robinson. Determined, Joey went back in tough, beating Rocky Castellani, Gil Turner and England's Johnny Sullivan. Chico Vejar, Castellani again, Al Andrews and Rory Calhoun all fell to the 'Adonis'.

'When I fought Calhoun, and I thought I beat him decisively both times [he lost the first and won the second], the promoter was Jack Ruby. He was later famous for gunning down the man everyone thought killed JFK, Lee Harvey Oswald. He was a fantastic cook and he would make us steak every night. But he was a killer.'

Points defeats to the useful pair of Yama Bahama, from the Bahamas, and Argentine Farid Salim had him on the outside looking in but, at 31, he had enough to slash open Cuban puncher Florentino Fernandez for a cuts win. That turned out to be merely a swansong and a disappointing loss to Denny Moyer followed in a shot at the vacant WBA light-middleweight crown. It was Giambra's first world title contest after a long, 77-fight career.

'Sonny Liston was the referee and after the fight he said to me, "You won it, baby. You won it."'

But, in losing a split decision, Joey claims he was screwed over in Portland, Oregon – where Moyer was from – and back-to-back defeats to Luis Rodriguez and Joe DeNucci, as well as a horrific car smash, spelled the end.

Now here we were in Vegas and Giambra was looking to the future and hoping it would involve the silver screen.

I had heard a lot of big ideas in boxing that never reached fruition. That is as much a part of the sport as championship fights.

Joey could say proudly that during the course of 65 victories against ten losses and a couple of draws he was never stopped, but he reckoned he was his own worst enemy as far as not getting chances at the title during his prime years were concerned.

'I wasn't with the Mob, that's why I never had a chance,' he reckoned. 'I knew all the Mob guys and they respected me because they knew I wouldn't throw a fight and I was always in shape.'

In retirement he operated a taxi in Nevada and worked on his autobiography. I got the feeling he took his books everywhere to sell a few copies here and there.

He seemed happy with his lot. He lived with his son, Joey Jnr, a racing car driver who inherited his old man's good looks, his proud dad said.

When I told Joey I was going to walk back to the Strip and later visit some of the gyms he would not hear of it and insisted on driving me.

Concluding the *Basic Instinct*-style interview, he threw on a T-shirt and some shorts and within 20 minutes we were outside the Nevada Partners gym.

Who would be there, Joey could not say. How I would get back, I did not know. But I was a firm believer in the old adage that the harder you worked the more fortunate you became and I was rewarded as soon as I stepped inside.

Joey drove carefully away, leaving me briefly back in the boiling Las Vegas extremes. Inside I recognised someone instantly. Richard Steele was a good scrapper in his day but made his name as a referee after he hung his gloves up.

He was in his office when I intruded. There was a large internal window looking out over the gym and its two boxing rings. On the walls were pictures of Steele with fighters, actors and politicians. Many of them had been signed and, wearing an open-neck Hawaiian shirt and with his gold teeth sparkling, he told me his story.

Steele was brought up in LA, joined the US Marine Corps when he was a youngster and only started boxing because he 'was too little to play football'.

'I broke my arm and I broke my leg, the damage was too bad for me and I was too slow,' he said. 'So my buddy in the Marine Corps said, "Why don't you go and try boxing where you can compete against people your own size?"'

And that was how the middleweight laced on gloves for the first time.

'I did good as an amateur,' he nodded, proudly assessing his 16–4 record in the unpaid code. 'I went to the Olympic trials in

1964. I didn't make the team but I got the experience and I turned professional, boxed for seven years and did pretty good.'

We spoke about the high-profile fights he'd officiated, such as Marvin Hagler's three-round war with Tommy Hearns, and the controversial bout in which he stopped Meldrick Taylor during the final seconds against Julio Cesar Chavez.

Steele had built this gym eight years before I visited and said it was being used by mostly 'local guys'.

'Right now we don't have any big names. But when a lot of fighters come to fight in Vegas they come here. It's also a recreation gym with more than a hundred kids that come after 3pm and work out. We take good care of them, make sure they do good in school and put them on educational programmes, life skill programmes, and we can help them become better citizens.'

'Who is that wearing the Bruno–Tyson T-shirt?' I asked, looking at a greying, ageing figure calling instructions to fighters inside the ring. I recognised his face but could not put a name to it. From the way he walked and snarled at the boxers it was apparent he was an ex-fighter.

'That's Hedgemon Lewis, he was a great welterweight.'

Steele let me use his room to interview Lewis, too.

Hedgemon had lived in Vegas for 20 years and said he came for one reason.

'I moved here because Eddie Futch was living here,' he said, swapping seats with Steele. 'I had a very good relationship with him. He trained me and trained my trainer. He was a father figure, that's what he was.

'The guy who started me off was Luther Burgess of Detroit and Eddie had been training him since he was eight or nine years old. Boxing wasn't happening too much in Detroit at the time so he called Eddie to take a look at me and he liked what he saw and he came and got me.

'I went to a recreation centre in Detroit for swimming and got there late. I was 11 or 12 and me and my friends would have nothing better to do than turn over trash cans and act like fools.

'The man who was taking the swimming lessons ran out and said, "Get your asses upstairs if you want to do that tearing up stuff. Go up there and work out. Ask for a guy called Duke Ellis."

'Duke Ellis was damn near 90 but he had trained Joe Louis.'

Hedgemon pounded on the speed bag, working alongside other fighters, enjoying every minute.

'A few months later we had a little tournament,' he continued. 'I was about 12, weighed 105lb and I boxed for the Northern Recreation Centre. I won my first few and my first loss was against someone from the Kronk, where Emanuel Steward was from, and I lost a fight to him in the amateurs.

'I was a pretty outstanding amateur. I had a lot of fights, 80 or so, but I lost in the Olympic trials to a boy named Charles Ellis, Jimmy Ellis's brother, and that was really the end of my amateur career.

'But let me say this, I won the nationals in 1964 and got to the Olympic trials but I kept on winning.'

After capturing national AAU titles in '65 and '66 he opted to join the paid ranks.

'I had heard Eddie's name all over boxing, all over Detroit and he was there on the West Coast. He told me he had brought a lot of fighters out from Detroit but nobody had stayed. I was one of the first that went and stayed.

'I would go back home from time to time. I was flying to and from Detroit and I came to LA for my ninth fight and Eddie had talked to a guy that worked for Jay Sebring. He was a barber for Hollywood clients and had a relationship with Sharon Tate, do you remember her? [Sebring and Tate were murdered by the Manson family.] He cut everybody's hair who was anybody in Hollywood.

'A guy who worked for him, Dale Jackson, put together a corporation called Fighters Incorporated. It was owned by Bill Cosby, Robert Goulet and a couple of other guys. They brought me out and saw me fight in my ninth fight and I scored a knockout in the third round [over Phil Garcia].'

Ironically, Richard Steele fought on the undercard at the Olympic Auditorium in LA.

'They were impressed,' Hedgemon continued. 'They wanted me to move to Los Angeles. I was a boy so it was kinda difficult. I wasn't ready to leave my mother. I was her only son. So I would go to LA and keep coming back. It took me a year to move over properly, but I had made the decision with Eddie.

'Eddie told me, "If you can just stay in town you can make something of yourself," and it was late '67 or early '68 when I finally decided.'

He racked up a 22-fight winning streak without having to work during the day.

In 1968 he was matched for the first time with Ernie 'Indian Red' Lopez.

'It was a pretty big fight at the time,' Lewis remembered. 'He was tough, strong and could take a shot. He beat me twice, I beat him once and I scored the only knockdown of the three fights. But I got stopped twice and I beat him once on points.

'He was probably one of the toughest guys I faced. He was one of the biggest punchers and another was Jose Napoles. He was one of the best. He beat me twice but I thought I beat him the first time. I was not impressed with Carlos Palamino. We fought a draw. I thought I beat him. It was near the end of my career and he was a favourite there in LA where we fought but I was hometown, too, back then.'

'How about John H Stracey?' I asked.

He smiled, acknowledging my English links.

'Stracey, it's more a blur now. He was a tough fighter but I wasn't impressed.'

I asked him what he would say to Stracey if he met his former rival today.

He pondered an answer and smiled.

'Congratulations John, you won the fight. Let's do a rematch!'

Stracey was his last contest. Lewis won 53 times, losing seven and drawing three in a decade.

Hedgemon retired because of a promise to his mother to quit at the age of 30, which he was when he met Stracey.

The main thing, Lewis said, was that he regretted nothing, especially because his purses allowed him to pay for his sister to go through college. She became a teacher.

'I can't complain,' smiled Hedgemon, looking tired and worn. 'It's been a good life.'

Chapter 15

THERE was enthusiasm in the old man's eyes as we spoke of his contemporaries. He wanted to know what Saad Muhammad, Dwight Qawi and Vonzell Johnson had said about him. He wanted to know what they were doing. He took immense pleasure asking me about an era he partly ruled.

Now there was more hair on Eddie Mustafa Muhammad's chin than there was on his head and he had become one of the sport's leading trainers.

We went to the front of the gym, away from the hustle and bustle of the increasingly busy gym floor. Steele returned to his office, Lewis to his fighters.

Eddie, the Brooklyn, New York, warrior, was now bigger, balder and softer than his fighting days of the late seventies and early eighties.

In retirement, he moved to Vegas and said his decision to quit the ring, aged 36, was triggered by his first loss inside the distance.

As we sat on benches in the compact and bland entrance hall, Eddie remembered, 'I always said to myself that if I ever got stopped, no matter if it was my first fight or my last fight, no matter what the circumstances were, I was going to retire.'

Like many, he was initially attracted to the sport so he could say he had done something for himself, without anybody else's help.

'Boxing is an individual thing,' he stated. 'I'm not a guy that needs to have a team to achieve. I'm a one-on-one individual and if I set my mind to it I know I can do it.'

He fought more than a hundred times as an amateur and was an alternate on the 1972 Olympic squad.

'I thought I was jobbed out of making the Olympic team,' he recalled. 'I fought Jesse Burnett who made the team. I knocked him down and beat him fair and square but I lost a decision. Millions of people saw it on TV and thought I won.'

As a pro, he came through with the likes of Saad Muhammad, Marvin Johnson, John Conteh and Victor Galindez but he learned his trade as a Brooklyn-born fighter who commuted to Philadelphia to beat the toughest available opponents, including local hardmen Bennie Briscoe and Eugene 'Cyclone' Hart.

'It was great I came up in that era,' he said, excitedly. 'It showed the world that I was a force to be reckoned with. I beat Saad Muhammad [in Philadelphia]. I beat Galindez over in Italy fair and square but they gave it to him. I beat a lot of those guys where I would go to their hometowns and it didn't matter what you did to them you couldn't win. In reality I thought I only lost about one fight in my career.'

His record was 50 wins, eight losses and a draw. He boxed as a pro for 16 years.

I asked why he took so many chances by going to Philly to beat Briscoe on a split decision and why he went anywhere near knockout artist Hart, who he stopped in four, in just his 11th fight.

'When I'm in the ring it's my home,' he said, confidently. 'I don't care where the ring is but when I step inside it that's my home. I had to fight hard. I fought Briscoe in Philly. I beat him. He was tough but I was tougher. I knocked "Cyclone" out. I respected these guys but if you're going to be a champion you've gotta fight the best. You've gotta go in their hometowns and fight the best and that's what I did. I went there, I fought there and I beat the best.'

He boxed Saad, who was then Matthew Franklin, as co-feature to 'Cyclone' versus Vito Antuofermo.

'I beat all three of them,' Eddie, then known as Eddie Gregory, went on. 'I beat Antuofermo in the amateurs twice. I knocked out "Cyclone" and I beat Saad and we were all on the same bill.'

Matthew decked him with a crunching right.

'Saad hit me so hard in the first round he split my trunks,' Eddie laughed. 'But I got up and won a decision in his hometown. He hit me so hard, man. I didn't know I was down until I saw the referee and I didn't even hear him count. That was the first time I had ever been down.'

He had to use some replacement trunks for the rest of the fight.

Beating Matthew earned him a bout with WBA champion Galindez in Italy. Eddie was 22–2–1, Galindez was a more seasoned 47–6–4.

'He was scared of me,' Eddie reckoned. 'I cut him up, beat him up and they gave it to him but I knew going into the fight that it was going to happen, even though I was a novice.'

'Why then go to Mali to fight Bo Sounkalo?'

'Because I had to,' he shouted, already sick of saying why he was always the outsider.

'This guy was supposed to be a champion, he was a good fighter and all that so I said, "No problem, I'll go out there and beat him up." I beat him from round one to ten and I knocked him down about four times to make sure they wouldn't take it from me.'

They didn't. They couldn't.

'I never had a promoter. I did it all on my own. I didn't need promoters paying for this, for that. None of it. I did it the hard way. No promoter. I did it with my fists. That's all. It would have made it easier to be with a promoter but my life has always been hard and I would have made less money because I would have been paying them. No doubt.'

He said Muhammad Ali was 'very influential' in his career. They were friends and had even trained together.

'He showed me how he was living and how he was so happy and so humble and it helped because I still feel, to this day, that if it wasn't for Islam I would not be where I am today.'

One man who needed a similar influence was inmate James Scott. Even though he was languishing in a New Jersey penitentiary on a murder charge he had still been allowed to fight with TV companies happy to broadcast his fights from the sports hall or inside the prison grounds at Rahway.

'He beat me fair and square,' Eddie said, with clear respect for Scott.

'He couldn't intimidate me. What was he going to do? They're inmates, what are they going to do? They would have got beat up. But Scott beat me fair and square.

'There's no telling what he could have done if he was a free man because I'm out there subjected to women and things like that and he didn't have that. I'm a ladies' man, I always have been and he didn't have those distractions.

'I would have brought ladies into the prison if I was in there. God bless him. I wanted to give him a rematch after I won the title but the WBA said I couldn't. He was so well conditioned and he tried to intimidate you but he couldn't intimidate me. Please, I'm from Brooklyn.'

Apparently, Eddie had occasionally sent Saad Muhammad some money but he would not say whether he had, only that 'I wish him all the love...'

'So how about Jesse Burnett?' I asked, changing lanes. 'If he stopped you going to the Olympics did you have something to prove when you fought him in the pros?'

'I didn't have anything to prove against Burnett. I knew what I could do. I can box, I can punch and I was a very good professional fighter and I went there and did my thing.'

Eddie was involved in one of the biggest scandals to hit the sport in the eighties when he was involved with Harold Smith.

Smith, who basically wanted to trump Don King all of the time, would throw enormous sums of money at fighters to get them to box under his promotional banner. He gave a lot of boxers a lot of money only for it to later be revealed the funds, thought to be between $200 and $300 million, had been embezzled from the Wells Fargo Bank where a Smith acquaintance had worked.

'He was good, rich, and he kept me busy and he kept money in my pocket. He paid me well, I got no problem with Harold Smith,' Eddie joked. 'No problem at all.'

A rematch between him and Saad, with Saad as the WBC champ and Eddie holding the WBA belt, was going to be huge. Madison Square Garden was the venue, the place where I had paid for tickets so Matthew could actually get in years later, and both were due to make a record light-heavyweight purse of $1.5 million each.

Ken Norton was matched with Gerry Cooney, Saad and Eddie would go at it again, Tommy Hearns would meet Wilfred Benitez and Aaron Pryor was scheduled to clash with Saoul Mamby on a card billed definitively as 'This Is It!'

'About a week down the road the fight is called off,' Eddie remembered. 'They say Smith did some things that were unlawful but I don't know. All I know is what I was privy to. To me he was one of the best promoters because he paid so well.

'It would have been a huge card. It would have been everything and it would have meant everything to everyone.

'I had beat Saad once. I could have whupped him again. This time it would have been in my territory, in Madison Square Garden. I would have beat him easy. If I beat you once I'll beat you again.

'People say he changed his style after he fought me but it wouldn't have made a difference. He might have got knocked out next time.'

He spoke of the best fighters of his day.

'Yaqui Lopez?'

'Tough, tough, tough, tough, fighter. He was a warrior. I was sitting ringside when he fought Saad the second time. I was right there and I had blood on my tracksuit just looking at those guys.'

'John Conteh?'

'Very smart individual and a good tactician.'

'Dwight Qawi?' Who I interviewed a week ago.

'I liked him. I caught up with him at some fights at Philly one time and he asked me, "What would have happened if we ever fought?" I said, "I would have knocked you out." He looked at me laughing and said, "I just had to know." I'd have knocked him out, no problem.

'What did Qawi say about me?' Eddie probed.

'He said he would have beaten you.'

'Nah, he's too short. I would have got him easy. He would have had to come into me.'

'Oh,' I replied. 'He said you were too tall and could not keep him away.'

Eddie smiled.

'What about Marvin Johnson?'

'Me and Marvin were room-mates on the Olympic team. We slept in the same room never knowing we were going to fight each other for the world title. At that point I was 147lb and Marvin was 165lb and never in my life did I think we would fight. We were friends.'

I asked Eddie to recall their 1980 world championship fight, mentioning I might be talking to Marvin in the near future as I considered another Indianapolis stop on my return leg.

'He had to come into me and he was a strong fighter. He would throw a variety of punches and barrages, which was cool. I just sat there, waited and knocked him out. That was it.'

Body shots did for poor Marvin, who was stopped in the 11th.

'Tell him I still love him and that he's always going to be one of my favourite fighters,' Eddie added. 'I will always respect him. I respect all these guys, don't get me wrong. I respect these guys to the utmost but I know what I can do.

'I would have knocked out Conteh. I would have knocked out Yaqui. I would have knocked out Qawi. I was too strong for these guys. I was a good body puncher. I had a pinpoint shot. I could take a punch and I had the biggest punch out of all of them. I knocked out 40 guys.'

As the champion, he wanted to give Scott a rematch but ended up defending against Jerry Martin because 'The Bull' had gone to Rahway and untracked the prisoner, stopping him in 11 rounds.

Eddie had weight issues, though, and found himself in the heavyweight division.

In a non-title fight, he fought Renaldo Snipes who 'ran all over the place' and 'didn't want to fight'. Snipes won a split decision.

'I went up to heavyweight because I knew I could fight with these guys,' he said. 'I was smarter than a lot of them and I would beat them up in sparring. I had boxed a lot of heavyweights.

'It was speed. They're not going to see it coming. I'm not going to let them bang on me. I'm going to be in striking distance. If you miss I'm going to make you pay.'

However, when he accepted a challenge from Michael Spinks he left it too late to shed more than 20lb in eight weeks before their fight for Eddie's light-heavyweight crown.

'I think Michael is a good fighter when he's not fighting dirty,' he said. 'He hits you one, two, three, bang,' he said, twisting his elbow towards my forehead.

'But, God bless him, he did what he had to do to win the title from me.

'He was OK. We were supposed to have a rematch and if he was that good he would have fought me at my best and the second time we were supposed to fight I was at my best.'

As his career wound down, he made an unhappy trip to Italy and lost to Slobodan Kacar. Unsurprisingly, he had an answer ready to explain the controversial split decision.

'Let me tell you this – and you can come to your own conclusion – after the fight they took him from the ring to the hospital with internal bleeding because I beat him to death. I thought I really hurt him. I beat him up for 15 rounds pretty bad. He didn't fight again for 15 months and when he did he was beaten up by Bobby Czyz because there was nothing there.'

Eddie took three years out before trying again but it was not to be.

Since then, though, he had invested his money and was doing well as a trainer, working with the likes of Chad Dawson, Al Cole, Johnny Tapia and Herbie Hide. He was also trying to make sure fighters had something to fall back on when they fell away from the sport.

He had set up JAB, a union for boxers.

'It's a long time coming,' he proudly said. 'It's so at the end of their career fighters have pensions, insurance, health benefits, retirement packages, the whole nine yards. Just like an ordinary job.'

Eddie had been married to Simone for 22 years and they had five kids, with two grandkids on the way.

'You're not old enough to be a granddad,' I teased.

'I'm 51. I know I don't look it but I'm 51 years old. I take care of myself. I work out in the gym every day, this is my livelihood. This is a young man's game and you've got to keep up with the younger guys.

'I've been blessed. Every day I wake up and do what I want to do. I love my job. Boxing is my life. If it wasn't for boxing there's no telling where I would be.'

Then, he transported himself back to his prime years.

'Fighters from our era respected each other because the bottom line is we came to fight. We didn't have to put tassels on our shoes or do anything fancy. We came in a pair of trunks, shoes and ready to rumble.'

By now, his fighters were waiting for his wise words.

'I've got work to do,' he said, as we embraced and he went back into the gym.

I made the long walk back to the Strip and went to sleep. The Vegas adventure had been worthwhile, but there was just five days to get back to New York for my flight.

Chapter 16

THERE was no breeze and there were no clouds. Vegas was its sweltering self. What looked more fatigued, the Greyhound bus or me, I don't know. I should have felt revitalised after two nights in a hotel but I was exhausted.

As the first on board, even climbing the steps was a chore.

It started filling up and I'm sure it buckled under the weight of an enormous woman as she hauled herself on deck. She was so big it did not matter that she turned sideways to fit down the aisle, she still hit the seats on both sides on her way down, plonking herself next to me. Her behind was so big part of it was on my lap.

The sweaty flaps of skin behind her arms drooped casually over my shoulder.

I was pinned by the window and there was not much space for the passengers on the other side of the aisle either. Certainly no one would be coming past.

Everything was squished. There was not space to read a book or even to have an itch.

As we slowly left Vegas, and I say slowly because I think the freight was particularly heavy, I was optimistic.

I was able to loosely arrange two interviews on my way back to New York. A friend in Minnesota, Jim Carlin, was big pals with Ernie Terrell and said the former heavyweight champion would be available if I could get to Chicago.

One year at the Hall of Fame I had met Frankie Pryor, wife of the legendary light-welterweight champion Aaron. She'd insisted if I was ever passing through Cincinnati they would welcome a visit, although one wondered whether she actually believed I would show up outside their apartment with all of my worldly possessions in a single bag.

A couple of uncomfortable hours into the journey I began to get cramps in my legs. I could not move properly and was fed up with being flattened while the women drifted in and out of sleep, leaning over and on me as the bus ploughed around winding corners to the left.

Greyhound's finest was getting just as weary as I was and as we made our way up a steep hill in the middle of nowhere, with only dusty mountains and pale brown desert in sight, the engine toiled and finally cut out.

The driver made reassurances but it was not long before he told us the air-conditioning was not working either.

He could not let anyone out due to the dangerous bend we had broken down on. To compound our misery he announced the sunroofs would not be opened as it would make it even hotter inside to allow the overpowering sunlight into the vehicle.

Meanwhile, the woman next to me slept, snoring like a warthog with a sinus problem. And she was getting hot. The sweat from under her arms dripped on me but still I dared not move in case I woke her.

The one-hour mark came and went and the restless passengers were told another coach was coming from Sin City to fetch us and take us on our way.

Eventually, we piled off and on to the newer, shinier vessel and I was confident fate would intervene and the lady would sit next to someone else.

But I had dues to pay and when she smiled and said, 'I was sleeping so peacefully, you don't mind if we try that again,' I had no option but to smile, breathe in and prepare for another leg of a sweat-soaked journey.

As she backed in to sit down, her arse squeezed against the seat in front and the back of her chair. She rested it on the seat, my eyeline dropped by a couple of inches as the chair moved with us, and that big wedge of skin between her soggy and saggy right tricep and shoulder pressed itself over my collarbone, within inches of my face.

She peered over her chunky slab of flesh and smiled, 'Kinda cosy, ain't it?'

Yet the prospect of Terrell and Pryor made the discomfort, the snoring and latterly the smell not so bad. Despite my burly and hungry companion making a point of getting out at each stop to retrieve Big Macs, Whoppers, milkshakes, fries and all of the other rubbish you could imagine, I was surprisingly upbeat.

I simply and silently protested against Greyhound stopping at nowhere other than Pizza Hut, Taco Bell, McDonald's, Burger King and Wendy's by fasting again. If they were only going to give me the option of crap then I wouldn't eat.

The buzz of moving around America trying to trace lost heroes was almost enough to keep me going.

Nearly two days went by before I arrived in Chicago and I hadn't eaten a crumb. Sometimes the challenge of not eating drove me further. If I didn't have a meal for 24 hours I tried 30, then 36, 48 and so on. It was a risky game. Some do not recover from playing with their diets like that. I had no idea what I weighed but at least I stayed clean by washing and shaving in the restrooms at various bus stops. It was the sleep deprivation that really hurt though, only grabbing an hour here and there. In more than 20 days I had spent six nights in a bed.

My instructions were to call Ernie as soon as I arrived but it was gone 7pm so I thought I should first find a place to stay.

Again, I looked for information from the free phones at the bus station, unperturbed by the shitholes and dives I had stayed in having used them before. Sure enough, there was an available dump just a 30-minute local bus ride out of the city where I could stay for less than $30 per night.

Seeing as this was Chicago, I figured that wasn't bad.

Upon check-in, though, I could tell why it was at the bottom end of the market. In fact, $30 was steep for what I was getting and I quickly surmised why they were so keen to debit my card over the phone to secure the reservation before I got there.

It was one of those wonderfully enclosed rooms with no windows, a toilet that was brown and a shower cubicle that was green even though the suite was supposed to be white. It had an ancient, small, white TV with 14 channels, which you changed by turning a broken knob, but, alas, there was no picture; merely loud black and white fuzz. The bed was a lumpy single, but the lumps were hard.

It felt like I was trying to relax with muscle spasms and, when I rolled over, one lump pushed against my thigh, another dug into my ribs and there was one firmly in my cheek. There were no pillows. Perhaps they were in the deluxe rooms.

I didn't much care. Not really. I was horizontal for the first time in three days.

I called Ernie at daybreak.

The bus to Cincinnati was due to leave in the late afternoon so I was businesslike but courteous.

Ernie was the same with me.

He asked where I was staying and he was keen to come and collect me rather than let me become a Chicago crime statistic by attempting to find him.

Where I was, he told me, wasn't where tourists go.

That much, I told him, I could tell.

Less than an hour after putting the phone down there was a knock at the door. Obviously there was no peephole. I guessed the rooms with those also cost extra. I opened the door and a huge man, donning his trademark fedora and a pleasant grin, smiled inquisitively.

He placed his hat in his hand. His big round face was made to look all the more spherical once he removed it, thus revealing his balding dome.

He was tall, too, every inch 6ft 6in and every ounce still a heavyweight.

'Are you Tris?'

'Yes,' I replied.

'Then let's get something to eat,' he said gently.

He threw my bag on the back seat of his car and began to talk shop.

Ernie had a contract cleaning business with hundreds of staff on the books. His company provided cleaners for schools, police stations, shops and just about everything else you could have cleaned.

He took me to a nice place on the outskirts of Chicago. It was a buffet-style restaurant in a quiet suburban area and we helped ourselves before sitting down and putting my tape recorder through its paces.

I had been to Chicago on vacation before. This time, however, I had seen another side to the city; specifically the South side.

Still, in Ernie's gentle, puppy-dog eyes it was the 'greatest city in the world' and he started retelling old stories of his amateur days as a Golden Gloves champion who finished his unpaid career with just two losses in 34 fights.

Like a generation of kids who grew up when 'The Brown Bomber' was still boxing, Ernie's early hero was Joe Louis. He listened to his fights on the wireless with his family.

'I can remember I wanted to be just like him,' Ernie began. 'I remember the effect he had on households when he fought. Everything would stop because he was fighting. He had a couple of fights in the late 1940s when I was just a baby and I remember how it was for all of the homes in our neighbourhood and I thought that if I ever had a chance to do that I would like to.'

While Ernie looked up to Louis – and later became friends with him – after he turned professional he found himself hanging out with the anti-Louis, Sonny Liston.

'I knew him well,' Terrell recalled. 'We trained together a lot. Sonny Liston's camp and my camp were associated. Sonny was nice to the folks he knew. He didn't think he could trust people to get close to him but once you knew him he was all right.

'One time we were driving around here in Chicago and we were passing by various upper-class neighbourhoods and I said, "Look at these buildings. When I become champion I'm going to buy a building like that."

'And Sonny looked at me and said, "Are you crazy? You must think I ain't gonna fight nobody but you when I get the championship."

'That's the way he was, he could come out with some funny lines when he wanted to and I always felt comfortable around him.

'He was going to fight a guy, Roy Harris, in Cut 'n' Shoot, Texas,' Ernie continued.

'Harris, at that time, was a very prominent guy. There was a middleweight named Jesse Smith who always trained with Sonny and myself. Sonny was talking to us and he looked and saw a crowd gathering around the bus when we got there and like a fool, really, Sonny picked up a paper that someone was reading. So he had the paper looking like he was reading it but he couldn't read.

'I said, "Come on Sonny, let's get off the bus," and so we got off and he brought the paper with him. We walked in there and they had all the boxers inside and Roy Harris was there and he was sitting down looking kind of jolly because all of the attention was around him and Sonny's still "reading" the paper.

'Then someone shouted, "Let's put 'em on the scales."'

'So they put Roy Harris on the scales and he weighed 190-whatever it was and then they said, "Let's put Liston on the scales."

'So he got on the scales and the paper is still up there with him and the officials told him to strip to his waist for the official weigh-in.'

'Yep,' Ernie remembered, shaking his head with a wry smile.

'And he had a suit on and a hat so the commissioner said, "Our regulations call for you to at least strip to your waist for the official weigh-in."

'Sonny hadn't done that. He had a suit on. So he took the paper and threw it down, took off his hat, threw it down, took off his coat, threw it down and he reached for his tie. All the while he was getting more agitated at being the exhibition and the centre of attention and a reporter asked him, "Sonny, we understand you could have chosen a neutral referee, aren't you afraid of a hometown decision?"

'And this is the only time Liston said anything.

'He said, "A decision? I've come here to kill this man. If it's a decision I don't want it."

'And that was Sonny Liston,' Ernie laughed.

'That's all he said and that was the end of the whole thing. He won that fight right there and then.'

Harris was destroyed in one round.

'Sonny had a good jab and he was a good fighter in every sense of the word. I cannot explain some of the controversy that went with him because I never knew. I didn't know that part of him. You know how I would describe Sonny? He was a gentle giant. He was a nice guy who had a hard life and we were friends. We went out together. He was always full of jokes and Sonny liked to play with kids. Whenever we sparred he would go to a school and see kids.'

Ernie actually boxed Liston in an exhibition and said Sonny would have been a tough fight, but he believed he could have beaten him.

They all say that.

While Liston's legacy is a generally unsavoury one, Terrell's, albeit indirectly, also damaged the sport.

He became the pioneering WBA champion and was the first beneficiary of the title that governing body created to reward a new heavyweight champion after Cassius Clay (later Muhammad Ali) was stripped. In the ensuing years the sport became more and more fragmented.

'Do you feel partly responsible for there being so many sanctioning bodies?' I asked.

'Yes, I do,' he said regrettably, in the knowledge that the damage was probably irreversible.

'There's only one world and it can't have that many world champions. I told the people during a speech once that I didn't even know how many champions there were now and I was the start of it.

'But there was no other association at the time, just the WBA. The rest of it came afterwards. I had to do something because Floyd Patterson fought Ingemar Johansson for three years. Nobody else got a shot because they beat each other.

'You had people who had been there for years like Eddie Machen, Zora Foley, Cleveland Williams, Sonny and myself who didn't get a shot.

'All these guys were top-ranked fighters; we were all at the top. A lot of them didn't get a shot at the title unless they got a shot at Ali.'

When Terrell did eventually get his, against Machen, he made the most of it.

'Joe Louis was in my corner,' he smiled. 'Being around a legend like Joe, it's so hard to show your appreciation. People are always around. People are always interrupting. Joe belonged to everybody. He was a god. Some people are so rude that they would stop him no matter what. Joe didn't know how to handle it. He was training me but people would just interfere with him.'

Ernie formed a close relationship with his boyhood idol that he cherished until Louis died. In 1967, however, Terrell fought a notoriously bad-tempered affair with Ali in a one-sided bout that left Terrell with nasty facial swelling and made Ali even less popular than he already was.

It was over Terrell's alleged refusal to address Ali as Muhammad Ali, instead opting to call him Cassius Clay during press conferences and in interviews during the bout's build-up.

'Did you not call him Clay to hype the fight?'

'I didn't know if it would provoke him or not but it did,' he explained. 'However, you must realise that I had known

Micky Ward relaxes at home in Lowell after his bruising first fight with Arturo Gatti

Micky Ward (right) and Arturo Gatti shared three incredible battles (Press Association)

Matthew Saad Muhammad hangs out with friends in the Atlantic City ghetto

Saad, during happier times with his first wife in 1980 (P. K Trace Photography/Boxing News)

Saad works the heavy bag in preparation for a world title defence (Boxing News)

Rocky Castellani stands proudly in front of his house on the Atlantic City outskirts

Castellani weighs-in as opponent Sugar Ray Robinson looks on (Steve Lott/Boxing Hall of Fame Las Vegas)

Joey Giardello, ready to rumble in the car park of a diner in Cherry Hill, New Jersey

Giardello cuts a more menacing figure in his heyday (Boxing News)

Jeff Chandler is kept in line by his manager, the diminutive Becky O'Neil (Boxing News)

Chandler goes through his repertoire of punches at his home in Philadelphia

Harold Johnson stands proudly, an isolated figure in a Philadelphia care home

Light-heavyweight ruler Johnson celebrates another victory (Associated Press)

Johnson, in fighting shape, back in 1961 (Steve Lott/Boxing Hall of Fame Las Vegas)

Charismatic Marvis Frazier reflects on his career from his father's gym in Philadelphia

Many felt Marvis (right) was haunted by the pressure of being Joe Frazier's son (Press Association)

Jimmy Young sends George Foreman into retirement (Press Association)

Former heavyweight contender Young puts on a brave face

Dwight Qawi, in an impoverished section of Atlantic City, remembers his struggles in and out of boxing

Qawi leaves rival Saad Muhammad battered, bruised and defeated (Boxing News)

Saad Muhammad and Chuck Wepner stand united at ringside in Atlantic City

Dwight Muhammad Qawi, champion at light-heavyweight and cruiserweight (Boxing News)

Matthew Saad Muhammad once stood on top of the boxing world

The boxing world is stunned as Buster Douglas sensationally topples Mike Tyson in Tokyo (Press Association)

Douglas, with his sons, enjoys the fruits of his labour in Columbus, Ohio

Vonzell Johnson, the former light-heavyweight contender, reports for duty as a trainer

Johnson strikes a fighting pose in his 1980s prime (Boxing News)

Don Fullmer shows off the gloves that retired former middleweight king Carl 'Bobo' Olson

Don was a force to be reckoned with and carved out his own successful career (Press Association)

Gene Fullmer struck championship gold in a magnificent career

Gene Fullmer swings a violent right towards Carmen Basilio (Press Association)

'Uncrowned' middleweight champion Joey Giambra is still dreaming big in Las Vegas

Giambra in a training publicity shot during his pomp (Steve Lott/Boxing Hall of Fame Las Vegas)

Giambra is on the receiving end against old rival Joey Giardello (Boxing News)

Hedgemon Lewis, former welterweight champ, training fighters in Sin City

Lewis and old mentor Eddie Futch pictured deep in conversation (Boxing News)

Aaron Pryor tracks Alexis Arguello to the ropes and lets his punches fly (Press Association)

Aaron Pryor, with his championship belt, strikes a familiar pose in his Cincinnati apartment

Big Ernie Terrell cuts an impressive figure on the streets of Chicago

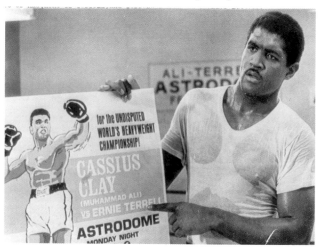

Terrell gets involved in the hype ahead of his fight with Muhammad Ali, whom he still referred to as Clay (Boxing News)

Stanley Hayward, at work in the Philadelphia court buildings

'Kitten' Hayward was a handful for anyone in his prime (John DiSanto/PhillyBoxingHistory)

Bandy-legged Watts was a terrific mover and a nightmare to fight (John DiSanto/ PhillyBoxingHistory)

Bobby 'Boogaloo' Watts was never a champion, but he fought the very best middleweights

Drayton patiently learned his trade as Marvin Hagler's sparring partner (Boxing News)

Still in shape, former IBF light-middleweight champion Buster Drayton works out

Jose Torres shadowboxes in the fresh New York autumnal air

Torres takes centre stage as opponent Dick Tiger hits the scales (Steve Lott/Boxing Hall of Fame Las Vegas)

Chuck Wepner is on the receiving end against Muhammad Ali, but his gallant showing inspired the Rocky series (Steve Lott/Boxing Hall of Fame Las Vegas)

Wepner, pictured in an Atlantic City casino, with wife Linda

Richie Kates runs a tight ship in the PAL gym in Vineland, New Jersey

Kates feared no one, but came through in a tough era of light-heavyweights (John DiSanto/PhillyBoxingHistory)

James Scott. While waiting for a trial he had been allowed to fight inside Rahway Prison, starring in televised bouts until he was finally convicted in 1981

Scott, boxing in front of inmates in Rahway Prison, sends another opponent packing (Boxing News)

The author is pictured in Northern State Prison with former light-heavyweight contender Scott

Scott's mugshot, from the New Jersey Department of Corrections website

Chico Vejar, photographed in around 1954 when he was a staple on TV (Steve Lott/ Boxing Hall of Fame Las Vegas)

Vejar, outside a restaurant in Stamford, Connecticut

George Chuvalo, in Toronto, tells his remarkable story

Chuvalo with sons, from left-right, George Jnr, 2, Steven, 4, Jesse, 8 months, and five-year-old Mitchell (Boxing News)

Chuvalo and Ernie Terrell looking tough ahead of their close fight (Boxing News)

Florentino Fernandez looking spritely by his home in Miami

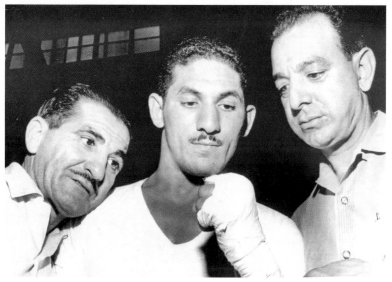

Former middleweight puncher Fernandez is flanked by Cuban manager Higino Ruiz and trainer Angelo Dundee (Boxing News)

Duane Bobick, photographed in Minnesota, still has boxing in his blood

Long-haired Bobick turned pro with much fanfare, but his career failed to hit the heights (Duane Bobick)

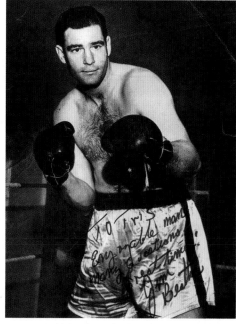

Jim Beattie, self-confessed Mob heavyweight, ended up working in the gold business

A Beattie publicity shot in his days as a fringe contender (Jim Beattie)

Johnson became the first three-time light-heavyweight champion (Boxing News)

The reclusive Marvin Johnson eventually comes round for a picture

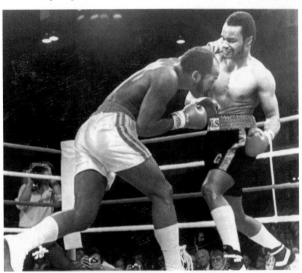

Eddie Mustafa Muhammad (right) finds a way to stifle Johnson (Associated Press)

Yaqui Lopez, with his friend and cutman Benny Casing, at his home in California

Lopez sportingly raises the hand of talented Liverpudlian champion John Conteh after losing to the Englishman in Denmark (Boxing News)

Old warriors and rivals Saad Muhammad, Marvin Johnson, Eddie Mustafa Muhammad and Yaqui Lopez are finally reunited (Larry Tornambe)

Leavander Johnson is all smiles ahead of his tragic fight with Jesus Chavez (Press Association)

The Johnson family stand beneath the statue of the late Leavander Johnson

Muhammad Ali for a while. We were amateurs at the same time. He would come here to Chicago to fight in the Golden Gloves so I knew him and he was Cassius Clay.

'We had sparring sessions in Miami when he was Cassius Clay in Angelo Dundee's gym. Now all of a sudden he was Muhammad Ali and we signed for the fight here in Chicago and the promoter at the time, who was Irving Schoenwald, said, "Ernie we want you back in town two weeks before the fight to help with the publicity, is that all right with you?"

'I said, "It's all right with me as long as it's all right with Clay."

'Irving says, "It's Muhammad."

'I said, "OK, it's all right with me if it's OK with him."

'Muhammad Ali then said, "Why are you calling me Clay when everyone else is calling me Muhammad?"

'I said, "Look, if you want to be called Muhammad that's all right but when I met you you were Clay and that's how I was introduced to you."

'And he said, "I ain't talking to you. You're just an old Uncle Tom."'

At the time there was a lot of talk about Muhammad Ali's Nation of Islam associates. An old copy of *The Ring* once featured the headline, 'Terrell fears Muslims', so I asked him what was behind the story and whether the sometimes ominous and odious characters around Ali bothered him.

Apparently, around the time of the fight the FBI was following the Ali people closely.

'We were in Texas,' Ernie explained. 'The fight is on so there's no need to do more hype because it's on. What's going to happen is going to happen. He was trying to get in my head so what they did was call my room and said there was some sort of emergency and I got all of my trainers and everybody out and someone in my room said, "You go to bed Ernie and lay down, it's mid-afternoon." I laid down and waited for them to come back.

'Then there was a knock at the door and there was about 20 or 25 girls who had sneaked their way in to the hotel.

'They burst in and started going through my things. One started going through my clothes. I said, "What are you all doing? Get out of here."

'Then they finally went out. The thing that really bothered me was I had a gym bag and they took my mouthpiece out of there. It was laying on the bed right there. This was the day of the fight.

'That was the only thing I was going to put in my mouth that day and I guess they did something like that to unnerve me.'

Needless to say, in the aftermath of their aggressive barbs Ali's mouth went into hyper-drive and Ernie, a kind man, was not the sort to retaliate.

The verbal exchanges adopted barbaric tones during the fight when, unable to match Ali for speed, Terrell took a shellacking.

'What's my name?' ringsiders heard Ali shout as he fired off quick combinations and moved away from a hapless Terrell in an ugly spectacle.

Many thought Ali could and should have mercifully put a stop to the fight.

Instead he was like someone who takes a magnifying glass in hand on a hot summer's day in search of ants.

But Terrell dished out his own share of punishment in a 16-year, 54-fight career.

As we downed mouthfuls of chicken, rice and vegetables, he told me his hardest opponent was Cleveland Williams, a man who had stopped him in 1962 and who Terrell outpointed on a split decision 12 months later.

'He was a good, hard puncher, strong and musclebound,' Ernie recalled.

I asked him whether he thought Ali's dazzling performance against Williams, widely regarded as the best pure boxing exhibition ever meted out, was just that.

He did not think so.

'When Ali beat him it was after Williams had got shot by a policeman, but he continued his career. I had to fight him before he got shot. I heard he was in a racist area in Texas and he was with a woman and a policeman shot him and it was lucky he lived,' Terrell said.

After Ernie called it a day he managed to stay in the limelight as a singer. The butterflies he would feel in the locker room before a fight returned behind the curtain as he awaited his cue to sing as the lead attraction of Ernie Terrell and the Heavyweights.

'We went all over. We went to Miami Beach and Vegas and we played clubs all over the world,' he recalled.

'What happened to the group was I had one older brother and one younger brother and after we had been gone so long they wanted to get married and stuff like that. That's what usually happens to groups.'

Ernie has his own strong family values, which were instilled in him by his parents.

He beamed proudly when we talked about his sister, Jean Terrell, who made it big as a replacement to one of the original Supremes, Diana Ross. She was spotted by former Motown boss Berry Gordy while performing with Ernie on the road in Florida.

Ernie was at his most comfortable talking about the love of his life, wife Maxine. The very mention of her name turned the former heavyweight into a blushing, bashful giant.

Still, when the band stopped, Ernie looked for other things to do and inevitably was drawn back into boxing as a promoter, manager, trainer and mentor.

'I did pretty good,' he smiled. 'I developed Alfonso Ratliff, who became the cruiserweight champion, Leroy Murphy, another cruiserweight champion, and James "Quick" Tillis.

'I also developed some good local talent like John Collins, he was a popular fighter here. Luke Capuano, he was a good local fighter, I also worked with Randy Shields and Mike Rossman. I had some good fighters up here.

'I matched John Collins with another of my fighters, Lenny LaPaglia, and they drew the biggest non-title gate in Chicago that we had ever had.

'I put on Tillis–Mike Weaver, Marvin Hagler and Mustafa Hamsho. I had quite a roll.'

It was only after that when Terrell really started to clean up with his janitorial business.

'I've had as many as about 850 employees,' he mentioned modestly. 'I've got about 450 now. I've got contracts for Chicago public schools and I've got two police districts, a total of 12 stations. I've got about 250 schools. I have had the business since 1988 and I've been doing well since about 1996.'

Terrell also travelled with the Calvary Missionary Baptist Church, visiting prisons with the church's 100-strong choir. The group sings for inmates and groups of disadvantaged people across the country.

I asked him what he thought the differences were between the boxing days of yesteryear and today.

He shook his head ruefully, sad that it had deteriorated, fragmented and divided in many ways.

'I think that was the best era of boxing, when I was boxing. If you come from the 1930s to the 70s you had excellent fighters. Today people just don't train like that anymore.'

'So, Ernie,' I asked, as a waitress cleared our plates, 'do you think we will ever have one sanctioning body again or have you ruined it for everyone?'

'No,' he sniggered. 'I don't think there will ever be one. If we do, it will probably happen when the world has one president!'

Following the meal, which Ernie paid for after looking at me in a derisory fashion when I offered, he took me to the bus station so I could get there in plenty of time. He posed for a couple of pictures outside the restaurant, shook hands with a few locals and threw my bag in his car where I saw a box full of fan mail. He had received it all in the last couple of days and we sifted through it.

Some of it was from the UK, some from Brazil, other letters were from America and Canada. They were nearly all autograph requests.

When we left, the traffic was bedlam and the heat was fierce. Even though the air-conditioning was on in the car I could feel the temperature rising.

It had gone 2pm and I was getting anxious. We were driving at about 10mph when we could, the rest of the time the Chicago streets were gridlocked so we made small talk.

He kept reassuring me it would be OK, that we wouldn't miss the bus, and after about half an hour I started to believe him. Then steam began emerging from the bonnet of his car. It was overheating.

He knew someone close by who might be able to fix it.

'In and right out,' he said we would be.

However, at 3pm I realised I wasn't going to make the bus.

Ernie had a plan B, though, and had already made a call.

He found out the Greyhound stopped on the fringes of Chicago on its way out and said he would take me to that stop. We had some more time. We even popped to his office briefly as we waited for a part for his limping car to be fitted and by 3.45pm I was waiting for my bus to Cincinnati.

The race was still on to get back to the East Coast for my flight. I wanted one more interview, Aaron Pryor, and then I would return with one last, long bus journey.

US journalist Martha Ellis Gelhorn, who covered wars around the world for 50 years, once wrote, 'My definition of what makes a journey wholly or partially horrible is boredom. Add discomfort, fatigue, strain in large amounts to get the purest-quality horror journey, but the kernel is boredom.'

But I found solace in her view that 'the threshold of boredom must be like the threshold of pain, different in all of us', as I was certainly becoming hardened to it.

On the bus to Ohio I sat next to a guy who had his headphones blaring rap music so loudly the bus driver, a good ten rows up, had to keep asking him to turn his music down.

His requests – they weren't forceful enough to be classed as orders – were met merely by grunts and when I arrived in Cincinnati at 3am, I was beyond dishevelled. I was more fatigued than ever before.

I hadn't slept properly for the best part of a week and my eating had been almost non-existent, inconsistent at best. The trip was taking a physical toll.

It had been a hard way of living but never once was I pleased to be on the home straight or homeward-bound. I had loved it. I was living a dream I did not want to end. I tried to find a decent place to spend the remaining hours of the night in Cincinnati. I needed a few hours' sleep, a shave and a shower. I needed some proper sleep, some time out of the eyes of the world. The only place I seemed to get any privacy was on a toilet and even then, in America, the doors are hung about a foot off the floor with gaps between them and walls so wide a small child could put their fingers through.

Although I had a policy that I would not pay for a room after midnight, when I arrived in Pryor's hometown I had little control over my body and had gently been losing control of my mind.

The lines between the rest of the world and my own were becoming increasingly distant. I could hardly remember being with Ernie.

My eyes were horribly bloodshot, my hair was unkempt and I could feel myself ageing, emotionally and physically.

Stubble turned into hair, my skin felt unclean, my clothes needed to be washed. What I really needed was three square meals and ten hours of sleep.

At the bus station I made my way to the phone in the wall with posters advertising places to stay in and around the city and saw one that claimed to offer a room for less than $40 per night. Better still, it was only five minutes away.

Normally I wouldn't have bothered. I would have made do with catnapping on the station floor.

But I hadn't experienced these levels of utter exhaustion before. I must have been delirious when I called the place and when I walked to it as I couldn't recall much about how I had got there the next day.

When I checked in, and I won't call it a hotel because that puts images of Marriotts, Hiltons, Quality Inns, Comfort Inns and Travelodges into one's mind, it was not long before I realised I was staying at the worst hotel I had been unfortunate enough to visit. Calling it a dump would be dressing it up.

Outside there were drug deals going down, and the hustlers weren't discreet. I was offered an array of substances as if they were sweets.

After refusing from the first guy, another came to me and said, 'Do you drink?'

'No.'

'Do you smoke?'

'No.'

'Cocaine?'

'No.'

'Do you take pills?'

'No.'

'Do you inject?'

I ignored him and carried on as he shouted, 'Wasssup, man, ain't you tryin' this shit?'

I looked back and saw him waving a white rock.

He didn't seem anything like as bored listening to my answers as I was giving them to him, though he did sound genuinely surprised by my negative responses.

Anyway, back to the building.

The valet was a 10lb rat. Unfortunately, his friends were staying inside.

I buzzed on the door and a Hispanic guy stinking of musty booze and nicotine with his belly hanging over his shorts and out of a string vest came to the door. It was hot and he was greasy, but I was in no position to judge on that score. I walked through a dimly lit corridor. Certainly it was a case of the less I could see the better.

He went into a cage and locked himself inside, addressing me from behind a metal grate in the hallway.

I paid cash, they didn't take cards.

He seemed amazed I would stay there and even knocked five dollars off for me.

There was no lift and the room was on the top floor.

I ascended a narrow spiral wooden staircase, which got so thin near the pinnacle, getting hotter and hotter, I had to carry my bag in front of me.

The room was four flights up and down another long, thin corridor.

All I wanted was to wash my face and sleep.

There were seven hours before I was due to meet Pryor.

The door had to be forced open with my body and bag pushing against it in one momentous last effort and as I fell through I heaved my rucksack on to a couch.

I went to turn the light on, but the switch was broken. There was no bulb in it anyway. Only the streetlights outside allowed me to see what was what, albeit in dark shadow form.

The floorboards were rough and uneven; I could see stains on a rug.

There was a dining table and chairs in a corner; each chair was different. Some had bits of card underneath them to stop them rocking unevenly. The table was metal and would have been more suited to a garden.

There was a huge bay window behind the bed and three of the four sashes were open, which was good because I needed to cool down.

Torn net curtains blew softly in the breeze and a large cockroach scurried across the bed sheets before leaping on to the floor with a thud.

I was able to hear its feet as it tip-toed heavily towards me before squeezing underneath the door and scuttling down the hallway.

I continued my investigation. A sick, uncaring smile crossed my face. I wasn't even upset with how shit the room was.

It was the bed I was interested in.

The paint was coming off the walls, and so was some of the mix and match wallpaper.

It was filthy. The bins were filled with waste, including used condoms and needles. When I went into the bathroom I was surprised the light worked. I just wished it hadn't. It was rank in there.

The white toilet was brown on the inside, and the sink had deteriorated to match. The shower had two or three spots where you could stand on tip-toes without being on the damp mould or the disgusting browny-green colour that also rose up the wall.

The tiles on the floor were broken, naturally, and there was a pale space where a mirror used to be. I turned a tap to wash my face and yellow, gunky liquid came out. I turned the tap back and it came off in my hand.

The other tap turned so a trickle came out, more yellow stuff, and I washed my face and brushed my teeth. The water was warm. Disgusting.

I would save the shower for the morning because 4am was fast approaching.

I undressed, folded my clothes and went to close the windows having cooled down. One was being propped open by a coke can filled with cigarette butts, the other by a beer bottle. The third was managing to hold itself up.

Funny thing was, none of them closed, even without the can and bottle in support.

I lay on the bed and thought about what I had done and where I had been. Apart from that, there was nothing else in my mind.

I turned over to sleep on my side, my mind now fatigued with blankness.

Then the bottom right leg of the bed gave out and I limply rolled down towards that corner.

I didn't even care.

I fell asleep on a slant to the ground.

Finally, I could rest, albeit with my right leg closer to the creepy-crawlies on the floor than the left leg.

Chapter 17

TRAFFIC buzzed several stories below. The sleep had not been as deep as required but there had been a degree of peace. Daybreak had arrived in light speed.

I woke early knowing there was a local bus to take and managed to explore some of the city on foot before heading off.

Again the sun was bright and the heat increasing but not to the levels of Vegas. Frankie had given me directions and the bus swept through some pretty awful-looking places. But Cincinnati was known for its unforgiving ghettoes. These were the streets that had spawned boxers including Tim Austin, Pryor, Ezzard Charles and Bud Smith, hungry fighters with something to prove to the world.

I eventually disembarked in a leafier neighbourhood with a few apartment blocks and homes scattered casually around. I walked on a steep pavement that curved with the road from left to right and finally showed up on the Pryors' doorstep.

One gentle knock provoked a commotion from inside.

'Hawk-time,' came the cries. It swung open. Frankie and Aaron warmly greeted me, with handshakes and embraces.

'You made it,' Frankie said, apparently impressed.

Aaron was on form from the start. Although he was nearly 50, he had childlike qualities. He was playful.

'Hawk-time,' he kept calling out, as he had done in his glory days, in reference to his 'Hawk' moniker.

Their apartment was open plan with the lounge leading into the kitchen and dining room. It was busy but tidy and Aaron and I took our seats on a soft couch.

He wore a cream shirt, open at the neck, and spoke well, even loudly at times. Tinted spectacles disguised a wild past and gave him a degree of sophistication.

Pryor was a fighter who had had more than his fair share of battles in life and in the ring.

He became a hard-drug junkie when he was still boxing and even as a champion he would live for weeks at a time in crackhouses.

He ran through his money.

He split from his wife, who had led him into the murky world of pimps, drugs and dens of iniquity.

Life had been difficult on Aaron from almost the beginning and it was pretty much all downhill from there.

Until now, that is. It was not long before my visit that he had become a deacon in a nearby church. Frankie disappeared, leaving us to talk. Aaron slouched so far his backside was almost on the floor.

Aaron found boxing when he was 13. He was too small for football, too short for basketball, did not enjoy karate but was good at boxing from the moment he put gloves on.

'When you find a sport you're compatible with not only do you know it but the people that know you know it,' he said. 'Faith is what a boxer has when he first goes in the ring. Faith. You have to have faith.'

Pryor had missed out on the Olympic team even though he believed he was more than capable of bringing back a gold medal that would have seen him become an overnight superstar.

'I really wanted to go to the Olympics,' he recalled. 'I was the champion of the world way before I became a professional champion of the world. I was the champion of the world all the way from '73 until '76 as an amateur when I lost in the Olympic box-offs. I won every international and area tournament that led up to the 1976 Olympics from 1973.'

He had more than 200 unpaid fights and actually fought in the Olympic trials in 1972. 'Remember Tim Dement and Duane Bobick?' he asked, testing my history. 'They were on that team. I boxed in the Olympic trials and I lost but I came back in '76 and I lost in the box-offs to Howard Davis, who went on and won the gold medal.

'Then I turned professional in Cincinnati making $200 a fight and I became Sugar Ray Leonard's sparring partner in about '77, '78 and '79. And I was Howard Davis's sparring partner. These guys were millionaires at the beginning of their careers and I'm making by now $600, $700, $800 in my local fights. Then I started knocking guys out and I built up a good record.'

Few people knew who he was, though. He certainly wasn't a matinee idol like his great rival, Leonard, who many believe avoided Pryor as a pro. Nor was Aaron tipped for the same superstardom as Davis, even though they were evenly matched as amateurs.

Pryor was desperate for a good deal and a helping hand so when restaurant owner Buddy LaRosa agreed to give him $125 a week to train, in exchange for 50 per cent of future earnings over the next ten years, Aaron enthusiastically asked where to sign.

It was a terrible deal.

Although it must have been hard to say, Aaron told me he did not bear Buddy any ill will.

'And the big thing about it is he's a really nice guy,' he explained. 'He was only being a businessman but I, I, I...' He slowed down, thinking back. 'I just wish that he could have been a little bit more understanding with me.'

Pryor said LaRosa now owns around a hundred restaurants and that he has 'made a lot of money'.

Even though so much wealth and no small amount of opportunism separated them, Pryor didn't find it hard telling me how well the man who took half of his career purses was doing. In fact, he seemed proud Buddy had made it.

'We still talk, we're good friends actually,' Aaron nodded. 'It's been 12 years since I've been clean from drugs and now I have been ordained as a deacon at the New Friendship Baptist Church here in Cincinnati. What I have been doing with Buddy is working with the Cincinnati Golden Gloves for maybe six or seven years. I have been working with the kids since coming back off the drugs.

'Buddy franchised all of the Cincinnati Golden Gloves and when I was getting my life back together they gave me a little job working with some young amateur fighters but,' and he said this to make a point that he clearly wanted me to pick up on because his eyes looked directly into mine, 'I had to take a urine test once a month and they said that as long as I stayed straight I would keep the job. That was one of the things that helped me. So even though he took advantage of me on one side, he helped me out on the other.'

When Pryor came out from his severe drugs ordeal, which had lasted years, he learned to forgive and started with a clean slate.

He did have some friends looking out for him in his fighting days, though, and they were the ones he remembered most fondly.

Ken Hawk was one of them, the man behind 'The Hawk' nickname that Aaron used.

He was a Cincinnati businessman who had seen Aaron fight as an amateur and was convinced Pryor could make it as a pro. He backed him, like a dad would a talented son, and filled the father figure void in Pryor's life.

Ken bought him boxing gear. In return Aaron would always cherish the one man who showed belief in him and backed it up with kindness, rewards and love.

Finally, in August 1980, in his 25th fight, Pryor was given the chance to show he had what it took, that he was as good as he said he was. He had to make his mark against 100-fight veteran (87 wins) Antonio Cervantes, for the WBA belt.

'I've got it on tape. Do you want to watch it?' he smiled.

Aaron leapt up, grabbed a video and put it on so his famous night unfolded before us. He started talking over his ring entrance.

'On August 2nd 1980 Muhammad Ali promoted Aaron Pryor and Antonio Cervantes at the Coliseum here in Cincinnati. Also on that night Pipino Cuevas and Tommy Hearns were fighting at 8pm in Detroit. Hearns knocked out Cuevas and I knocked out Cervantes; Muhammad Ali promoted them both,' he began.

It was on the night when infamous promoter and money-launderer extraordinaire Harold Smith became the first promoter to have two different televised shows on the same afternoon and evening, though the net was closing in on his company, Muhammad Ali Professional Sports.

'He was like a young Don King,' Aaron said. 'He was a Don King for fighters who almost made it to the Olympics and had to get to where they were with hard work.

'He went to prison and stuff, he did what he did. He loved his boxing and if there's anything that I could do for him because of the love he had for boxers I would honour him.

'Me and Tommy Hearns and a few other fighters, we were the guys behind Ray Leonard and Howard Davis and the guys that went to the Olympics that year,' Aaron went on.

'I wanted to be lightweight champion of the world and I was just sitting there and I couldn't get a shot so I had to move out of the lightweight division.

'"Boom Boom" Mancini, they wasn't gonna let me fight "Boom Boom" and they wasn't gonna let me fight Sean O'Grady and Hilmer Kenty [over whom he held several amateur victories] wasn't gonna fight me. Howard Davis wasn't gonna fight me. Sugar wasn't. There was no one gonna fight me as a lightweight.

'But it's funny because the same people I looked up to, God brought me to them and they made me champion of the world.

'When I was little I remember Joe Frazier and Muhammad Ali fighting. I was maybe 11 or 12 and the TV was broke. There was no picture but I could listen and then, in 1980, Muhammad Ali and his organisation, [Ali had little to do with it once he agreed they could use his name] made my world title fight here in the Cincinnati Coliseum.

'Ali brought it here. He promoted that fight and today me and Muhammad Ali are good friends and every time he sees me he knows who I am because he had a lot to do with "The Hawk" becoming "The Hawk". He opened doors for me.

'It was a great atmosphere winning the title at the Coliseum downtown because I can remember selling hotdogs there when I was a kid. To be able to fight for the title there meant a lot to me, but Cincinnati really wasn't a big boxing town.

'At that time the junior-welterweight division wasn't looked at that highly because it did not have the highlight fights in it. I was No.3 in my division but I had to move out of my weight class to fight the old guy Cervantes, who'd had all these title fights, about 12 or 14 of them, and he'd been champion since I was a teenager. I wanted the shot so bad though because everyone else but me had done made it. Howard Davis done made it. Leonard done made it. Kenty done made it.

'I beat Kenty in the amateurs and Kenty done made it. We fought about 12 times. I beat him about nine times but he had won a world title.'

Wanting to impress, Pryor planned on giving Cervantes hell for the first two or three rounds but things did not start as he'd hoped.

He thought he could 'take advantage of the old dude' and raced in.

'He knocked my ass straight down,' Pryor laughed.

Sure enough, within seconds, he was on his backside in front of us on the screen.

'He shocked me. I didn't think he still had that kind of power. I don't go down like that.'

As we watched, however, the young lion mauled the older man into a fourth-round submission.

Pryor, the new world champion, had firmly shut the mouths of the naysayers, and the look on his face now was eerily similar to the one then, an overjoyed contentment that he finally deserved to be mentioned alongside the Olympians.

'Suddenly I had more friends than I had ever met in my life. It was like…' He paused a few seconds to catch his breath, reliving the thrill of being champion. 'I remember when I was with friends thinking about this. What happens is when you start saying thank you in your life instead of please, you become another person. You're not like these people who were with you at the start. Then, when your family members come and ask you for money, they beg you for the amount they heard you made in the fight. They want to see all the money instead of the money you paid taxes on. So there is a conflict in the way you answer people about what they ask for.

'You know you pay your manager. You pay your trainer. You know you pay taxes. You know what you got left over. But they are still looking at the big numbers. If they see you made $100,000 they want to borrow it.'

He spoke of his championship reign and his war with Dujuan Johnson just over a year, three fights, after winning the crown.

'Emanuel Steward and Tommy Hearns were in his corner that night and that was one of my toughest fights,' Aaron recollected, excitedly. 'I didn't know nothing about this guy but they all did,' as if they had been keeping the very capable Johnson a secret.

'But,' and Aaron's voice slowed and went quieter, 'after he fought me he got himself killed but he was just a helluva fighter, you know. He knocked me down in the first round. He was Tommy Hearns's sparring partner. He was shot dead in a robbery less than three years later in Detroit.'

It was another example of the narrow line between success and utter doom that boxing often vividly highlighted.

If Aaron had stayed down for the count would I have been in Detroit with Dujuan?

Having seen Pryor's famous night against Cervantes, Aaron spoke up, 'Do you want to watch one of my tapes, let's watch this one that was just on HBO, one of the greatest nights.'

It was his Legendary Night, as rightly billed by HBO, in a series of hour-long shows documenting the best bouts televised by the network in their 30-year association with the sport.

It featured his infamous, brilliant first clash with Nicaragua's heroic banger Alexis Arguello.

Aaron Pryor–Alexis Arguello I is one of the best, most popular fights of all time and now I was sitting with the winner on his sofa about to watch it.

As the show began, a host of commentators and historians gave Arguello sterling character references.

'He was a good guy, he was a good fighter too,' Aaron agreed.

Meanwhile, Pryor was introduced to the viewers as one of one seven children from a Cincinnati ghetto.

'I was not born in no ghetto,' he interrupted.

He talked on camera about how, when he fought all over the world as an amateur, people back home in Cincinnati never even realised he was gone.

It was an emotional story, well told, about how he missed out on his Olympic dream, how he was up there with Howard Davis and Sugar Ray but didn't get the breaks.

It was about his dysfunctional family, unhappy childhood and how fighters dodged him, making his already difficult life harder.

Arguello was tall and rangy with pencil-like arms that worked like powerful pistons, rarely allowing opponents any respite.

'Did you want to go to war with him? That was generally a tactic of yours.'

'That's what I do,' he nodded. 'Yeah, I wanted to go to war with him like that but I didn't have to because I was a better boxer than that. I had to box him. I can box and punch and that's what you need to be able to do when someone can deal with you on one of your levels.

'Alexis could deal with me on one level but he couldn't deal with me on a boxing level. He caught me with some good shots, he got me.

207

'But he couldn't handle me moving on my toes, that took me to another level because he never knew when I was going to start boxing and when I was going to trade leather.

'I thought they were going to try and take the fight away from me no matter what happened. I thought during the fight they were going to stop it on a foul or something irregular.

'I just was going to fight my heart out and whatever happened happened. That's all you can do anyway.

'I would say things to hype the fight and I would use my dad not being around; Ken Hawk having to get me boxing shoes, that anger that I had inside me, it had to come out.'

A few rounds in and he explained to me why his head was repeatedly jolted back by Alexis's punches.

'Yeah, he hit me with some good shots when I was standing in front of him. They were big shots.'

'Roll,' he shouted at the screen, urging himself to get out of the way.

'Roll,' he cried again, as the guy who looked a lot like he still did two decades on tried to avoid Arguello's rangy bombs.

Then the commentator picked up on Pryor, the angry, resentful brawler, changing his approach, starting to outbox Arguello as he promised me he would.

In the 14th and decisive round of their breathtaking duel Aaron, having boxed as well as brawled, pinned Arguello on the ropes. Alexis's head was frequently and brutally snapped backwards. His neck muscles relaxed alarmingly, lending him the appearance of a bobble-head doll.

'Now he's tired, now, now, now,' Aaron shouted, urging South African referee Stanley Christodoulou to jump in.

He took over from Arguello's perspective, 'I'm tired now.'

Returning from his lapse into his rival's psyche, Aaron returned as the aggressor. 'Stop the fight, referee. Stop it. He's taking a licking in there.

'He's looking at it,' he said, analysing the referee.

'He's looking at it,' he repeated, and then finally Christodoulou intervened.

'He's too late. They stopped the fight too late. They wanted him to win so bad they almost got him killed.

'They almost got him killed,' he said again, as slow-motion replays showed the exaggerated violence.

'I never had to hit a guy and not want to hit him before then. Look at him.'

Arguello was prone on the screen. Within moments of Aaron's hand being raised, however, the narrator spoke of a mysterious black bottle as the mood darkened on screen and in the lounge.

The bottle used by Pryor's controversial trainer, Panama Lewis, was being questioned. In between rounds, Lewis had been heard calling to cornermen to get him the specific bottle for Pryor to drink from between rounds in the incessant cauldron in Miami.

'When I beat Alexis I woke up the next day crying,' he added. 'I didn't wake up happy because they said in the papers, "Pryor won the fight but he won it illegally. He had something in his system."

'They made me feel bad and I had never had a drug problem or anything at that time of my life. I had never done nothing. It was only after the second Arguello fight and then my life went into turmoil.'

'What was in it?'

'Nothing.'

'Just water?' I asked.

'It was something like schnapps.'

'What did it taste of?'

'It had never happened before in the history of boxing, that's why commissioners are there, to run the fight and if they're not doing it there's something wrong with it. Why did the commissioner come to the fight? Why in the hell did the commissioner come to the fight and then say there was something in the bottle?'

If it was Eddie Futch or Emanuel Steward in the corner there would have been no controversy but it was not. It was Panama Lewis, a shit-stain on the sport who had done nothing to benefit boxing.

In fact, he had done the opposite.

Another year would pass before Lewis's most shameful act.

On 16 June 1983, on the undercard of the Roberto Duran–Davey Moore championship fight, Lewis was in the corner of Luis Resto in a bout he was supposed to lose against the undefeated and popular prospect Billy Collins Jnr.

Prior to the opening bell, Lewis removed the padding from Resto's gloves, allowing him to inflict grotesque facial damage en route to a ten-round points decision victory. Collins's father, Billy

Snr, felt Resto's gloves at the end of the bout as he congratulated the winner and immediately alerted the New York State Athletic Commission.

In October 1986, Resto was convicted of assault, conspiracy, and criminal possession of a deadly weapon – his fists. He served two and a half years of a three-year jail sentence. As an accessory, Lewis did one. The postscript to the tragedy was written when young Collins, having sustained such serious eye damage, never fought again. He fell into a pit of depression and alcoholism.

He died in March 1984 when, driving under the influence, his car careered off the road.

His father said it was suicide and that his son had made only partial physical and emotional recoveries from the fight.

'Panama Lewis,' Aaron said, thinking carefully about the character whose very name conjures controversy.

'I got to 38–0 and all that and nobody ever accused me of doing anything before that in my whole career. After this fight it changed my whole life. They had me painted as the loser.

'He was a good trainer, I really liked him, but he did a lot of damage for my fight by carrying the black bottle. It did a lot of damage.'

Pryor also had wanted to fight Duran but because of Lewis's close links with the Panamanian he talked Aaron out of chasing a showdown with him, something I could see Pryor held a manifesting resentfulness about.

Like Hearns, Leonard, Kenty, Mancini and Davis, Duran was yet another big name that eluded him.

Arguello was the great he needed for his career to be appreciated as legendary.

'He was the man that he is and that's what makes him a great fighter,' Aaron replied, when asked what made Arguello great and what made them the best friends they had become.

'What he did was take up a challenge to fight me and even then, afterwards and now – to this day – because he lost those fights with me, it doesn't mean he's not great. To me he's a living legend, definitely in my eyes.

'When it comes to him doing what Ray Leonard wouldn't do, what Howard Davis would not do, doing what Tommy Hearns wouldn't do, and doing what any of those punks wouldn't do, I give him more respect than any boxer I know.'

A rematch with Arguello was inevitable and ten months after their first encounter they were at war again. This time the fight was shorter, more one-sided and there was no controversy.

Aaron was ahead on all three cards when referee Richard Steele stepped in to separate them and raise Pryor's hand.

'I retired after my last fight with Alexis,' Pryor said.

'I retired because my manager was taking 50 per cent of my money. He had a 50-50 cutback for ten years and I didn't want to agree with that contract and my wife at that time was divorcing me so when I fought Alexis the second time, my manager and I were in court and my wife and I were in court.

'Panama Lewis was also going to court. So the second time I fought Alexis I hired Emanuel Steward, who trained me. He knew what I was capable of which is why I didn't fight Tommy Hearns [who was trained by Steward]. But after that fight I didn't have a trainer, I didn't have a manager and I didn't have a wife, so I just retired.'

The downward spiral had a head start.

'Then things happened in my life. I got started on drugs and I got really upset in my life and everything. But I won't forget how at that point in my career everyone really wanted me to get the respect I deserved.'

Pryor came back several times afterwards, fighting on-and-off until 1990. He only lost one of 40 fights but his downfall was long, slow and painful. He blew his money on crack, lost his dignity, lost his self-respect, danced and shadowboxed in the street for handouts to get hits and would spend days out of his mind and lost in Florida drug dens. He dropped to around eight stone [112lb] in weight.

It was a miserable existence and no way for one of the all-time greats to end up. Thankfully, 12 years before my visit to his home, he was in rehab where he met another recovering addict, Frankie.

They clearly now had a nice life together. There were pictures of their families on the walls and their home was quiet and welcoming. Aaron's life was nothing like as exciting as it was, but he was enjoying the slower pace. His life had been wild even by boxing's delirious standards.

But he, like just about all of the others, could not shake boxing.

'Last year I weighed around 220lb and this year I got my weight back. I went to Germany last year to train Larry Donald when he fought Vitali Klitschko and I was in training but I just couldn't lose it and I forgot that you've really got to run. I was hitting the bags and everything but I wasn't running and you've got to run to lose the weight. Then I went running when I went to Germany with Larry and right now I weigh 165lb. It's not bad for my age.'

He'd learned from his errors.

'I did graduate from them but I made a lot of mistakes in my life. What happens is that...' he went quiet for a moment, 'You make a lot of mistakes.

'If you don't have anyone that loves you or looks after you financially you're going to have fun but you're going to lose out. You'll pay for it in the end and I did.

'My son Aaron Jnr is a 2003 Golden Gloves champion in Cincinnati and my other son Stephan is 27 and 8–0. He's been on TV a few times and I work with them very hard because, I said this to myself, I have to look out to them because I had no one looking out to me.

'Even though I don't have the riches no more I really don't want them. Thank God for taking them. I got shot twice.'

'Shot?' I exclaimed, asking him to expand.

'With a gun, boom, boom, boom. I got kidnapped. So I've been through a lot in my life. My point is that God took me through that, showed me how to live life and more importantly how to love life.'

With that, Frankie walked back in and smiled. The two held hands as I prepared to leave.

Frankie, who religiously collected as much memorabilia from Aaron's fighting days as she could during their time together, only realised after a few months together that she had been dating a Hall of Fame fighter.

Aaron was now a proud dad, husband and ex-fighter who finally had the credit he deserved.

It was something he was rightfully proud of.

'I really wanted to show people that God had answered my prayers... again,' he smiled radiantly.

The Pryors said they would keep in touch and both hugged me as I left to begin the final leg of my race to New York.

That nameless shithole I stayed in was the last 'hotel' I visited before I flew home.

CHAPTER 17

I travelled overnight, of course, slept on the hard floors of the Port Authority bus station the following evening and that morning took the subway back to JFK, flying back to my English normality.

The journey was over, after more than 20 interviews in ten (though I had been to many more) cities in less than 30 days.

I had experienced more in a month than I had done in years in the UK.

I had seen poverty but had met legends.

I had been hungry and tired but was uniquely satisfied.

Back in Britain that feeling did not last long.

I decided to try to do a similar thing, without the incessant travelling. Terry Downes and John Conteh both wanted money and Dennis Andries would not speak. Their attitude was so different to the American fighters I had spoken with.

Piece by piece, I sold stories from my trip and took menial jobs.

I worked as a bouncer by night, driving for a local stationery firm delivering supplies to schools, offices and businesses all over Dorset, Somerset, Hampshire and Wiltshire by day.

When I was out on the road I would sometimes call the fighters I had met.

More often than not, someone saying, 'Hey, it's the crazy English guy' greeted me on the other end of the line.

Life as a freelance sportswriter became increasingly surreal. One moment I was at Lennox Lewis's retirement press conference in London with the then heavyweight champion of the world and his mum, Violet, and within hours I was stood on the door of a night-club turning away thugs who thought they were Lennox Lewis.

I yearned to get back out on the open road and return to America.

Driving around the rolling countryside in rural southern England, I constantly thought of new places and fighters to visit Stateside. The list was long and I couldn't wait to go back out there. All I needed was to make enough money for the plane fare and a magical Greyhound ticket.

I had lived a dream and was desperate to do it all over again. I even missed having an empty stomach and sleeping on the buses.

The frustration of my career not progressing and dozens of job rejections, from those at least courteous enough to respond, meant there was nothing to lose by going back.

Maybe another trip would pay dividends. As Mark Twain once wrote, 'The man with a new idea is a crank until the idea succeeds.'

I may have been seen as a crank after the last trip but if I kept working at it maybe it would lead somewhere.

The temp job lasted a couple of months and then a call came to work for a newspaper in London for a while which was also short-term.

I had grown to begrudge living in a small city, small community, knowing that there was more exploring to be done.

I wanted to see faces light up, like I had with Jimmy Young and Jeff Chandler. I missed Saad, too, and there were so many more like him, anonymous in the neighbourhoods where they lived.

I wanted the fighters to feel like champions again, that they were still worth something to somebody and that they had not been forgotten.

By September I had made my mind up and by mid-October I was on my way, flying to Newark where I planned on jumping straight back on the Greyhounds and returning four weeks later from San Francisco.

I made my contacts aware of my plans and so it was, a few months after my last visit, I was back on the road to nowhere.

Chapter 18

AH, Philadelphia. How I had missed you. I was within touching distance of my old acquaintances, near the Rocky steps, on the roads where Saad had been abandoned, amongst the gyms. It all felt homely, as though I was walking on the set of a film I'd seen a thousand times.

After a brief layover in Zurich, my ever-dependable chauffeur Tom Jess collected me from Newark and drove me back to the City of Brotherly Love.

As we chatted about who we might find and where we would go several names came up. Johnny Carter, whom former rival Chandler had affectionately talked about, Meldrick Taylor and Rocky Lockridge, too, were contenders.

Stanley 'Kitten' Hayward, Tom said, was working in one of the Philadelphia court buildings. If we invested some time and effort we could find the former welterweight contender.

Hayward had whipped Curtis Cokes inside four rounds and Cokes had since been inducted into the Hall of Fame.

Hayward was perfect. I had not heard anything about him for years but had seen several of his fights on tape. He was a determined, gritty battler with a mean streak that was apparent in his willingness to march through punishment to dish it out.

After parking in a multi-storey, we sucked in the air of a clear and dry autumnal day and made our way to the courts. Tom also wanted to meet Hayward so he could sign a poster of just about every great Philly fighter you could name.

Hayward's face was tucked in proudly and deservedly among them. There were signatures from many of the others already on there.

We found an administrative type downstairs and asked if she knew where we could find 'Kitten' Hayward.

'Hayward? Sounds familiar,' she deliberated. 'But what's the first name again? "Kitten"?'

'Yes, that's right,' I said.

'No,' she replied. 'I don't know a "Kitten". The only Hayward we have here that I know of is Stanley and I don't know if he's in.'

'Stanley "Kitten" Hayward, that's his full name, that's him,' I said.

She was clearly surprised at my delight.

'He works on one of the upper floors,' she offered. 'But I'm not sure he's in. Go and take a look.'

Tom and I piled into a lift, questioning two smart-looking men with security passes. When I asked the first if he knew who 'Kitten' was he said he had never heard of him but the second cracked a wry smile and said, 'I know him. He works on the third floor. You can't miss him.'

As we gained momentum, Tom and I grew more eager.

We patrolled the long corridors with their high, white ceilings and marble floors. We asked more questions and unfortunately our endeavours began to look less likely to bear fruit.

After around half an hour, Tom perked up.

'I think that's him over there,' he said. 'I only caught a glimpse of his face but it looked just like him.'

The man he pointed to was going into a courtroom with a bundle of papers stacked under his arm and I could only see him from the back.

He wore a suit that was a shade somewhere in between emerald and sapphire. He had deep, shiny black hair and seemed about the right height to be a welterweight.

It rapidly dawned upon me that it was neither the time nor the place for an interview and that he was probably too busy to talk to us, perhaps even a little embarrassed by two strangers coming in off the street to reminisce about the old days.

We waited patiently for the door to reopen only for other people to disappointingly trot out.

There was no sign of our man but we knew he would re-emerge at some stage. He had to. We edged closer to the door, trying to peek inside whenever it came ajar. It opened again and as we got ready to look inside our man came out.

'Excuse me, sir,' I said timidly. 'Are you "Kitten" Hayward?'

'That's right,' he said, with a bubbly and joyful expression.

A contagious grin spanned his face.

'You want to talk about boxing, don't you?' he asked.

'How can you tell?'

'Nobody has called me Kitten in years,' he smiled. 'I thought I had seen the last of Kitten.'

He shuffled us into a quiet corner of the courthouse and we stood and talked. He commended Tom and I on our alliance and said he was impressed that a wannabe writer from England and a fight fan from New Jersey had conspired to track down an ex-boxer in court.

In his heyday he was a crowd idol in Philly, a popular fighter who won respect the hard way. Evidently he was still popular now.

'Hey man, how are you?' he called out to a passer-by.

'Good, thanks,' came the reply.

I told him about the Philly fighters I had met and, like me, he had a soft spot for Matthew.

'When we sparred, Saad didn't know when to stop coming and I said to him, "Man, why are you having a war with me?"'

'Every sparring session's a war around here,' Tom said of the notorious city gyms.

'You don't mind having wars when you're younger but as you get older you get more professional,' smiled Kitten. 'Joey Giardello taught me how to be that way. I became smarter. That's why I lasted so long.

'Briscoe, "Cyclone" Hart, "Boogaloo" Watts, I would have ate them guys up in my young days but I was older when I fought them.'

'Hi Sandra, how you doin'?' he said, interrupting his flow to greet a top Philly barrister before continuing.

'When you get older you don't take them serious. Old professionals say about young fighters, "They can't fight."

'What was good about me is I had another side. My name is Stanley "Kitten" Hayward but my real honest given name that my mother gave me was Stanley Cornelius Hayward. Cornelius you never heard of but when I got hit in the ring Cornelius would tell the other two guys, Stanley and Kitten, to destroy the other guy. Kitten was the mean one. Oh, he would destroy you.

'That's the other somebody in my heart, the guts, the guy that would get in there and wear you down and throw all those punches.'

After just a few minutes Stanley Cornelius was enjoying the memories so much he had seemingly forgotten where he was.

Perhaps he no longer felt the constrictions of his smart suit, instead, picturing the man he saw in the mirror 40 years ago who was naked from the waist up and ready to unleash his inner Kitten.

I asked how his boxing journey had begun and he faked a left hook to my chin. My right came up in self-preservation and, as it did, Kitten threw another left downstairs.

'See that right there,' he said, raising his left. 'I had that good Philly left hook.'

But it did not start smoothly.

'I had one amateur fight and I got stopped in the first round. I wanted to become the best and because I thought I wasn't any good as an amateur I figured I would fight professionally. But it was all about money. I got into the boxing game not wanting to be a fighter but having to be. There was a guy named Candy McFarland. Did you ever hear that name?'

He carried on before I could answer.

'He was the best, man. But he had a different style. He was more of a boxer and mover. Stick and move, stick and move.

'You know what? On 35th Street and Halford Avenue there was a boys' club years ago but they remodelled it and everything's different now.

'We were playing basketball. I was a basketball player, you know? I loved it and these guys were going upstairs to the club and I'm like 17 years old so I say, "Come and play" and they say, "No, we want to see Candy McFarland box."

'I said, "That guy can't fight," and his father overheard me and said, "You want to put the gloves on?"

'I thought I was a tough kid so I said, "Yeah, I'll put the gloves on."

'We had these big 16-ounce gloves and when I put them on my hands dropped down to my sides. And when my hands went down he hit me right in my eyeball. It was a bad loss,' he laughed.

Humiliated, Kitten lay in wait for Candy when he left the gym. With a rock in his paw, he was prepared to blindside McFarland who, incidentally, would go on to become a good pro.

'Back in them days in the early '50s I said I was going to grease this guy. That's the word everyone was using and we were outside waiting for him to come out and get it on in the street and I'm like, "Where they at?" Anyways, his father came out with him and said, "Why don't you come back and try again tomorrow?"

'I said, "OK, I'll be back again tomorrow."'

So Stanley dropped the stone.

'But I was a street fighter,' he smiled mischievously, looking around the courts.

He returned to the gym the next day and, in his words, the place was packed. Everyone came to see little tough kid Hayward be taught a lesson by clever Candy.

Kitten's enthusiasm was lighting up the courthouse and Tom and I were hanging on his every word as he encouraged us to huddle in like scouts around a campfire.

'The next day the place is packed, the Westway Boys' Club. I'm no boxer guy and he blacked the other eye so I had two shiners now and I was really upset. It was raining and when I went out I picked up a stick and I was ready to wail his ass and he came out and his father said, "Why don't you come back again tomorrow?"

'So I said, "I will," and I came back the next day and he said, "The one thing I like about you is you got a lot of heart, but to whup up on him you got to try training. I've got to teach you how to fight and box."

'I said, "How long's that gonna take?"

'He says, "It won't take long."

'I said, "I want him."'

So I stayed around and trained and all that and whoever he had in the gym I started whuppin' them up.'

After training for two weeks, Kitten was ready to take on Candy and this time he passed the test. He did not get a black eye.

'I started whuppin' up on him and bloodying him up and I got my revenge. Then what happened was I didn't go to the gym no more and he and his father started looking for me. They found out where I lived at. He said, "Hey, why don't you come to the gym?"

'"I don't want to be no fighter."

'"Why not?"

'I said, "Ah, that ain't my bag. I do what I want to do."

'He said, "But you could make a lot of money."

'I said, "How much could I make?" He said "About $5,000–$10,000" and I said "I'll see you in the gym the 'morrow."

'That was a lot of money, but if they had said it was one or two million I would have been in there quicker. These fighters today make that much.

'The type of fighter I was, I took punches to make a fight. I was a fighter's fighter. You couldn't come to a fight of mine and sit down because it was always going to be action. They would say "Hayward's up next" and they knew there was going to be action. That's how Philadelphia fighters work. We would box anyone.

'But I always got nervous before every fight. Every fighter does. You're a fighter,' he said, pointing at me. 'You know what it's like. But the moment you get hit it's over with. You know that.'

A lady Hayward's age who was wearing a sharp grey suit walked by.

'This guy's from England. He wants to know about my history in boxing,' said Hayward, out to impress.

'Oh really,' she smiled, staring longingly at the ex-pug.

'You used to beat people up,' she said to Hayward while addressing me.

'You don't mix it up with him,' she warned me and Tom. 'You hear me.'

Tom already had his next question ready as she left us to get down to business.

'Who was the best you fought?' he asked. It saved me asking one of the obvious ones, at least.

'A guy just asked me that in the elevator and I would say, getting to the top was my hardest fight. That means you've got to be exciting and getting to the top is your hardest fight because every fight is a hard fight. "Cyclone" Hart was the hardest puncher. I took him lightly. But I'm a ladies' man. I was never in the gym.'

Funnily enough, a leggy brunette strutted by and, almost forgetting his court image, he purred, 'Hey baby.'

She said the same in return.

'You had to lock me up,' he whispered, checking the woman out from behind as she strolled on by. 'I fought for 21 years but I was never in the gym. I was number one a long time. If I had fought Emile Griffith when I was younger... At the time I was waiting for a shot it would have been a sensational fight. It would have been a knockout, either he knocked me out or I knocked him out. My style of fighting was different back then. I would take a punch to give a punch. But when I lost to Gypsy Joe I told my manager, "I'm not the dumbest man in the world, I have to change my style."

'You see where I'm at? You see how I dress? You see how I talk, right? Nobody would ever say I'm a fighter,' he continued apace.

'I had two classic fights with Bennie Briscoe. Two Philadelphia fighters will always give you the best fight because they want superiority and to be the top guy in town.'

Although the big contests came and went for Kitten, they were either too early or on the wrong side of his peak.

He was 39 when he retired.

'I can say that was my handicap and why I lost several of my last fights,' he explained. 'I was afraid of being in the ring. That's when I knew it was over. I didn't have a feel for it no more.'

Another important suit-wearing fellow walked by and asked Stanley how he was.

'I'm fine. Yourself?'

'Yeah, we have a jury.' The news was apparently pleasing for both men.

Although Hayward managed himself and admitted to squandering some of his winnings at the racetrack, it looked like he wasn't doing badly.

'Why keep fighting and losing all the respect you get from boxing just to make a few dollars? I knew I was handicapped by age so I got out.'

Refusing to remain downcast, he picked me off with a playful jab and got up on his toes.

'I never lost it. You see my movement, you see my movement. I'm 65 now, you see me.'

He danced, throwing punches as people stared at us.

'You never lose it.'

'You miss it, don't you?' I asked.

'Yes, I do. But my time has gone. I made it. I didn't make half a million in total, maybe about $150,000.

'I made good investments in property at Fairmont Park. I knew someone who renovated one of the places there so I said "I could do that", and I did. I bought a few places and I'm letting them out.'

He was a pensioner who still dressed to impress and swaggered around the courts as though he owned them.

'I'm not married and I like it that way,' he added. 'We had a guy in here the other day who was getting divorced for the seventh time. I said, "Man, didn't you learn from the first one?"'

Kitten still wanted to play.

'Feel my biceps,' he implored us.

He said he weighed around 139lb. He fought at anywhere from 140lb to 160lb and certainly looked bigger than 139, although not in a bad way.

'I've been working here for 34 years. I know all the guys and all the top cases, you know, like the Mob cases. I knew the Mob guys through fighting and when the Mob guys see me they say, "Damn, Kitten, you look good."'

A security guard walked by, jangling a hefty set of keys.

'Hey, how you doin'?' Kitten asked. 'Locked anybody up today?'

'Not yet,' he laughed. 'But it's early.'

Hayward switched his attention back to us. 'I'm blessed that I was taught to do the right thing. My mother was a teacher but she was more than that. She was a very educated lady and a pioneering council woman at one time in Philadelphia, a big name, like that lady over there now,' he said, acknowledging an executive woman strutting through the corridors.

As we prepared to leave, Tom handed over his poster to be signed. Kitten was pleased to see his image of 40 years ago returning a menacing stare.

With the marble pillars of the courthouse in the background, Hayward waved goodbye.

'Wherever you go next, good luck,' he smiled.

Chapter 19

ATOP the narrow wooden staircase that led up to Augie's Gym in South Philly, shadowboxers were whispering 'tsche, tsche, tsche' after each punch. They paused to move their heads, circled the floor and outwitted their invisible opponents.

It was different to the confines of the Philadelphia courts.

I instantly recognised one man, Bobby 'Boogaloo' Watts, courtesy of his trademark wide-brimmed hat.

A well-built specimen cut a solitary figure as he skipped by himself in the corner near a large window. His hard, chiselled physique made for a musclebound silhouette. He was the only one no one was telling what to do or when to do it.

He wasn't a puppy in terms of age, but his swollen arms, thick chest and slender waist told me he wasn't that old.

He reminded me of how another Philly boxer, Buster Drayton, once looked.

Boogaloo warmly introduced himself. So did the man the gym was named after.

Augie Scimeca, a veteran manager and trainer, spoke with the conviction that whatever he said was right.

Boogaloo was quiet, even shy, but if he'd chosen to he could have bragged about his draw with Marvin Hagler or showdowns with city rivals Bennie Briscoe, Willie Monroe and Eugene Hart.

I expected flamboyant but got modest. I thought he would be boisterous, but as we chatted on the ring apron in the dark, musty gym, I had to ask him to repeat himself because he wasn't speaking loudly enough over the background din.

He wore a blue and grey sweater, baggy tracksuit bottoms and the hat he would often remove to scratch his greying-dark hair.

He told me how his cousin, Jimmy Young, had 'encouraged' him to start boxing and from that point on we had some common ground.

'I met Jimmy earlier this year,' I said.

'Oh yeah, you're the guy from England that has been finding all the old Philly guys?'

He had been pleased I had gone into deepest darkest Philadelphia to try and shed some light on his cousin. He was from real fighting stock. Another cousin, this time younger, David Reid scooped boxing gold at the 1996 Olympics.

As we talked about Philly fighters he pointed towards the muscular boxer in the black singlet training in the corner.

'I'm sure Buster Drayton would be happy to talk to you,' he said, optimistically.

Even though the fighter he showed me looked like Drayton, Buster had to be about 50 now and he appeared to be nothing of the sort.

'I started boxing because of my cousin, Jimmy,' Watts recalled.

'What a nice guy,' I interrupted.

'Yeah, he got me started. We wasn't with no gang or nothing like that then but if you're not in a gang people would harass you. So later I joined them and started going to the gym and from then on I was a fighter.'

He had a 45–3 record as an amateur but still needed to work as a longshoreman to pay the bills once he turned pro.

'I liked the game,' Watts went on. 'I did well in the amateurs and I had just recently got married. I had a couple of kids so I decided to give pro boxing a try.'

The speed bag was taking a pasting in the background and a high-pitched alarm tolled to tell the fighters when each three-minute session had expired.

I asked Boogaloo who was the best of the Philadelphia famous four; him, Briscoe, 'Cyclone' Hart or Willie Monroe.

'Well, I think me. But I didn't get my opportunity because I never had a promoter. "Worm", Bennie, Hart and all, they had a promoter.

'Before I fought Worm and Hart I had fought guys who were world-rated like Armando Muniz and Ralph Palladin, so I fought a few big-name guys over the years. And don't forget, I fought Marvin Hagler. Twice.'

The first contest with the future middleweight king was a famous Philadelphia controversy with many believing Bobby had been gifted a draw.

A total of 6,167 watched it at the Spectrum.

'To tell you the truth, actually I overtrained,' he reflected. 'You know, because two years before that I fought Worm and Hart at 158–159lb, two years later, for Hagler, I came in at '55 and a half.

'I overtrained. I thought I won. I was smart enough to tie him up so he couldn't get off and I got off and then I'd tie him up when he came back at me. He put up a good fight but I didn't consider him at that time a real tough fighter. It was just that I had the strength to handle him.'

Regardless, it was a dubious decision. Even promoter Russell Peltz said afterwards, 'How am I going to get decent fighters to come here after results like this?'

Outraged, Hagler fumed, 'He was just trying to steal the fight and they let him.'

'I actually fought Marvin the second time on seven days' notice,' Watts went on. 'The money was there and I couldn't turn it down.'

Two one-sided rounds later, Hagler's hand was raised and he accelerated towards a world title fight with Britain's Alan Minter.

Boogaloo, who earned his nickname because he was apparently a great dancer back in the day, was also a good mover in the ring. He wasn't the stereotypical Philly fighter but boasted the well-renowned heart and desire.

Sadly his chin let him down. Of his seven losses he was stopped six times.

'Having fought Worm and Hart I wanted to fight Bennie Briscoe but at the same time I didn't want to fight Bennie because we lived around the corner from each other. Our kids used to play together, so I did and I didn't want the fight.

'But, for me, I always wanted to be known as the best at whatever I do. I didn't have a problem with those guys although us fighting each other meant we knocked each other off. But I never had a choice because I never had a promoter. If I did, maybe I would have fought elsewhere.'

Now 54, Bobby looked good. He had won 38 of his 46 fights, lost seven and drawn one in a career that spanned from 1969 to 1983.

After a long spell at the top, Boogaloo was determined not to become a fighter who was used to pad a prospect's record and, barring one exception, he called it a day.

'I'd been retired for six months and I got a call for a good amount of money and I thought, "Why not?"'

He was beaten in four by Englishman Mark Kaylor at Wembley Arena and decided again to retire. This time he kept his word.

'I really got frustrated that I wasn't fighting the way I wanted and that the fights coming in saw me billed as the opponent. I didn't want to be a name for anybody. I was on the outside looking in and I knew it was time to quit for good.'

Bobby was content in retirement. Married to Judy for almost 40 years, they had three daughters in their 30s and he worked at the Philadelphia University of Art.

'I wanted to become a champion of the world and I never gave up on that dream but it didn't happen. So after I retired I started training fighters and I trained Charles Brewer and he did something I never did by winning the world title. So now I can say even though I never became a world champion, I made one.'

With that in mind, he waved over his friend, Buster, to talk to me.

Drayton said he would happily chat once he had showered and promptly reappeared wearing a large white hoodie and black tracksuit trousers.

From the outset of our chat on the benches in the gym he made it clear that the success he enjoyed as a fighter was down to being Marvin Hagler's sparring partner over several vicious years. They shared hundreds of tough, highly charged rounds.

As Larry Holmes learned the trade from Ali, Buster learned the brutal business from the Boston-based middleweight.

'I stayed in camp with Marvin for four years and I seen guys get carried out, laid out and knocked out because they had the wrong attitude,' said Buster.

'They were thinking, "I'm going to knock Marvin out and beat him up," but my attitude was that I went there to learn. "Show me everything I can learn from you."

'After four years Marvin said, "You're ready to be your own champion now."

'I said, "I'm not ready" and he said, "Oh yes you are." It was like a father telling a son, "You're 18, now get out there." After being around Marvin I knew what to expect. It was just a case of when am I going to get my chance. That was my blessing, going to camp with him.'

Yet Buster didn't want to be a fighter when he was a kid. He went to the Philly gyms to watch boxers train, not to get involved. It was only after he joined the Marine Corps as a machine-gunner that he stumbled into fighting.

Following an altercation with a colleague, Drayton was told life would be easier if he joined the boxing team and that he could even enjoy some benefits. Despite initial success, he still wasn't keen and when he demobbed, in 1976, he was asked to compete in the Olympic trials. Having left the forces, the last thing he wanted to do was carry on boxing when there was no added motivation.

Almost inevitably in Philadelphia he fell back into the sport and while he furthered his academic education people from his neighbourhood were telling him it was a shame he had not taken boxing more seriously because there had never been a Golden Gloves champion from their area.

That was all Buster needed to hear to be tempted back and he started training with the goal of capturing the amateur title.

Back in the gym, he said he used to tear up the likes of Frank 'The Animal' Fletcher, 'Not because I was good but because of how bad I wanted it.'

He started knocking fighters out in competitions and his decision was soon made. He wanted to fight.

Although his mother named him Moses Buster Drayton she told him he had to drop Moses if he was going to be taken seriously as a fighter.

Buster then walked me through the highs and lows of his career. He was proud to have Hagler ringside when he captured his own world title, the IBF light-middleweight belt, after going 15 rounds with Carlos Santos.

Buster's record was not exceptional when he won the championship but he had a wealth of experience to draw upon. Travelling everywhere as the 'opponent' at the start of his career, he learned different fighting styles and adapted overseas having fought in Italy, England and South Africa.

He took a couple in England, against Mark Kaylor – the man who had ended Boogaloo's career – and Jimmy Cable.

Cable was knocked out in a round.

'Of all of my fights, the only easy one I had was when I knocked Jimmy Cable out because everyone I fought really were either former world champions or became world champions.

'They called me back a month later to fight Mark Kaylor at short notice but the gym was my life. I did everything in the gym, I even ate in the gym and when they called me back I was ready.

'They said Kaylor was a big puncher, that he was this and he was that. But you can be the biggest puncher in the world but how can you hit what you can't see?'

Buster's two-defence reign was then brought to a halt by game Canadian Matthew Hilton.

'I have to give credit to him because he went the whole 15 rounds,' Drayton recalled. 'I broke my hand in the third round so I didn't feel bad about the decision. I fought with one hand from the third to the 15th. With one hand. Even though I lost I was happy. I thought the only person who could do something like that was Muhammad Ali.

'People would ask me, "Why are you so happy you lost the title?" But I won something more than that. I learned something about myself.'

He conceded that the thunderous-punching Julian Jackson, who stopped him in round three of their 1988 Atlantic City clash, 'just plain and simple caught me', and he held only one person responsible.

'I blame myself. Wait for the hook, take the hook and come back with a hook.

'That was in my mind. But I had my hands out too far and he came around the side and I couldn't see it. I say to myself now, "Why didn't I slip that?"

'But in camp with Marvin I learned discipline, how to deal with a loss, how to deal with a win and how to deal with the public. I wouldn't have learned none of that if it wasn't for him.'

By Drayton's admission, when he lost to Terry Norris the Texan who fought out of California was 'coming up and I was going down'. The difference was Norris's conditioning and mileage, which a past-his-prime Buster couldn't match.

'I'd had my day in the sun. In my last fight I fought Derrick Rolon to a draw [recorded as a 12-round points loss for Buster]. I took the tape home and watched it, watched it and watched it again and as the fight went on I could see things I didn't do that I would have done if I was at my best. After that I could tell it was over.

'I'm satisfied. I couldn't be more satisfied. I'm happy most of all that, number one, I came out with all my marbles and, number two, I always said there's life after fighting.

'When you don't consider those two things, then when your career is over you got problems. Whether it is walking straight, standing up or talking, you've got problems.

'Every time a fighter gets into that ring for his first fight they should always remember there's life after this. If you go into the sport not knowing that then, when it's over, you're not going to have anywhere to turn.

'Right now I couldn't be more happy.'

Rap music blared in the gym. I asked Drayton, besides keeping in shape, what he did with his time.

He reached around in his tracksuit bottoms and pulled out a leather wallet, flipping it open to reveal a shiny metallic badge.

'You're a police officer?' I asked, clearly surprised.

'Yeah,' he smiled proudly. 'Remember I told you I went to school and everything... God has blessed me. He's been so good to me.'

Buster had been one of Philadelphia's finest for almost 20 years and graduated from three police academies, two federal and one municipal.

He'd been married to his second wife, Sylvia, for more than five years and his oldest child was 24.

'You don't look old enough to have a kid my age,' I joked.

'How old do you think I am?'

'Early 30s? No more than 40.'

I knew that didn't make any sense because he had been a champion 20 years ago. He just didn't look any older than that.

'Fifty-one.'

'You're kidding me.'

'I wouldn't kid you.'

'Augie, how old am I?' he said, waving over to the gym owner.

'Fifty-one,' he said, backing up Buster's story.

'It's a good day today,' Buster smiled.

I couldn't have agreed more.

On my previous Philadelphia visit I had the positive recollections of Marvis Frazier but the sad tales of Harold Johnson and Jimmy Young to report.

Here I was looking at three success stories. Hayward, Watts and Drayton were all getting on with life after boxing.

On this day, Philadelphia wasn't one of boxing's wastelands. It was a city where ex-fighters had been adopted by the community to play active and important roles in society. They were all working, sure. None of them could afford not to.

They hadn't made the super-money of the champions they had encountered and so perhaps they gave life after boxing, and what they did with their earnings, more thought than the better-known boxers who had frittered much more away.

They had not allowed themselves to think they would ever be comfortable enough to do nothing after their fighting careers finished.

Years ago, the three of them attracted crowds of thousands to Philadelphia's famous boxing arenas. Now they mingled daily with folk who didn't even know them, people who didn't know what they had achieved and who didn't much care, either.

Whether the trio liked it or not, and I got the feeling from all three that they weren't bothered, they had to look to the future as boxing was not going to fund their existence.

They accepted that.

It is so easy to be blinded by money, success and fame, but Kitten, Buster and Boogaloo – now there are three names you don't hear very often in the same sentence – were perfect examples of people who showed me there was more to life than the sport that they still all clearly held so dearly. What's more, they were content.

Chapter 20

THERE was a mesmerising draw to the New York skyline. It reminded me of that night in Madison Square Garden with Saad Muhammad. It also illustrated how far I was from home and caused me to excitedly hum the tune of that famous Sinatra song.

No matter how tough the going became, how hungry I was, how hard it had been to track down anonymous fighters in the biggest smoke of all, I always told myself that if I could make it there, I could make it anywhere.

It made me bite down and get on with the job.

All I had to do was picture what I might be doing in England, where I could be, what town, city or village I could have toiled in and what job I might be doing. If that did not inspire me to get a move on nothing would.

I wanted to start at the top and in New York that would mean speaking to the 'Bronx Bull', the Raging Bull, Jake LaMotta.

A friend of a friend messaged me his phone number and I called as soon as Tom and I arrived in the city.

'Excuse me Mr LaMotta,' I enquired, recognising the gruff, 90-year-old voice on the end of the line. 'I was hoping we could meet, do an interview and I could take a couple of pictures?'

'Well, time is money, kid,' he growled. 'So how much money you got?'

'Sorry Mr LaMotta. I don't have much money,' I replied.

'Well kid,' he said. 'If you ain't got the money, you ain't got the money.'

The phone went dead. Plan B was to talk to Emile Griffith but following a call to his manager, Howie Albert, I learned Griffith was in Wales. Jose Torres was up next.

The Puerto Rican star had been guided to the light-heavyweight championship of the world by Cus D'Amato.

Besides being a good fighter, he had also been the chairman of the New York State Athletic Commission and authored two books. His writings on Mike Tyson, *Fire and Fear*, and Muhammad Ali, *Sting Like a Bee*, were popular for different reasons.

The latter was adored by critics for his insight into the psyche of The Greatest and boxers in general.

But *Fire and Fear*, a gossipy book about alleged incidents in Tyson's chaotic life, was a superior seller.

Jose said he would welcome me in his apartment, giving me directions of the best way to his place in Greenwich Village using the subway.

Within half an hour or so I was there. His apartment was in an unremarkable block although in a sought-after location that would have cost a fair amount of money, I presumed.

Although he had said I should come straight over he still only greeted me in boxer shorts and a vest, as if it was a daily occurrence.

I wasn't fazed by the black and white striped boxers or the crisp white vest. After all, it was more than Joey Giambra had worn.

D'Amato was soon the main topic of conversation.

Torres told me about a conversation he had with Cus when he was just an eager pupil. It was about great heavyweights and Rocky Marciano in particular after D'Amato had given him some tapes of the Brockton banger to watch.

'I never forgot what Cus said to me,' started Torres. 'I said, "Cus, I've been watching him every day for a week, every day, and Marciano got hit *less* than Joe Louis, *less* than Muhammad Ali, less than all those champions and all I knew before that was he used to take punches to hit you once." But he was actually so smart. He was awkward but he was smart and he got hit less than most heavyweight champions.'

'Sonny Liston was an intelligent fighter too?' I ventured, knowing Torres would appreciate the former champ who traded on fear.

'Of course,' Jose agreed, his face lighting up. 'Of course. But what happens is there are fighters who are good and entertainers. Sugar Ray Robinson was an entertainer, he knew the way to fight that made him look better. I think Cus was the person who knew boxing better than anyone in history, the way he explained things and the way he understood it. I asked Cus one time, "If Sandy Saddler beat Willie Pep three out of four times, how come everyone talks about Pep being the best but nobody says anything about Sandy Saddler?"

'He would say it was because the fight when Pep beat Saddler was not filmed. He said it was the greatest exhibition anyone in the world had ever seen from a fighter so everybody remembered that fight better than the three he lost.

Jose, 'Chegui' to his friends, started boxing when he was in the army.

He volunteered to join the military but instantly regretted it.

'The sergeant, who knew I didn't like it, came to me and said, "You look like an athlete. If you join a sport it will make life better." So I went for track and field and the season was over. I went for basketball, season was over. I tried baseball, season was over. "What's open?" I asked.

'He said boxing, I said OK.

'I hated the army so I became a boxer. In my first fight, I knocked the guy out and it gave me the incentive to keep going. I said, "Holy shit. I can knock guys out."

'Second fight, I knocked the guy out. I used to be a big fighter in the street. When I was a kid we just loved to fight and any kid who came from the next town we just targeted.

'Me and my friends would make out we were just little helpless kids and one day there was this guy who was bigger than me so I threw the punch first. Bang, boom,' Jose shouted, firmly losing control of any inhibitions he might have had with a stranger in his lounge.

'But we never used any knives or weapons. We were street fighters in my hometown.'

Jose made swift progress in the ring.

His 29th amateur fight was the 1956 Olympic final, which meant he was inexperienced for the stage he found himself on, particularly against a quality operator like Hungarian Laszlo Papp, who was gunning for the third of three Olympic golds.

Somewhat unsurprisingly, Torres left with silver.

Back in America he met D'Amato, who wasn't driven by money.

'He said, "Let's put you back in the amateurs." So he put me in the [New York] Golden Gloves, and I won the Golden Gloves. Then I won the national Golden Gloves and then I won the AAU title, all in one year. I think it was 1958. Cus could not believe I went to the Olympics after just 24 fights.'

Torres clearly recollected knocking out Gene Hamilton in a round in 1959 on his debut.

'For my first fight they gave me $500 but Cus D'Amato gave me $1,000 in cash,' he said.

'The second fight, $500, he gave me $1,000. I knew I was only being paid $500.

'The third fight I made $1,000, he gave me $2,000 and then, when I started to make real money, he didn't take one cent. He was making money with Floyd Patterson, who was the heavyweight champion.'

They had a handshake deal.

'He never took one penny from me,' said Torres. 'He took zero and *he* gave me money. I used to box with Floyd every day and I learned so much because he was a good champion.'

I enquired after Floyd's health. I had heard he was not doing well, and had severe memory problems.

'Not good,' Jose admitted, tinged with sadness before going on to say that, like Ali, Floyd's condition was not boxing-related.

'Floyd's parents both had Alzheimer's and they never fought. Floyd is now at the dangerous stage where he's forgetting how to swallow.

'Willie Pep also has it [Alzheimer's] and he never got hit.'

Whichever direction our conversation took, it was never long before it reverted to the man who meant the most to Torres.

'Cus would teach me about the intellectual side of boxing, the emotional side, the psychological side. His training was not all physical. It was all mental. Then I had Joey Fariello working with me who was also a student of Cus.'

When he started punching for pay, Torres thought he might become a champion but D'Amato, a mastermind of instilling self-belief into his charges, said he knew Jose would.

'I wasn't even thinking about it,' Torres continued. As time went on, though, Cus made him certain.

I then asked Torres about the books.

'I did one on Tyson,' he started, enthusiastically.

'Yeah, *Fire and Fear*. I read it,' I said.

'Did you like it?' he asked.

'I preferred *Sting Like a Bee*,' I replied diplomatically.

'I liked *Sting Like a Bee* better than the Tyson book,' he agreed. 'But the Tyson book sold more because of the gossip and the shit and the Tyson attention. But I like the Ali book.

'When Tyson came to Catskill he was only 13 and I was very impressed because he was so smart, he was so intelligent,' Torres explained. 'You know, the reason he was the best was because Cus taught him. Cus knew Tyson was a pick-pocket. He said that when Tyson would get on to public buses the drivers used to warn people, "Watch yourself, watch your wallets and your pockets because every day we get complaints about people who take things from the public."

'Cus told me Tyson used to wait until the chauffeur warned the people, then he stole the money. Cus thought that was a good quality.'

Jose laughed loudly before going on, 'He thought it was good that Tyson used to steal the money after the people had been warned.'

Back to his own career and Torres said the late Papp, his amateur rival, was the best he faced and that hard Nigerian Dick Tiger, whom he fought twice, was his toughest opponent.

'I hurt him once or twice but I could not knock him out,' he said. 'They were both close fights. The second one I lost by one point and I thought it was an unjust decision. But if they had given it to me he would have thought it was unjust. It was that close. I always feel that I hit him more than he hit me, but he hurt me a couple of times.'

Jose regarded Archie Moore as the best light-heavyweight of all time and Ali as the best boxer he ever saw. He captured the title against Miami-based Ali stablemate Willie Pastrano in one of his finest displays.

'He was a smart boxer and one of those that looked good doing it,' Jose thought. 'The referee stopped the fight and asked Willie, "What's your name and where are you?" He said, "My name is Willie Pastrano and I'm in Madison Square Garden getting my ass kicked."'

The referee stopped the fight between the ninth and tenth rounds.

But Torres admitted that being one of D'Amato's boxers meant he was not in a hard fight every time. Cus was known for accepting the easiest available options for his fighters, particularly his champions, for the highest monetary return.

While we were on the subject of Cus I asked about Joey Giambra, who said D'Amato had trained him a little.

'I interviewed Joey Giambra,' I said. 'He was recently inducted in the World Boxing Hall of Fame.'

'Were you there?' 'Chegui' asked me excitedly.

'No,' I replied, letting him down.

'Oh, I was there,' said Torres.

'But I went to his home in June,' I went on.

'Oh,' laughed Jose. 'Did he sell you a fucking book? Goddamn it. He sold me a fucking book.'

Jose could tell I had purchased one.

'You bought a book, didn't you?' he boomed.

'He signed me the book,' added Torres, 'gave it to me and I said thank you. He said, "That's fifteen bucks." I said "holy shit",' smiled Jose.

'What do you mean holy shit?' I interrupted. 'He charged me $20.'

'Ohhh,' Jose laughed happily, realising there were bigger mugs out there than him.

I'm sure I heard him mutter 'sucker' under his breath.

Jose had two sons, one lived in New York, the other in Virginia. They were in their thirties. But Torres is on a shortlist of fighters who knew when to stop and left the sport with a win. Charlie 'Devil' Green gave him the scare that triggered his retirement.

'When he knocked me down in the first round I knew it was time,' he remembered. 'He used to be my sparring partner, so I knew it was the end.'

As the interview came to a close, Torres picked up my tape recorder and asked, 'Is this digital?'

'No.'

'I paid 200 bucks for one almost like this.'

'Oh really?'

'$200. I don't know where I put it, I lost it. Then I bought another one, 75 bucks. Small too, but a little bigger and I don't know where I put it. Too many fucking fights,' he laughed. 'I'm telling you, too many fucking fights.'

I asked Jose to stand for some photos and he slid open the glass balcony doors and strode out into the bitter November New York air.

My imagination can be vivid at times but never did I think I would have a former world light-heavyweight champion dancing around, shadowboxing in boxer shorts and a vest on his balcony to keep warm while I took pictures.

'You're not getting the shorts in are you?' he asked.

'I'm trying not to,' I said.

'I'm sure people don't want to see my boxer shorts.'

'I'm sure they don't,' I smiled back.

Shortly after leaving Jose I received a call from a member of one of the charitable ex-boxers' organisations in New York.

Torres had rung and told him what I was trying to do and Jules Feiler offered a list of names of old-timers he might be able to put me in touch with.

Midway through our conversation, he said, 'Hey, are you the guy that turned up at Rocky Castellani's house?'

I confessed and was ready to be reprimanded for whatever it was I might have done wrong or, worse still, written. However, he said Rocky's daughter had told him my visit had meant a lot to the Castellanis.

I told Jules I would look in on Rocky as I was heading back to Atlantic City and he encouraged me to contact Chuck Wepner, who was hanging out at the Tropicana.

Chuck was the guy who inspired Sylvester Stallone to write *Rocky* when, as a huge underdog, he lasted into the last round against Muhammad Ali. He had also fought Sonny Liston and Ernie Terrell in a long, hard and bloody career.

I had recently read he planned to sue Stallone, claiming Sly had never paid him a bean for his part in planting the *Rocky* seed in the then out-of-work actor's head.

I travelled to Atlantic City, that place I had such a strange, sickly affinity with, that afternoon and the phone was ringing almost as soon as I was back through the door of the ghetto apartment I'd shared with Saad Muhammad that I had so often called home.

Chapter 21

'**G**ET me Tris Dixon,' barked the voice.

'Who is this?' I shot back.

'What do you mean, who is this? Get me Tris Dixon.'

'He's speaking to you,' I said, agitated.

'Tris. Hi. How are you? It's Chuck here. Chuck Wepner.'

'Hi Chuck,' I replied, off guard.

'Tris, I understand you have interviewed some great guys and I was hoping I might become one of them. I'm down here in the Tropicana at the VIP with my wife, Linda. Why don't you come down, we can talk and I can get you lunch or a drink. Whatever you want, you can have it.'

'When do you want to do it?' I asked.

'Well, we're in town for the weekend, they treat us real good here. But come now. Can you make it?'

'I'm on my way,' I said, stretching the phone cord to its limits as I reached for my notepad and tape recorder.

'I'll wait out front on the Boardwalk for you. I'm wearing...'

'I know what you look like, Chuck. See you in 20 minutes.'

I walked to the part of the Boardwalk nearest where I was staying and strolled briskly, about a mile and a half up to the sea-facing side of the Tropicana.

I spotted Chuck on his cell phone and a lady by his side. I introduced myself to Linda and Wepner cut off his conversation to shake my hand. His ham-like palm stretched out, crushing my far daintier mitt. He sported cauliflower ears, a flat nose and scar tissue around the eyes. The likes of Ali and Liston had left their signatures, particularly Liston.

After fighting Sonny, Chuck – who was known as the 'Bayonne Bleeder' in the trade – required nearly 100 of his career 326 facial stitches.

Once off the phone, he insisted we went into his VIP area in the casino. Linda joined us. She had thick lips and big boobs and her face was heavily made-up. Her eye-shadow was deep and dark, almost gothic, but she had an endearing smile and a charming, inquisitive way.

Chuck was larger than life. He was big, loud and brash but he had an apparently kind and generous nature.

'Make yourself at home, help yourself,' he said, pointing towards jugs of iced drinks and trays of hot finger food.

'Eat, eat,' he went on. 'Help yourself. They got shrimp, they got crab, they got steak, they got everything.'

I got stuck in.

'Hi honey. How are you?' Chuck said, as one of the waitresses asked if he needed anything.

'I'm great, how are you?' she said, fluttering her eyelids.

Linda shot a territorial smile.

As well as motivational speaking Chuck worked in New Jersey's thriving liquor trade. His son did some marketing for the same company and was also carrying out some investigative work on the Stallone case.

'And I tap him up for ideas for the motivational speaking engagements,' Chuck said, before going on about his boy like any proud dad.

'He's a member of Mensa, in the top five per cent in the USA. His wife is a psychologist and my granddaughter, who is 11, is in the top three per cent in the United States. She hasn't got less than 99 in a test in the last three years.

'I guess they take after my son and my daughter. I just about got out of high school. They certainly don't take after me. After I got out of high school I joined the Marine Corps for three years, then I got into security work for an electrical firm and from there I went to Allied Liquor where I am now 36 years on.

'I turned around $209,000 last year in liquor sales. I made $168,000.

'We have more than $3 million a year turnaround and we get five per cent of that. I bought my wife in with me this year. She will do a million this year, so I live large. I've got a brand new Cadillac, white with big wheels and with the gold packaging. We live in a $250,000 condo and we got a place in Florida. I do very well. I got a good life.'

He still does some protection work for a pharmaceutical company and although he's advancing in years he looked and carried himself like a hard man.

He spent years studying karate, becoming a black belt and he was well versed in judo. As an amateur he won the New York and National Golden Gloves and AAU youth championships in 1964, triumphing in the final of the latter tournament in Madison Square Garden.

Wepner, who looked up to fellow East Coast fighters Rocky Marciano and Ernie Durando, turned pro the following year and boxed until 1980.

He was invited to a trial for the Olympics before deciding to turn over because there were two guys, Buster Mathis and Joe Frazier, vying for the same spot. Aged 25, Chuck figured he didn't have time to waste and took the vest off.

Mathis was the original Olympic pick but when injury forced him out Frazier stepped in and won gold. Wepner still owned the letter of invitation to try out for the team and Mathis would later stop Chuck as a pro.

Rocky Graziano worked Chuck's corner that night but a cut-prone Wepner was sliced open so badly the scrap had to be stopped.

Before the fight, Rocky instructed Chuck, 'Go out and smoke that fat guy.'

After feeling Buster's surprising speed Chuck returned to his corner and barked, 'Rocky, you go out and smoke him.'

'He had hand speed like… Forgedaboutit,' Wepner admitted.

Chuck, never one to be intimidated, said he napped in his dressing room before the biggest night of his life, against Ali, and it was easy to see the fighter's spirit had not deserted him. He loved the machismo of being a boxer.

He apparently thrived upon his reputation as a tough guy, but in a genial way. He didn't try to live up to it. He just enjoyed discussing it.

His fighting spirit was rekindled in the aftermath of the 9/11 attacks when boxing and boxers united to raise funds for the families of the victims in New York.

Wepner, in his sixties, laced up gloves and shared the ring in Gleason's Gym with old foe and since-turned referee Randy Neumann.

He beat Neumann in two of their three fights and they put on a real show for the charitable evening.

'We are very good friends nowadays,' Wepner smiled. 'In fact, I was 63 years old when we did that exhibition and we banged it out. Everyone had gone in there and pawed at each other, kidding around but we went right at it from the opening bell. We did it for real. We had 14-ounce gloves on and headgear but... Oh boy! People clapped. They didn't clap for nobody else but they clapped for us.'

Chuck lost one of his fights with Randy on points, won the rematch on the scorecards and ironically stopped Neumann on a cut in their rubber match.

'We came out of the clinch and I hit him with a right hand,' said Wepner. 'It was in the fifth round and there was blood all over the place. I said to the ref, Arthur Mercante, "Arthur, Arthur, please don't stop the fight, my manager will take care of this."

'He said, "You're not cut. Neumann's cut."

'I said, "Oh my God, that's a terrible gash, stop the fight right away!"

'It was a close fight. Randy thought he was ahead. I thought I was.'

It ended in the sixth.

Chuck brought colour in and out of the ring and clearly his bashful days, if there were ever any, were long gone.

'I might have been with like 200 women, which is a lot of women,' he said. 'Nowadays you can't do that because of the viruses.'

But Wepner was just one of many bad boys around at the time.

'I once went up to Sonny Liston,' he recalled, 'and I said, "Hey Sonny, I'm Chuck Wepner" and he wouldn't even shake my hand.'

Despite the crimson gore over his face, he reckons he should have been allowed to finish the fight against Liston. Instead, it was stopped in the tenth with blood oozing out of Wepner from just about everywhere.

'All around, Ali was the best fighter I faced,' he said. 'You couldn't hit him. I fought a lot of great fighters. I have had fame and notoriety. I fought the greatest fighter and man that ever lived and I can say that was a great honour.

'Jerry Quarry, Ernie Terrell, Ali, Frazier, Norton, Earnie Shavers, any one of these guys would be champions today with all these titles. They only had one championship then. Now there's seven or eight. It's ridiculous.'

He asked me about some of the fighters I had seen, his fellow seventies contenders to be specific.

'How's Jimmy Young doing? I hear he's not doing good. Is he a garbage man or something?'

He also wanted to know more about Ernie Terrell and was genuinely thrilled when I said Terrell's doing well and mentioned Ernie's cleaning empire.

'No kidding. Really? Good for Ernie.

'We had a close fight.

'If I fought him in Chicago, he wins that fight. I fought him in Jersey so I won the fight. I've got it on video and it was close. He was a tough guy.'

Then Chuck focused his questions on me.

'So does your paper send you over here or do you do it on your own?'

'I'm on my own.'

'But they're paying all the expenses?'

'Not really, no. I'm being paid nothing.'

'Who do you work for?'

'Erm.'

I told him that I was living on Greyhound buses and expected to spend at least 25 of the next 30 days on the buses or in their shelters.

I then added that I had no idea if our interview would ever see the light of day.

Chuck said he was trying to work on his autobiography. *The Real Rocky*, of course, would be its title.

Chuck's public profile was still quite high. He went to events, autograph signings and charity functions involving ex-boxers. He had even arranged one or two in his time. He staged one in an Atlantic City casino and invited fellow former fighters and champions along to sign autographs and meet fans.

But some of the money from the event went missing at around the same time Jake LaMotta left the venue.

'Jake goes upstairs to his room, I followed him and I knocked on his door and he was sitting on the bed with the cash and he said, "By the way, you guys owe me a thousand bucks, ten per cent."

'So Jake said, "All right, we'll send you a cheque."

'"You'll give me the cash right now or I'll break both your fuckin' legs,"' Wepner steamed.

'Jake said, "I'm not gonna fight you, you're too big."

'Both Jake and the late Rocky Graziano, God rest his soul, they're my dear friends but two cheap bastards.'

Chuck grinned.

Even though they eventually came to an agreement, Chuck still lost money on the show but he put it on as a reunion event to get boxers some recognition for their careers and didn't mind.

As far as the *Rocky* and Stallone case was going, Chuck had an East Coast law firm with West Coast connections on the case.

'I don't want to go after Stallone,' he reasoned. 'I just want him to pay me for using my name for 20 years to promote this movie and have me make appearances with him. I mean, there are a lot of broken promises there.

'After people saw the movie they said, "Chuck, great movie you'll do great out of it."

'I didn't get a dime.'

Another glamour-puss waitress, wearing a sparkly lilac number with such a low neckline it was almost pointless, came and asked Chuck if he wanted crabs.

I was sure Atlantic City was the place for that but he politely declined.

'I'm OK thanks, Dani,' he smiled.

'You're not suing Stallone for the money, are you?' I asked.

'No,' he boomed. 'It's the principle. You wanna know something? I don't need the money. It would have been nice if the guy had done something for me, anything, over all these years when he has used my name to promote the movie and we've been together. I'm disappointed. I like Sylvester Stallone. I have always liked him but he's a multi, multi-millionaire and that movie promoted all of his other movies because he would have been nothing without that. Everything came from *Rocky*.'

Chuck hoped to settle out of court, to bring Sly to the table and reach a verbal agreement and for him to say, '"You know, Chuck, you're right. You were the inspiration, we used your name for 28 years to promote the movie." Just to come to some sort of agreement. I always liked the guy.'

I wondered if, bearing in mind he was the other fighter involved in the fight that was used to draw inspiration from, whether Ali had ever thought of suing Stallone for the Apollo Creed character.

Regardless of what I thought, Wepner asked whether there was anyone else I particularly wanted to talk to and when I said light-heavyweight Mike Rossman his ears pricked up.

'You know what? You can probably interview Mike. You can probably interview him this weekend. He's my dear friend.'

Chuck had now called many A-listers his dear friend and I wondered exactly what categorised one. After all, I was starting to feel like a friend by now.

He picked up his cell phone, which was almost lost in his massive hands, and was soon ringing Rossman.

The number was no longer in service.

Instead, Chuck insisted on giving me numbers for people he thought might be able to help on my journey.

We said our goodbyes and I headed back to the ghetto while Chuck and Linda returned to their high-priced suite.

I stayed overnight in the old apartment and left early the next morning. I had a lead. A former top contender was training fighters in Vineland in New Jersey, a 30-minute New Jersey Transit bus ride away.

Chapter 22

RICHIE Kates was a ring general who, over the years, had become a cult hero. The middleweight stylist eventually grew into a light-heavyweight banger, linking two eras. His contemporaries insisted he would have worn a world crown today but back then he was a championship-level gatekeeper and dangerous contender.

Having started out in the smaller division in the late 1960s, he filled out and was involved in some thrilling ring struggles. His fight with Matthew Saad Muhammad was violently dramatic and his South African war with Victor Galindez was an all-time classic. Kates had last been seen in Vineland and given its proximity to Atlantic City it was at least worth having a look.

It was a dry, autumnal morning in Vineland, an archetypal American suburb with a main street, a couple of cafes, a few stores and a few hundred houses.

I stopped in a couple of the shops and asked if they knew Richie Kates, 'the ex-boxer'.

The responses were negative.

I door-knocked a handful of residents who looked at me as though I had dropped out of space. One or two wanted to know more about Kates and his career. Another kept me talking for a good half an hour. He knew Kates and had even been to see some of his fights. He was a fan. But he had no idea if Richie was in Vineland or not.

The search continued.

I was in no great hurry and would rather explore every avenue than leave and realise later I might have missed him.

In fact, considering it was only a short bus ride from Atlantic City it had almost felt too easy so I fully expected to have to put in some hard work.

Nothing was ever straightforward.

I deliberated about going into the police station. It might have been the first place members of the anti-boxing brigade would have looked. They might have thought an ex-fighter was bound to have been in trouble. It was because of that stigma I initially resisted the urge to try.

Lunchtime was approaching and, running out of options, I found myself in conversation with the officer in charge at the front desk.

'I'm looking for Richie Kates,' I said. 'I understand he lives around here. He used to be a fighter.'

The man raised his eyebrows and said, 'You'll have to speak to Detective Bennie Velez. I'll just get him for you.'

I had no idea what to expect.

Velez was a short, important-looking Hispanic man and he came out with a look of concern on his face, which didn't ease my fears.

'You're looking for Mr Kates?' he queried.

That triggered the spiel I had given to countless others who had stared at me with an unsubtle blend of contempt and bewilderment.

'Well,' he said, shaking his head, 'I can tell you where to find him but I can't tell you if he will speak to you.'

I was halfway.

'OK. Where do I have to go?'

'You don't have to go far,' he said. 'But what you will have to do is wait. Mr Kates works at the Vineland Police Athletic League gym every day after work.'

'What does he do?'

'He's training young fighters. He's doing a great job and is very popular there.'

'Where's the PAL and what time should he be there?' I asked.

'Try around 5pm,' he said, and then scribbled a small map for me to follow.

With several hours to wait, I ducked into a store with an Internet terminal and checked my e-mails while scanning the boxing websites.

I printed off some details about Richie's career along with his record and headed over to the PAL.

It was locked so I sat patiently.

I would be lying if I said time flew by.

In fact, it dragged. Perhaps it was the uncertainty of not knowing if he would speak and that my time and efforts had been wasted.

There were no guarantees that an interview with him was even going to be printed and I definitely wasn't going to be able to claim any expenses for time, the return bus ticket, camera film, mini-cassette tapes for my tape recorder or batteries.

It took these quiet spells for me to contemplate what I was doing and what I had taken on. The challenge was immense.

Sure, I thought it might sound a little crazy to people, eccentric even, but the only part of it which daunted me was the number of fighters I might miss before it was too late.

The boredom in between interviews didn't concern me. I suppose the only thing that was lacking was a little more conversation but as Dylan Thomas penned in a letter once, 'I don't think it does any harm to the artist to be as lonely as an artist.'

Some writers thrive on solitude.

As 5pm neared excited youngsters of all races congregated in front of the building. A few looked over but didn't say anything.

Then one of the larger teenagers put the call out.

'Kates is here.'

He got out of his car and passed the gym keys over to the fighters, telling them to wait upstairs as he fixed his eyes on me.

He wore cream trousers, a red shirt with a dark tie and he carried a hat.

'Can I help?' he asked.

He looked big, strong and powerful and his outfit added an authoritative air.

'Yes, you can,' I eagerly replied.

After listening to my proposal he invited me upstairs to watch the youngsters train. As we talked he would point at fighters, explaining who was doing what and how long he had been working with him.

Former heavyweight contender Darrell Wilson was punching away, trying to get his career back on track.

Kates had also taken on ex-WBA heavyweight champion and one-time Mike Tyson victim Bruce Seldon, who was attempting a comeback.

Yet Kates was community-minded and apparently received as much enjoyment from helping the raw amateurs as he did the seasoned pros.

He told me he had just finished a shift in Trenton for the day, where he worked as a programme development specialist for the New Jersey Department of Corrections. He was initially employed there in the late sixties after graduating from high school. He left several years later only to return in 1996.

'I've always been a people person, someone who believes you might be able to help turn someone's life around by giving him the proper instructions and guidance,' he said.

'I'd like to think that through my job I've been able to make a positive impact on a significant number of people.

'If an inmate has treatment needs I make the assignments and different programmes for them.'

I asked if he had experienced any dealings with an inmate by the name of James Scott, his former opponent who defeated him in Rahway State Prison in 1979, halting Kates in round ten.

Richie said there had been one further encounter, when he tried to help the prisoner get on a new programme. But he said Scott was 'talking fantasies' and it was simply a 'great shame' that anyone had to serve 30 years in prison.

'A waste,' he called it.

Kates, however, could easily have taken the same path.

'Where I was brought up you had to fight,' he reflected. 'I got seven brothers and sisters and in a big family you've got to fight.'

He eventually decided to try his hand in the ring and, in his words, 'I got involved and I loved it.'

He had around 70 amateur fights, losing just five.

He 'won' the Golden Gloves in Philadelphia but got 'robbed' of a decision in the nationals in California and decided to turn pro. He was 18 years old and made $50 for his first four-round fight.

'And my cutman got $15 of that,' he smiled.

Kates was now 56.

Somebody put the gym's sound system up full blast so I couldn't hear him and he couldn't hear himself.

Rap lyrics boomed when Kates yelled, 'Turn that thing down.'

Tranquillity was promptly restored and the sound of speedballs being thumped, heavy bags being walloped and skipping ropes fizzing away took over once more.

'I was a hard trainer,' he said, looking at his boxers. 'I always took it seriously. I tell kids the right way to do things. I don't just train them, I take it a step further. The kids don't come in cursing, with their pants hanging by their butts, wearing doo rags or hats that are twisted to the side. I don't allow that. I send them outside and tell them not to come back until they get rid of the doo rag, pull up their pants and speak proper English. This isn't just about boxing. It's about life.'

As a middleweight Kates fought my old friend Don Fullmer, who outpointed him. Looking at Richie now, it's hard to believe they were from the same era because 'Mr Kates', as everyone called him, was much bigger and looked years younger.

'He's a good guy,' Richie recalled. 'I remember being a little intimidated by him. He'd fought for the world championship and had so many more fights than me. These little things add up in your mind.'

Kates said he learned from Don how to tie opponents up if he was caught by a good hard shot, because he landed plenty on Don – who kept holding.

'I remember I wasn't supposed to beat Len Hutchins and in 1971, when I fought him, I went in as an underdog,' he recalled of a breakthrough bout before he took on Fullmer.

'I went to Joe Frazier's camp as an amateur and sparred with Joe in '68 and one of the guys there was Len Hutchins and we sparred. I did real good with him.

'My manager turned the Hutchins fight down and said, "You're not going to beat this guy."'

Kates kept asking for it and was rewarded with victory.

It also moved him into that golden era of light-heavyweights in the mid-to-late seventies and it wasn't long before he earned a title shot, almost a decade after turning pro, against Argentina's WBA king and future Hall-of-Famer Victor Galindez.

It was 15 May 1976, in Johannesburg, South Africa, during apartheid. The title fight was only the second time in the country's history that a black man had been allowed to face a white opponent in a licensed bout. The ringside seats were occupied by white fans, the black supporters were confined to the final two or three rows.

'At the time, I wasn't educated about the politics of apartheid,' Kates remembered. 'I was there to fight. That was my chance to win the championship and I wanted to take advantage of it. I also believed that when the people saw I was a human being and really no different than any of them that my presence could make a positive difference.'

The Argentine was left dripping in blood following a Kates left hook in round three. Richie carried on, wielding away and the champion seemed unable to fight back. Referee Stanley Christodoulou jumped between them.

'I assumed the fight was over and I was the champ,' said Kates. 'I was as happy and excited as I ever was in my life.

'They stopped the fight for about ten minutes but it felt like a century to me.'

A crowd of more than 35,000 was going wild and the ring filled with spectators, reporters and photographers.

Christodoulou insisted the cut was caused by a head clash, not a left hook. Kates argued it was a punch. The fight resumed.

'When they first stopped the fight for the cut I thought the announcer was giving me the belt,' Richie recalled. 'Then I thought they were trying to decide if it was a punch or the headbutt, which I didn't do. They put stuff in it like cement.

'I was thinking about how they were taking the championship away from me. I was having trouble coming to terms with it. I went from the highest of highs to the lowest of lows.

'Emotionally, it tore me apart.

'Looking back at the fight now, maybe I should have made more of a protest but I was in a foreign country and, man, they stopped it with one second left in the 15th round. I thought I was ahead but it turned out he was.

'The truth is, I was never the same after that fight. I'd train hard and I was still winning but I didn't have the same determination. I wasn't making the same sacrifices I made earlier.'

The controversy earned Richie a second crack at Galindez, in Italy, and again Kates was left wondering what might have been.

'Galindez wasn't the best I fought but it was a hard fight for me,' he went on. 'In our first fight he was very cocky and arrogant but in the second fight he was a nice guy. I thought I won that second fight, too. People at ringside thought I was ahead but hey, they gave him the decision.'

Then came a shot at Matthew Franklin, later Saad Muhammad, for the vacant NABF title.

Franklin went down and was out when a Kates right ricocheted off his chin, planting him face-first on the canvas. Matthew woke up from the impact of landing on the mat, was back on his feet marginally before ten was counted and then was saved by the bell.

The same thing happened in reverse at the end of the next round. Kates hit the deck and the bell rescued him. When Richie teetered out for the sixth, however, he ate a booming right that caused him to lurch from one side of the ring to the other with no control over the direction his legs were wobbling in. It was all over.

'Even in that fight I was supposed to fight on a Monday night and there was a real bad snowstorm and it got postponed for a couple of days,' he lamented. 'So on the Monday I was ready to go. I remember, after knocking him down, his cornermen going out there, grabbing the guy and taking him back to the corner, you know what I mean?'

'But the bell saved you in the next round, too?' I countered.

'Yeah, definitely. You've got to give the guy credit because he took a licking and kept on ticking. It was my toughest fight. When I flattened him I thought that was it. It was over. Goodnight. It was a flat punch, boom. But he had good recuperating powers.'

Kates was one of a handful of fighters who took up the Rahway challenge to fight Scott in prison. He said he allowed himself to be psyched out and conceded it was an 'intimidating situation'.

'It must have been like fighting in his own cell?'

'Exactly, the inmates were in close to the ring but even with that considered I think they stopped the fight prematurely. He wasn't one of the best fighters, he was banal. He was in good condition but they wanted him to win the fight because it was good TV to have a guy like that on a show. He had all of the opportunities.'

It was ironic to hear that about a guy who was firmly behind bars, but then this was boxing.

'I kind of felt bad about it but looking back over my career that first fight against Galindez took a lot out of me,' Kates reflected. 'It changes you more than words can say. For a long time I was winning fights just to put me back on track but I think the best thing for me was to take some time off. I retired from '79 and I came back in '82. I won five fights before I retired a final time and I had boxed and beaten a couple of guys who became world champions in Murray Sutherland in '79 and Jeff Lampkin in 1983.'

Richie went out with a win, against rugged Antiguan Jerry Martin, who had given Saad all he could handle for the title and who'd whipped Scott in prison.

'I wasn't in the fight. Personal problems,' said Kates, despite getting the decision. He also realised he could no longer motivate himself.

'Martin was once my sparring partner,' he shrugged. 'I used to destroy him and when you struggle with a guy like him you get out.

'I felt the years were starting to hurt me. My hands were starting to hurt. I had been successful. After boxing, some of the other guys are not aware of their surroundings. I wanted to know when it was time to get out. I didn't want to be one of the fighters who sticks around too long. Boxing had been good to me.'

Kates was 32 and still ranked in the top ten when he walked away.

He was pleased his name stood alongside comrades Galindez, Saad Muhammad, John Conteh, Marvin Johnson and the others.

'It makes me feel pretty good because you had to make a lot of sacrifices to be associated with those guys,' he continued.

'But there are also people who say you came along at the wrong time because there were so many tough guys. You don't choose the time you come along. It was the best era. I don't think there will be another like that again. It was special and back then we fought 15 rounds.'

Now here Richie was, a father figure to amateur fighters, boys and girls, and surrogate dad to a handful of pros he was trying to steer safely through boxing's murky waters.

He finished with a 44–6 record in a 14-year career that saw him challenge for the world title twice and quit near the top. In that sense, he was one of the lucky ones.

He made the decision – not a doctor, his physical condition or his age.

He had been married for more than 30 years and had five children.

'I try to be a good husband, a good parent and a good citizen,' he said. 'I'm a church deacon. I have a variety of interests. I've seen so many fighters, including ex-champions, who are unable to put sentences together, who are begging for handouts. I take a look at my life and I consider myself fortunate.'

Although I had not travelled far it was about 7.30pm when I left Vineland. It had been another long day without much food but it was nice knowing I had a place to stay back in Atlantic City.

I spent one more night there before meeting up with Tom Jess. He was taking me to a boxing event in Pennsylvania but little did I know that in a couple of days' time I would be in prison.

Chapter 23

ONE of the great former world heavyweight champions, Larry Holmes, was holding court, thanking his friends and old fighters for sharing a big night with him.

We were at a charity function inside a Holiday Inn in Bethlehem, Pennsylvania. Each year he invited guests for cocktails and a plush dinner to raise money and for them all to reunite. The previous evening Tom had taken me to a small theatre in New Brunswick to watch Eric Idle perform live. The full house loved his very British ways and his *Monty Python* skits.

I spent the night sleeping on Tom's office floor as he worked a night shift.

We hung out the following day until the afternoon and then he took me to the Days Inn. He had to work again that night and said he would collect me in the morning.

Anyway, I opened my e-mail shortly after checking in and couldn't believe it. For months I had been trying to contact the New Jersey Department of Corrections to set up an interview with James Scott, who still resided in one of their prisons.

I never really believed it would come to anything but always thought that if it did I would fly to the USA to make it happen.

Anyway, the e-mail said I could interview Scott the next day and it gave me an address and details of who I needed to see.

I excitedly called Tom, who said we would travel to Northern State Prison in Newark the next morning.

I was buzzing again.

He had also been right when he said there would be some good ex-fighters at the function. Holmes was there, so too Iran Barkley, Harry Arroyo, Saoul Mamby and around half a dozen others, all in demand with fans wanting anecdotes, autographs and photos.

A few minutes after it began I saddled up next to Barkley, who was tipping drinks back in a corner and who I had met a couple of years earlier in Canastota. He was the former warrior who I'd given a few dollars to for the picture.

He was a thickset bulldog who looked to have come off worse in a couple of violent scrapes. He had wide shoulders, a heavy chest, a hefty waist, scar tissue around his eyes, a flat nose, a bald head and arms like fire extinguishers.

He used to squeeze his frame down to middleweight but was now not in shape and clearly couldn't make it even into the cruiserweight division.

And Iran, nearing 45, was slow in his movements. His speech was slurred at times and he tried to hit me up for another ten bucks to talk but started rambling anyway.

He had a chip on his shoulder the size of an oak tree and made what I initially considered a throwaway joke about a far-fetched comeback.

I asked him why he decided to call it a day when he clearly felt he had something to prove.

'I didn't stop,' he snapped. 'I decided to take a break and rest and let my eye heal and do things I wanted to do with my family and, you know, the passing of my mother. I was, like, grieving over her and everything so I was going through a rough time.

'My eye is fine now. This over here is the scar tissue and that ain't never gonna be removed until I'm finished.'

'The Blade' still owned a menacing stare. It was a weapon he jokingly tried on people as they came up to him asking for photos and signatures. He was particularly taken by a fan's *KO* magazine poster of him and wanted to keep it, but the fan said he had to sign it and hand it over. He did so without further complaint.

Someone said he was a warrior and I asked him what it meant to be held in that regard.

'It means a great deal. I'm glad,' he said. 'It shows all the good work I have done in this game is appreciated.

'I would have to say the best opponent I faced was Roberto Duran. I knew what he was bringing to the table.

'But it felt great stopping Tommy Hearns. They wrote me off for that fight and they wrote me off in the second one, too.'

He said he felt Hearns's body shots and would have crumbled if he had not been 'in great shape'.

'But I thank God that I held up.'

He reckoned Nigel Benn – who stopped him in a round – 'wasn't a bad fighter' but a 'dirty' one and he would love to have fought Hagler and Ray Leonard. 'Ray told me he would never fight me because I hit too hard,' he claimed.

He no longer sounded like the guy with the vicious take-no-prisoners attitude he used to have, even if he still had the look.

Barkley, at this point, sounded like a nice guy. However, he was still terribly deluded. He actually really did want to fight again. Surely any commission in the world could tell he was in no physical condition to box?

'I knew from day one I was destined to be a champion, you know what I'm saying,' he tried to explain.

'I was a throwback from the old fighters. I used to like to watch Joe Louis, Jake LaMotta, those guys.

'Being exciting was just a gift that God gave me. Not even to excite people, it was just a rage that I had in me that I felt I was being taken advantage of. You know when you back a rat up into the corner it will come out biting. That's the way it was for me.

'I don't like to look back. I try to look ahead and just look at all the good things I am doing and have done in the game.

'I would hope fight fans remember me as a great warrior, a great champion and a respectful champion.

'I'm gonna get the votes,' he said of a possible induction into the Hall of Fame, knowing full well any fighter going in had to be retired for five years. 'But I'm making a comeback. I ain't ready to go in there yet. I've got three more fights.'

'No,' I protested. 'Surely not?'

'I need the money,' he said, quietly looking around to see who was listening.

'I've got to get paid.'

I spent the remainder of the evening as a fan, trying to enjoy it while knowing that I would finally come face-to-face with James Scott in the morning.

Chapter 24

GREY skies cast sombre shadows over Northern State Prison. It was not long after 9.30am when we drew up outside the high walls and Tom drove off, leaving the spray of a morning downpour in his wake.

I was alone. It looked like a fresh storm was coming. I hoped it wasn't a metaphor. The barbed wire atop the bored grey walls menaced intently. The armed watchtowers loomed ominously – in case someone made a run for it. For me, well, it was a long way from the New Forest.

The interview with James Scott was more than two hours away but I went into the reception to make sure they were ready for my visit.

I was on their ledger, amazingly, and promptly told I was far too early.

Upon leaving the compound a tall white building, a Holiday Inn that was bizarrely situated next door, seemed like a suitable place to stop for a bottle of water. I picked up a copy of the previous day's free paper and sat on a bench inside the front door.

I then heard a recognisable voice joking with hotel staff as he checked out. I looked up and saw a big guy who must have weighed around 250lb. He wore shades and as he walked past we respectfully nodded to one another.

I knew who he was. I was sure of it. From his reaction I thought he knew me but we couldn't place each other. His glasses covered much of his face and a beard disguised the remainder. A black bandana hid his hair, if he had any. Judging by the thick curls of skin on the back of his neck I assumed he was bald.

He left the hotel and I considered going after him as I saw him load his suitcase into the back of a rental car.

Thousands of miles from home, no one here knew me. I had nothing to lose so I followed him out. Who would know if I made a fool out of myself by calling a random name to find out who he was?

'Eddie,' I said, in what I thought was a shout but probably more of a whisper.

No response.

I tried again, slightly louder.

'Eddie.'

He looked up and beamed a flashing smile.

'My man, how you doing?' he said.

He knew me, he just didn't recognise me right away.

It was Eddie Mustafa Muhammad, who I had stayed in touch with after interviewing him on the last trip. Eddie was the man who had raved about James Scott, his former opponent.

'I remember, I remember,' he said happily, although some kind of vagueness was attached to his smile.

'Are you here to see James?' I asked.

'James who?'

'Scott. James Scott,' I said, excitedly, the words tripping into each other.

'No, where is he? Is he out?'

'No, he's in the prison next door. Over there,' I pointed.

'You're kidding,' Eddie replied, concern and amazement rapidly spreading across his face.

He had said in Vegas he would love to meet James again.

Naturally I assumed that's what he was doing here on the outskirts of Newark.

Instead, he had been in town preparing former cruiserweight champion Al Cole for a fight with old heavyweight Hasim Rahman and had no idea he'd been staying at a hotel next to the guy he fought in Rahway more than 25 years earlier.

Eddie asked me questions about Scott but there was little I could tell him yet. He asked me to call him once I had spoken to James. He would have tried to join me but had a plane to catch, back to Vegas.

Eddie urged me to give James his phone number and address and told me to make sure Scott knew he would be there for him on his release. He scribbled it down on a scrap of paper for James with a short note.

We talked for about 20 minutes before Eddie left with neither of us quite believing the coincidence that had reunited us after several months and on the other side of the continent.

When Eddie headed to the airport I familiarised myself with Scott's records, criminal and boxing, but had not had the time to do as much homework as I would have liked. I was doing what I called a 'naked' interview, one with very little preparation.

Northern State housed many of the East Coast's most violent and unpredictable personalities. It was not a place where I wanted to do anything 'naked'.

Scott had been in New Jersey's prisons for almost three decades. He had faced murder charges after a botched robbery back in 1975. While waiting for a trial he had been allowed to fight inside, starring in televised bouts until he was finally convicted in 1981.

Time passed quickly enough, aided by the apprehension of what I presumed would be a hostile environment.

Now it felt like I was going to become the subject, that I would be the one under the microscope.

The jail's entrance hall was compact and there was airport-style security.

I walked through the scanners and emptied out my dictaphone, camera, batteries, wallet and phone.

I carried Eddie's number and address separately and had scrawled 'EMM' on my hand so I wouldn't forget to pass it over when I eventually met Scott.

Nicholas Calenicoff, a smart screw who seemed to be to the prison system what Doogie Howser was to doctors, met me on the other side.

To put things into context as we left the civilised world behind and walked into the underbelly of the prison, it felt like I would be the one doing the saving if anything got out of hand.

Behind these walls some of New Jersey's worst criminals had been decaying – or rehabilitated – for decades.

The rest of Newark could have been in Timbuktu as far as the inmates were concerned.

We walked down some long, narrow corridors, with lots of white and lots of yellow paint. Many of the doors were activated by either security cards, locks, or both.

We moved beyond a thick glass wall where a group of cons sat waiting to watch people walk by.

They stared at me while I looked at the floor, choosing not to see if any of them were making any form of gesture.

Had it been a ghetto in Philly or New York one couldn't have shown such weakness, but these guys had no way of getting out and there was no way to hear any possible sly remarks about fresh meat being brought in.

Within a couple of minutes we were in a small interview room in what felt like the nerve centre of the prison.

'I'll be back in a minute,' said Nick, turning and retreating.

So here I was.

I looked around to see what weapons could be used.

I had obviously watched too many films.

But among the apprehensive feelings of fear, uncertainty and surprise at being able to get into this absurd situation in the first place, I was terrifically excited.

My heart rate was beating the same way it did before a fight.

Nick returned empty-handed, saying he couldn't find Scott. He pulled a face that put me on edge even more than I already was, as if to say, 'It's not the first time Scott had been acting up.'

When Nick left again and once more came back with nothing there seemed a very real chance that I could be out of there with no interview.

Two minutes turned to five and five to ten before I heard voices and footsteps approaching.

I stood and puffed out my chest, acting as if I wouldn't be intimidated. My loose-fitting jeans disguised slight tremors in my knees. Nick came around the corner, flashing a smile.

'Here he is,' he said, announcing the prison-system celebrity.

And in walked the former light-heavyweight contender.

Scott bounced hurriedly in, placing a pile of books and papers on the table. A deadpan face stared straight at me, overwhelmingly unimpressed.

He wore ridiculously baggy cream fatigues and carried a matching flat cap in his left hand.

He was about my height, 6ft 1in, but thinner.

He didn't take his eyes off me from the second he walked in until the moment I extended my hand.

He seemed surprised by my willingness to make contact.

Of course, I gave it my firmest squeeze doing the whole don't-show-fear thing, but his soft-spoken words surprised me.

He raised his eyes a little. He looked friendly but didn't smile. His face was open, long, and his eyes were dark.

His hand was large but his grip was surprisingly meek.

There were deep scars down his cheek and across his neck. Prison wounds, I assumed, trying not to look too obviously at the thick dark lines that branded him for life.

'Sorry I'm late,' he said, excusing himself. 'Class ran over. It's nice to meet you.'

Although his words reassured me something about his manner didn't put me at complete ease.

I wasn't kidding myself.

He didn't know me and he definitely didn't trust me. That much was mutual.

He said I was his first visitor in about seven years, and I could tell he was trying to figure out what I wanted and what I was doing. At about the same time I was thinking along similar lines.

After all, it's not as if I had even pitched an interview with him to any editors. This was another of my bright ideas.

No one knew I was here apart from Tom Jess and Eddie.

'Why did you agree to meet me?' I asked.

'I didn't,' he fired back, too rapidly for my liking. 'I didn't know anything about it until they just came to get me.'

'What about the form you had to sign?'

'What form?' he said, fixing Nick with an awkward and – frankly – uncomfortable stare.

Oops.

Calenicoff palmed off the query, saying it was the prison that made the first and final decisions about which inmates get to see what visitors.

With that in mind and James already riled, I moved swiftly on.

What a start.

'On my way over I saw a guy I recognised,' I said, with an uneasy blend of nerves and enthusiasm. My pulse was quickening. Sweat was ready to drip from my forehead and my hands were so, so clammy.

'There's a Holiday Inn just over there,' I said, fully realising just how peculiar that sounded and what a strange name it was for a place next to a prison with more than 2,000 inmates.

'He told me to give this to you,' I continued, handing him the slip of paper with Eddie's name, address and phone number on.

'He's here?' Scott asked, excitedly.

'He just left. He's been training a fighter here. He said if you need anything give him a call.'

'I can't make no phone calls,' Scott again hastily shot back. 'I don't get no phone calls. Tell him to come and see me.'

Oops again.

'He can write a letter,' offered Calenicoff, trying to bail me out.

'OK, I will ask him,' I said.

Scott was now disappointed. Within several tense minutes I had raised his hopes, pissed him off and upset him.

'I interviewed Eddie earlier this year and he said you were the only guy who beat him legitimately,' I said, desperately.

'Well, it's nice to hear him say that,' Scott nodded, as we finally sat down on some plastic seats.

'He became the world champion though. I didn't.'

Scott started to make small talk and I figured, hoped even, he was trying to put me at ease. I asked what he thought the result of this interview would be when committed to paper.

'Well,' he considered, 'you could do what everybody else does.'

He suggested, 'Grey skies cast sombre shadows... it's raining outside and I'm scheduled to go to prison to do an interview with an ex-pug.

'I don't know what it's going to be like behind the brick walls. Stone walls don't make a prison. Sitting before me is the former number two contender.'

Seeing as the skies were dark grey, it threatened rain again and his description was fairly accurate I said that was all logical, that there was no excuse for melodramatics.

I asked how he would write it if he was me.

That appealed to his creative side, which soon took over once more.

'It was dark and gloomy outside and I did the inevitable. I went into prison to be held in custody for several hours.

'When are they going to let this guy out? That's a very interesting paradox. Why? How come? Maybe you can answer the questions? Write in.'

With the fun stuff out of the way I decided to press him about his career.

I knew he had to quit because of his conviction but I wanted to hear what he thought about it.

'Why did you decide to stop boxing?'

'I didn't decide to stop,' he snapped. 'The administration decided for me. The prison system made the decision for me.'

'OK, why did you begin?' I said, going back to basics.

'I was working at the Department of Corrections in Florida and I had to transfer from Florida to New Jersey to promote myself to get a championship fight and I got arrested. So because I was working at the Department of Corrections in Florida they let me continue the boxing programme in Rahway. I was rated at the time anyway.'

'Because you had just beaten Jesse Burnett, right,' I interrupted.

'You did your research,' he winked, knowingly.

'I know a bit about the light-heavyweights from your era,' I continued.

'Oh yeah. Those were good guys. Yaqui Lopez, Saad Muhammad, Victor Galindez. Those were real warriors. Even if you won you got hurt.'

A quiet fell on the petite room as he paused and reflected.

'Conteh,' he exploded from deep in thought. 'John Conteh. Is he still alive?'

'Yeah, he's doing after-dinner speaking.'

'How does he look now? Does he still straighten his hair?'

'It's a little bit greyer than you might remember.'

James laughed. Time goes by on the outside as well as in.

'How's Bunny Johnson?' he asked of a former foe from the UK.

'He's doing OK. He's training fighters.'

'Oh, he's a trainer. Good,' he said, as if he was a teacher and one of his pupils was doing well after leaving school. 'Give him my regards.'

'Have you stayed in touch with any of the fighters?' I probed.

'Well, here's what happens,' Scott started, decisively. 'When a person is popular, everybody's in touch with him. And when he's unpopular everybody's out of touch with him.

'You know, one minute you're the warden of the prison and the next minute you're just a guy in the background.

'Look at the governors. Nobody talks about George Wallace anymore. You know what I'm saying? Look at Maggie [Thatcher];

she's not as popular anymore. Bush and Blair are pretty tight, they hobnob together, but pretty soon when Bush gets out of office they'll have nothing to say.

'That's the way it goes. When you're on top they like you, when you're on the bottom people don't like you.'

His only exposure to boxing prior to turning pro was 'fist fights'.

'They weren't organised,' he explained. 'We just put the gloves on and boxed. You'd be surprised that some of the best fighters have not turned pro.

'It's the same thing in baseball and football.'

Scott thought he would be a champ from the beginning. 'That was the goal,' he stated.

He looked up to Bob Foster and Archie Moore, two of the best light-heavyweights the division has seen.

'I think Archie would have won in a fight between them. He had tremendous defence and when he fought Rocky Marciano he was cheated on the count. Marciano was down but they managed to get Marciano back up.'

Moore was eventually stopped in the ninth.

'History says that Moore was one of the best light-heavyweights of all time. He was an old man. They called him "The Mongoose" and he's still got the greatest amount of knockouts in boxing history.'

'And you were being managed at the start by Hank Kaplan,' I said, drawing another smile from the convict.

'You did a lot of research,' he conceded.

'You know your stuff too,' I laughed with him.

'No, you know yours,' he replied quickly, as we briefly signed up to a mutual appreciation society. 'Look at the questions you're asking me.'

As we went on, prison boss Lydell Sherrer checked on us.

'Hey, how you doing? How's this going?' he asked.

'Fine, thanks,' I said.

'How you holding up?' he asked James.

'He's good,' Scott said, pointing at me and looking at Sherrer.

'That's great. I'll leave you guys alone,' Sherrer winked.

He nodded approvingly at me before disappearing.

My fascination with Scott's era of light-heavyweights meant it wasn't long before I probed about his fights and the champions.

It started with Yaqui Lopez, a man I was hoping to interview if I made it across to California in time.

'Lopez was a good fighter,' James recalled of one of several contenders he upset in Rahway. 'He was used to fighting people that would run or stand toe-to-toe with him.

'I just came forward and that caused him to back up. So with me being shorter than him and getting inside, he wasn't used to it. Anyone that beat him beat him inside, not outside. He was very skilled as an outside fighter.

'It was like Frazier and Ali, The Greatest. Once Frazier got inside The Greatest was hopeless.'

'Did you think you had an advantage over the guys that came to fight you in prison because of the intimidation factor?' I asked.

'The ring is the same wherever you box – all over the world. People boo and they cheer. They cheer for the other guy or they boo the other guy. Sometimes the hometown boos are for you and cheers for the other guy are coming from the streets. Either way you look at it, all the rings are the same.'

'Was there extra pressure on you boxing in front of the other inmates?'

'No, no. I used to train pretty hard. It's like the old saying, what you put in a glass of water is what you get out of the glass. If you fill it up all the way you get a full glass out of it. If you fill it up halfway you get a half glass. So what that means is if you train hard, you're ready. If you don't train hard you're not and that's why they gave me the nickname "Superman", because I used to do a thousand push-ups a day, 20 sets of 50 in a clip.

'I would run one hour every morning, from seven o'clock to eight, come inside, do the push-ups, go to bed, come back out at night-time and beat the bag until the bag got tired and that worked. All the old timers used to do that.

'The more modern society becomes the more sophisticated people become and they come up with different ideas. Like in the old days guys would practise for hours shooting in a basketball court and nowadays you know them guys are doing all different things like slam-dunking.'

Going off on a tangent, James started a mini-rant.

'I'm the first person in the country to fight for the title [he didn't] behind the walls and I beat the number one contender. The WBA stripped me of my rating when I beat the number one, which is kind of odd. But that's down to promoters, Don King, Bob Arum. It's about who's going to control the champion. Bob Arum got me stripped then Don King took over and he got me my first loss. He promoted the Jerry Martin fight. All the boxers I know of, and I've studied boxing a little bit, Don King is responsible for their first losses. Sugar Ray Leonard's first loss, The Greatest of All Time's first loss [Ali's – no he wasn't], Tyson's first loss… [yes, King was]. He always does it. He builds you up and then finds a fighter to bring you down. He probably wouldn't like me saying that but, you know, very few people retire from him undefeated.'

'Or unscathed,' I added, controversially.

'Unscathed, that's a good word,' Scott agreed. 'They got a story about him that he's not a liar, he just doesn't tell the truth.'

I told James I had seen letters he wrote to *The Ring* magazine and *Boxing News* from prison, calling out different champions.

'Did you get any responses?'

'No,' he said, bluntly. 'See, first of all, basically there was a kernel of truth in the idea that I was the uncrowned champion, because if I wasn't why would they strip me of my rating? They [the WBA] said they didn't know I was in prison. I came to jail number seven and every fight I had after that was inside the institution. After that I got rated number three, then number two and then number one in the United States; that was all in prison. They knew I was here. But see, there's always been a battle between the WBA and WBC and Don King wants to control one part and Bob Arum wants to control the other part. Even the magazines admit that. Flash Gordon [who used to produce a tell-all boxing newsletter], one of the best boxing writers, told the truth. He was good.

'But you know, there are other things to look at. For instance, the game is about making money. That's what King wants to do. He wants to make some money but the only problem is he's making it off the backs of people who have suffered.

'When they say, "You've got a ten-rounder coming up" and you've got to get up every morning and run for one hour and you've got to beat that bag and the trainer tells you to hit it again; he don't have to hit it so he tells you to hit it.

'One time I was so worked up at being ordered around I wanted to punch my trainer, David Taylor.

'The reason I went along with him in the first place is one time he said, "Hit my hand" and he kept moving it. I said, "I can't hit it. What do you keep moving it for?"

'He said, "That's how I want you to move your head."

'I said, "Wow, that makes sense. I liked the way you showed me that."

'From that point on I was with him and he was good.'

'You're good,' he said, again nodding in my direction. 'You know stuff I don't and I'm older than you. You should write a book.'

'No, you should,' I shot back. 'Did you think of writing one?'

'Yeah, I wrote one,' he said, somewhat wistfully. 'I learned something about books. The first book I wrote, the editor wrote back and said, "It's more like a diary. This is not a book." So I started ordering books from *Writer's Digest* and I found out about characters and how to create them. Then I started looking at cartoons; Popeye, Bluto, those are characters. Like the amazing green Hulk, now that's a character. So now you've got a character there's got to be a good side to the character and there's got to be a bad side so that the story has some interest. And when I went to school in prison that's what they had me doing.

'Because I wrote a diary before it was like, "My name is James Scott. My first professional fight was when I was an old man. I was expected to lose but the one thing I had going for me was determination."

'The editor was ruthless and they wrote back and, you know, you're a writer, they had taken this out, taken that out and he said it's too much like a diary. Then I started to read more books and guys like Hemingway and James Baldwin, them guys are good.

'The way they write and the things they say not only make sense but they use euphemisms. I was recently reading *Lady Chatterley's Lover*. That was very well done. A guy needs to read something like that in prison because there are no Lady Chatterleys around here. It's just all men in here.'

Moments later, we were talking about Richie Kates, who had fought Scott.

'Kates was the only guy who I fought who when he hit me said "excuse me",' Scott laughed.

'It got me so mad. I said, "What do you mean excuse me? You meant to do that." My head was bleeding and he rubbed it with his glove and he said, "Did that hurt?"'

Scott sympathised with Kates for the poor local officiating he received in the first Galindez fight but pointed out that Richie wasn't the first man to go to hostile territory to try to win the world light-heavyweight title.

'Battling Siki and Irish Mike McTigue,' James said, excitedly showing off his boxing knowledge. 'They fought for the title in 1923 and Siki would have lost his life if he had won the fight. He was the only black guy in Ireland, fighting Irish Mike McTigue on St Patrick's Day, and they fought 20 rounds. It's a miracle it went 20 rounds.'

Scott, like many others I had met, felt boxing should have the safety net of an organisation to protect fighters before, during and after their careers.

'It's one of the things we talked about in the old days, unions,' he said. 'There should be a union because when fighters are boxing you have the cameras on you, people calling for interviews, they want you on television. But then, after about ten years, nobody talks. This is the first interview I have had in years. I had one in Southport but other than that there have been none.

'There was an old statement once made about how you just fade into the background. One minute you are popular, the next minute you just fade away. In another three years they won't even talk about President Clinton. He was a popular president. What made him popular was the scandal at the White House.

'Jack Johnson,' he went on, focusing on another defiant fighter, like Scott and Siki and the first black heavyweight champion. 'He went to a Klan's meeting. A Ku Klux Klan meeting! They had the sheets on and everything and he made a speech. They didn't believe he came by himself so they hushed it up.'

Scott laughed at Johnson's boldness.

'He once got a ticket on the highway. He was going over the speed limit and the police pulled him over and he gave them a $50 bill when they only asked for $25.

'"Why are you giving me so much money, Jack?"' Scott said, impersonating the officer.

'"Because I'm coming back this way."'

I told James that former heavyweight contender Gerry Cooney and Eddie Mustafa had set up unions for ex-boxers. Cooney had started FIST, and Eddie had united with The Teamsters to form JAB. Unfortunately, neither lasted long.

'That's good,' Scott said, clearly interested. 'Fighters are waking up now because there's unions for everybody but fighters. Some of them wind up alcoholics.

'I would have gotten a union together if I had become champion. Fighters need a union. Everybody's got one but fighters.

'Fighters come and ask you, "Can I have a couple of quarters?" And you reply, "Weren't you the guy that was fighting on TV? Gee whiz. What happened to you?"

'That's what some fighters have to go through. They have to ask people so they can get something to eat. It should be mandatory that every fighter that quits the ring, they should take some money out of every fight they had so that when he retires he gets compensation, like a pension plan.

'Tennis players get it. Baseball players get it. Policemen get it. Firemen get it. Everybody gets it but fighters. I met Beau Jack, the former lightweight world champion from the 1920s and 1930s, in Florida when he was shining shoes.

'Here's a guy that was world champion and very popular and then he's shining shoes. Fighters can end up in really bad situations.'

I could see that looking at James. He took a moment to absorb what he had just said.

I decided the time had come to ask Scott about how he came to be behind bars and it provoked a strange answer that, unsurprisingly I suppose, gave nothing away.

I knew he was initially arrested for a botched $283 armed robbery and hoped he would flesh out the details.

'OK,' he said, raising my hopes that he might come clean and give me stacks of information. 'First of all Miami Beach, where I turned professional, didn't pay a lot of money. Most I made in Miami was $1,000. In 11 fights in Miami, that's $11,000. That was it.

'So I came up to New Jersey to promote myself. I was around great people. Hank [Kaplan] always used to do all kinds of things for me for publicity. I sparred Jimmy Ellis. He was pretty good, too. I worked with him before the Joe Frazier fight when they fought a rematch in Australia.

'So now I look at a guy who made the best of a bad situation. I was in jail, locked up, doing a lot of time and I found a way to write letters.

'I wrote to a guy named Bob Hope and he wrote back. His name was in *Parade* magazine and I wrote to him.

'I wrote, "Dear Mr Hope, the most important word in the dictionary is the four-letter word hope. I'm trying to get a boxing programme together so I can box in jail. Can you help me?"'

James had a chance because the famous comedian was a former professional fighter who still had a passion for the sport.

'Next thing a long letter came, he had written me back. And in it he said, "I'll see what I can do."

'I was allowed to box and I was on TV until I lost. He was very influential in helping me out.'

I tried to get James back on topic but he would not be drawn on the incident that saw him spend almost two-thirds of his 55 years in prison.

He then started talking about his time inside rather than how he got here.

I asked him where his knowledge came from; it was clear that he had done what Don King always advised prisoners. 'Don't serve prison time, make it serve you,' the promoter often said.

'Right now, I'm going to school and doing a lot of reading.

'When they finish with you, they really finish with you.

'The prison I put on the map [Rahway] they didn't reward me but sent me to another prison, Trenton. I got cut up in Trenton,' he said, showing me two long, deep scars. One was carved into his face and the other across the front of his neck.

Scott's power, ability and reputation would have seen him able to walk down just about any street in the world untouched but it singled him out as a marked man in prison. Still, his goals changed inside. They had to. His quest to be in superb physical shape in his fighting days was replaced by a thirst for knowledge.

'So then they sent me to Southwood. I went to school there and I passed everything but the mathematics,' he continued.

Scott had earned more than 60 college credits in the joints and was working towards his associate arts degree.

He was also aiming for general his diploma with a view to penning his life story in a different format than his earlier attempt hoping that, on his release, he could become a public speaker, travelling the country to discuss his unique life.

He perked up when we spoke of his eligibility for parole in January 2004. He conceded, however, that he wasn't getting his hopes up – even though he had less than two years remaining.

He had been residing in Northern State Prison for 20 months after the transfers from Rahway to Trenton to Southwood before arriving here, his final destination in the system.

I asked how he would cope on his release in a different world to the one he last saw.

'Before I got here,' he said, agreeing the change would be extreme, 'I remember when getting on the bus was 12 cents and if you had $200 you could live in a pretty nice place. Nowadays, the bus is up to $1.50 and rent is $600–$700 a month. And it might not even be a nice place. The cost of living is sky high. Inflation's unbelievable.'

'If you had won the title would your life be different?' I asked, perhaps a little insensitively.

'If you won the Pulitzer Prize would your life be different?' he shot back.

Inevitably, we were talking boxing before long. I felt Scott was most open and comfortable when we did.

He flashed his knowledge of boxing history once more, talking about how Rocky Marciano used a 400lb heavy bag, yet he remained modest about his own achievements in the ring.

Scott again heaped praise on Brit Bunny Johnson. Bunny's trainer, George Francis, thought Johnson had the advantage, being able to train wherever he wanted.

He wasn't expecting the superhuman fitness levels Scott had.

'He can't have any real stamina because he simply couldn't run up any hills in jail,' Francis reasoned in the build-up. But there are no hills in the ring, either.

Boxing News reported of the seventh-round finale, 'Johnson Does a Seven Stretch'.

Of course, there were fights James wanted that just never happened.

'Saad wouldn't give me a fight,' he started.

'Qawi didn't give me a fight [when he was champion].'

Still, America was enthralled by the real-life prison drama unfolding before them. His bouts were required viewing.

Saad ruled the WBC roost and told me later he never seriously entertained the idea of going back to prison to defend his title.

Politics made a difference wherever he was.

'Fighters are owned by promoters like cars are owned by people. When a promoter owns you you've got to do what they tell you.

'He navigates you to the top or he navigates you to the bottom. Either way, it's up to him.

'If you're a good fighter and the public wants to hear from you he pays you well, which is great because you're only in the game for the money and the recognition you're going to get.'

Yaqui Lopez was one of several men to fight both Saad and Scott, losing to James in prison and twice to Matthew, once when he was still known as Matt Franklin.

The *Boxing News* report of Scott's win over Lopez stated that the convict had a bust-up with promoter Murad Muhammad who then had the sole promotional rights with Rahway.

Scott apparently said he didn't want to fight for him again because he was unhappy with the way Muhammad was treating him.

Perhaps that was one of the sources for his frustration with promoters in general. He was just as disappointed with the boxers, namely the champions, who didn't put their gold on the line in Rahway.

'In my opinion,' Scott went on, 'when you become the champion the first people you are supposed to fight are the people that challenge you.

'I remember Mike Rossman saying in the papers he didn't want to fight a jailbird and that was a cop-out. Who cares where you have been?

'When you get in the ring all you've got to do is duck punches.

'Nobody turned out bad that came to prison.'

Of course, there was something extraordinary about how that sounded. It even drew a smirk from James.

Back then, James often wrote letters to the boxing magazines from the bland prison cells he called home, challenging the champions – who were living their flash lives with their expensive cars, big houses and taken-for-granted freedom.

Although they were fighting with the same golden goal in mind, Scott's life couldn't have been any more different.

Saad defended his title in the Playboy Casino in Atlantic City in front of thousands of fans and dozens of bunny girls. Why would he want to go to prison to fight a super-fit dangerman with a grudge in a hostile sports gym that sometimes sizzled at 100 degrees in front of hundreds of convicts?

One of Scott's many letters was aimed specifically at then WBA champ Eddie Mustafa Muhammad. It was headlined 'Come back, Mustafa'.

He implored Eddie to stop ducking him and go to Rahway and fight with his WBA title at stake. That was incredible given that Eddie had been next door earlier.

He signed off, 'James Scott, The People's Champ'.

None of the belt-holders bit at his goading.

Scott merely attracted hungry challengers wanting to make a name at his expense and Jerry Martin was the one who brought his big house crashing down.

Martin, a big Philly-based Antiguan, was solid and a rough night's work, despite what Richie Kates had said a couple of days earlier, and with a chance to meet Saad Muhammad he had everything to gain.

But while Jerry 'The Bull' trained for the fight of his life, Scott recalled how his preparations were hit by feuds and politics from behind the barbed-wire walls.

The inmates were up in arms about visiting hours and the warden wanted them to end their revolt.

James could help bring peace to the conflict.

'I did wrong,' he admitted. 'Here's what I did. The prison population was on strike because they took visits at the wrong time. So they wouldn't let me train. I came out of my cell and asked them, "Can I talk to the guys?" And I managed to persuade the prisoners to go back in so the work strike was over and they let the fight go on.

'But there's an old saying by Machiavelli, who said "the voice of the people is the voice of God", and I went out there and I lost. The reason I lost was because I broke the strike. If I hadn't broken the strike I wouldn't have lost. Why? Because I wouldn't have even fought.'

He said some inmates were actually cheering for Martin because he had broken the strike. *Boxing News* wrote how Martin 'burst Scott's bubble'.

There's no mention of how many actually watched the contest or indeed if there was any booing of the 'home' fighter.

Another former Rahway guest, an armed robber by the name of Dwight Braxton, also had no qualms about returning to his old stomping ground to face Scott. The man later known as Dwight Muhammad Qawi bulled his way through Scott to win a decision.

Having had years to dwell on his performance against Qawi, Scott recollected, 'I fought a different fight and they didn't accept it. This is a country that loves blood and gore. They put it on TV whenever they can.

'So what does that mean? It means they give me six-ounce gloves – I weighed 177–178lb, Qawi weighed about 179lb, and he's also got six-ounce gloves on.

'So I figure, why should I stand there and go toe-to-toe with a stocky guy?

'I practised dancing and moving around, jabbing. I didn't want to get hit that much. As you can see, the way I'm talking now I never took the punishment some of those guys did.'

That showed. His warm, lucid tones were fluent and accessible. There were no real signs he had been a fighter, only that he had been in fights and those were the wounds inflicted in prison.

'The most I made was $40,000 and the least I made, $2,400, was for the Eddie Mustafa fight. That was on HBO and they didn't pay a lot.'

'They do now,' I offered, explaining that HBO were the major power-brokers in world boxing these days.

'Thanks,' he said, letting me know my statement was of no use now.

'I put them on the map,' he went on. 'The most I made was fighting for Don King. But then the Public Defenders' Office sued me. The violent crime board sued me. The State got $2,000 a year for the cell and I had to pay $135 for the food to train on. So when they'd finished with the cheque I had $3,000–4,000. Out of 40.'

'So why did you go on?' I pressed.

'Like they say, it's just as hard for a quitter to win as a winner to quit.'

'Do you have any regrets?' I asked, sure he would mention something about the circumstances that saw him banged up for life, the trial, the actual incident, something. He sidestepped the question.

'I wish I hadn't broken the strike before the fight with Martin,' he said, offering me something but not what I wanted. 'I wish I hadn't broken the strike.

'Say a guard gets hurt. If the guards go on strike, if one of the guards goes out there and tries to get the other guards to go back, he's finished.'

I wondered if that meant James was not only finished as a force in the ring but condemned as an also-ran in the prison system.

Perhaps the scars were painful symbols of that.

'I shouldn't have done it. The warden appreciated it [so there's a good chance the inmates didn't] and said now we could get the fight on but I got one of the worst ass-whippings I ever got in boxing from Martin.'

He was still able to chuckle regretfully at that.

'So when I get home, James, what do you want me to tell the people in England?'

'Tell them people in America still like John Conteh and to Bunny Johnson I send my regards. If he writes to me I'll write him back.'

James was embarrassed when I asked him to pose for photos, asking, 'What do you need pictures of me for?'

I think he wanted the outside world to remember him as 'Superman', not the 50-something inmate dressed in a bland uniform.

He eventually agreed on the condition that I was in one and Nick was in the other.

We shook hands, Scott made no mention of keeping in touch, didn't seem bothered as to whether I sent him the article or not and strolled away with his shoulders hunched and cap in his hand, as though he was walking from just another prison duty.

In Sherrer's somewhat palatial office I talked to the prison's main man about inmate No. 0000873537.

'He's obviously done his homework,' I told Lydell, adding that I was impressed with his rounded knowledge.

I asked Sherrer to take me through James's record for background information and he produced a quite staggeringly large file.

This was Scott's previous.

He'd actually never been indicted on the homicide accusation but the robbery, combined with his many other crimes, had seen them withhold the key without quite throwing it away.

The volume of paperwork informed one that James had been a bad boy long before Rahway. It all seemed to begin on 2 May 1960, in Newark. Scott was just 13 years old.

Lydell started.

'First arrested as juvenile on charge of breaking and entering and larceny, subsequently defendant arrested on charges of truancy, assault and battery, possession of a dangerous weapon and violation of parole.'

Lydell explained: 'Breaking and entering, county judge gave him probation for one year.'

That was his first brush with the law.

'On June 27 [that year] his probation was extended because of truancy – extended for another year.

'On October 17, 1960, less than four months later, he got an enforceability charge not reporting, acting out, given probation continued.

'February 9, 1961 – possession of a dangerous weapon. He went to an institute, Jamesburg, from '61 to '62.

'Then there was violation of parole.

'Poor behaviour.

'He escaped Jamesburg in 1962.'

'He escaped?'

'Yes.

'1963 he was brought back into custody, transferred to more secure Annondale until June 1965. Now an adult. Released. Charged with an armed robbery 11 months later but not enough evidence to bring it to trial saw that charge dismissed by the grand jury.

'Couple more robbery charges pending, then went to another facility for about three years.

'Released in 1968 but on 12/5/68 he was charged with aggravated assault and battery and that went to trial. He was found not guilty.

'In 1969 he was charged with aggravated assault and battery, went to Newark municipal court and got four months at the jail.'

Then, down in Florida.

'7/10/69 he was charged with an armed robbery with a gun. It was deemed he stole a motor vehicle and was found guilty by jury and he got seven years.

'He was released on 1/8/74.

'Then, unfortunately, May 9 1975 he was convicted of homicide, robbery, robbery while armed and that's what he's doing time for now.'

'I didn't think he was convicted until 1981?' I piped up.

'He was in the county [jail] all that time waiting to be sentenced [until 1981].'

'Have you got information about the incident?'

'Of course,' Sherrer said, skimming through pages. 'On May 8 1975, this is the official version, at approximately 1.45am police were contacted to investigate a homicide at College Place in Newark, New Jersey.

'Upon responding to the scene, police officers discovered a victim was lying face down on the street next to the kerb. The victim was later identified as Everett Russ of 160 Prospect Street, East Shore, New Jersey.

'Police interviewed witnesses who said they heard what sounded like a gunshot and saw a car parked where the victim's body was found.

'It was a Chevy, late model. Licence plate revealed it belonged to Scott who was living at 732 Oakwood Road, Point Pleasant, New Jersey.

'Scott called the police asking if they were looking for him [on] May 8 at 4.30pm.

'He said he would be at the station in an hour but didn't go until after 10pm.'

By 7pm the next day, Scott had taken his last breath of freedom.

'Have you heard enough?' Sherrer asked.

'I have, but seeing as you're reading it out to me can't I just have a copy of the statements?'

'OK,' he said, easily enough.

'What do you think of James?' I asked, as he ran off a duplicate.

'He hasn't caused any problems while he has been here in the prison system. Overall his behaviour has been positive. He's a dangerous person due to having such good boxing skills. However, because of his age now, he's 55, born on October 17 1947...'

He didn't finish that line because the phone rang, but he started again as soon as he put the receiver down.

'But overall discipline has not been that bad. There were actually a couple of charges filed at the beginning but nothing major.'

'What, here in Northern State Prison?'

'No, not here.'

'How about those scars on his face, do you know about them?' He didn't.

'I guess there were buckets of blood everywhere because they were all across his face?'

'Absolutely,' Sherrer agreed, without expansion.

'The prosecutor still says he's a danger to society. That was very recent. The last parole board recommended he did not get released.'

'He's got two to three years left, hasn't he?'

Lydell's silence – and his facial expression – said it all.

I thought Scott would be in for another 30 years.

He was found guilty, pleaded not guilty and never confessed to the crime he was convicted for.

Lydell carried on, 'I was a correction officer at Rahway and James Scott and Rubin "Hurricane" Carter were at the same facility and I know because I talked with these guys, they are both very bitter individuals. They both claimed they were innocent and they claimed there was a lot of racism for them being found guilty. They would be in the same room and they were both well respected by the other inmates in the prison system and, overall, they were treated like everyone else. If you did anything wrong you got institutional process.'

Sherrer was in Rahway from 1981, just after James stopped fighting.

'I saw him sparring and you could see he was very powerful,' Lydell remembered.

Eventually, he walked me to the front of the building where I collected my rucksack and waited for a bus to the centre of Newark.

We accelerated past the Holiday Inn where Eddie Mustafa had been earlier in the day and the prison looked smaller and smaller until I could no longer see it.

I left James behind, just as the boxing world had done; as the world had done.

I was free again.

As far as I was concerned, New York City was the centre of America. The massive Port Authority bus terminal was often a place I referred to as home. If I could have, I would have had my mail sent there.

With a season ticket you could get just about anywhere in the country from there. And there was a 24-hour Internet cafe in the heart of Times Square where, in the early hours of the morning, you could go online for several hours at the cost of just a couple of bucks. While taking shelter there, I checked on the whereabouts of a couple of fighters I knew lived in Connecticut.

Former 1960s contender Chico Vejar was in Stamford while featherweight legend Willie Pep lived in a care facility in Hartford.

I found addresses for both. Vejar was in the book and I discovered the name of the nursing home where Alzheimer's-ridden Pep was staying.

I called Vejar late in the evening and he said he would collect me from the bus stop the following day. I would then head north to Pep's place and see if I could meet the old wizard.

By the time I left New York, with thoughts of James Scott fresh in my mind, I was shattered and asleep by the time the bus reached the other side of the Lincoln Tunnel.

Chapter 25

IT looked as though little Chico Vejar scarcely had enough strength to wear the enormous pale blue cardigan that hung loosely off him. As promised, he was waiting for me when my bus pulled in that afternoon.

He offered a late lunch and took me to Bobby Valentine's Sports Bar in the heart of Stamford, only about 50 miles from where James Scott was scoffing prison food.

I'm not sure he believed that a guy from England had called him, asking to meet up and talk about old times.

After all, he was never a champion. But I knew he had fought some of the best fighters at a time when there was just one champion for each division.

Surely he would have been a champ had he been boxing today, in an era of splintered titles and watered-down championships.

When I saw Chico, whose thick mop of grey hair was parted somewhere near the centre, instantly I had mixed emotions.

He introduced himself wearing that long, thick blue cardigan and baggy green trousers.

We shook hands and I could feel his arm trembling. Perhaps those 116 ageing battles that entertained so many people had made a deduction against his health in later life.

Inside Bobby V's, where the tinted glass gave it a dark feel, there were pictures of Connecticut sporting legends on the walls. There were sports games on the TVs. It was busy.

'I'm around here somewhere,' Chico said, glancing at the framed photos and lifting his hand tenderly to point to the walls.

No one in the diner made it known that they recognised him. In fact, it took around half an hour for our order to be taken.

Whatever Chico once was, he was clearly not that person any longer.

Yet he was the Micky Ward of his time with his fights frequently on TV or on the wireless. It's just he could never crack the big one and get a shot at the title. 'I was always the bridesmaid and never the bride,' he smiled, a hint of regret in his eyes.

As I guided him through some questions about his early career, how he got into the sport, his memorable fights and career highlights, he fixed me with a cool stare. I hadn't been able to ignore the fact that sometimes he would shake involuntarily.

'I think I've got Parkinson's,' he said, sadly, exhibiting the same sorrowful emotion with which he had told me he never made it to the absolute pinnacle.

'I was diagnosed four years ago. I'm not sure how far along it is, physically,' he said, with an expression which made me feel as though he was looking to me for help.

'At this point I don't think it's affected my life, not mentally anyway.'

The music was loud. Chico spoke so softly it was hard to hear him whether the rock and chart hits were blaring out of the nearby speakers or not. It had been nearly half a century since he was transfixed by boxing, moments after stepping into a gym for the first time. He amassed a proud record of 92 victories, 20 defeats and four draws.

'I walked in and two weeks later had my first amateur fight,' Chico smiled. 'The former heavyweight champion of the world, Joe Louis, was the main event. He was boxing in an exhibition and I was the opening bout.

'The first punch broke my nose and the second floored me. I got up, there was blood everywhere and by the third round we were so exhausted the referee had to hold us up by our trunks to stop us from collapsing, but I won.

'They were semi-pro fights that paid us around $15 for three rounds or $25 for five rounds.

'I won the Connecticut Fight of the Year in 1949. I went back to school and I did well. I didn't think I'd become a champion but I had the drive and wanted to be one of the most popular fighters in the world. I still hold some records as the most televised fighter.'

He turned pro in 1950 and one thriller he recalled was against the tough Italo Scortichini.

'They stopped the fight in my favour and blood was gushing out of both of us,' he laughed. 'I fought him in St Nick's in New

York and I was the first guy he fought in the States. He was a pretty tough hombre.

'I liked [Tony] Zale, the middleweight champion who [three times] fought Rocky Graziano. He was a sharp box-puncher. They were great fights with Rocky. They were televised and you didn't have to pay for them back then.

'I sparred with Graziano and he was like Gene Fullmer. He came right for me, even in sparring.

'I fought Chuck Davey on a Wednesday night TV show and he became boxing commissioner of Michigan. He beat the hell out of me twice. He died of Parkinson's after becoming a successful insurance salesman. He was a scholar from Michigan State. I didn't like him as a fighter, he was a southpaw, but as a man he was wonderful. First fight, he floored me three, four times. It was a unanimous decision. Chicago Stadium was packed. I got slaughtered; he kept hitting me in the stomach.

'A month later we fought again and he stopped me with body shots. So I got the reputation that I couldn't take it in the stomach. I took the whole summer off, rested and went back in the ring and was never hurt in the stomach again.

'Everybody I fought, Joey Giardello, the Fullmer guys – who could box like crazy and really worked with their body punching – they could never hurt me to the body.

'My toughest fight was against Giardello. We went ten rounds in a hard fight. I thought I won but I didn't get it. It was a split decision. We both hurt each other in a give and take fight. He was the hardest puncher I faced but Fullmer was the most devastating fighter. He wasn't a knockout puncher although, of course, he could knock you out. No, Gene wasn't a one-punch guy like Ray Robinson, but he was constant, bang, bang, bang. He could break you down like a bulldozer. He hit me in the arms until I couldn't lift them.

'I never got a shot at the title because I never beat the guys that mattered. If I'd beaten Giardello I'd have got a shot at the title. If I'd beaten Davey I'd have got a shot at the title. If I'd beaten Fullmer, I'd have got a shot at the title.'

He actually fought an eliminator against Tony DeMarco but was destroyed in a round so DeMarco got the shot.

'I fought Billy Graham in his last two fights. He wasn't the same guy he was ten years earlier. We were at a dinner some years later when he was asked to say a few words. He looked over to me and announced, "I knew it was time to quit because Chico Vejar could beat me."

'Billy had fought guys like Kid Gavilan, Henry Hank, but I was too aggressive. I had too much youth.'

Chico explained away his loss to DeMarco by saying he thought he could have continued despite shipping heavy punishment in the opening round.

'I don't know what happened,' he considered, still bemused. 'Tony hit me twice, he dropped me both times and they stopped the fight. I feel they could have let me continue but they'd have done the same thing if it happened to him here in Stamford.

'Tiger Jones was a tough guy. I fought all these guys as the opponent, never as the house fighter. Jones was a throwback. He could punch and he could take it as well as he could give it. He was a determined man, he was always punching.

'He was a great fighter and I'm sorry he never won the title.'

Neither did Chico, yet it's a mark of his status in the sport that he once had Muhammad Ali, then Cassius Clay, chasing him for his autograph.

Before a fight in Connecticut, a young Ali was able to talk his way in to Vejar's dressing room hoping to get a signature.

Vejar told him to come back after the fight.

'I lost and he never came back,' Chico chuckled. 'At a dinner years later he reminded me that it was him who asked for my autograph.'

Vejar, born in Chile, ended up being able to take his father back to their native land towards the end of his career when he was matched with Argentine champion Andres Antonio Selpa.

'My dad had never been home since he left, so I took a fight in Santiago so he could see all his old friends. We drew, they really gave me a hometown decision.'

Vejar modestly said he had deserved to lose.

Of course, he wanted to achieve more than he eventually did.

'I'd loved to have fought Sugar Ray Robinson,' he continued. 'It would have been a big payday. I'd have lost to him at his best because you just couldn't beat him. He was too sharp. I wasn't in his class. It's hard to say if he was the greatest ever boxer but he was a tremendous fighter. He had a good mind, good size, good reach, good power, good legs.

'He had everything going for him. But I was no sucker either. I fought a lot of tough guys. Back then, if you fought a guy in the top ten you weren't going to fight no fall guy.

'A couple of times I should have trained a little harder but really I don't have any regrets. I'm so grateful for my wonderful experiences. It means a lot to me to be associated with those fighters because that was probably the greatest era in boxing history. DeMarco, Zale, Graziano, Pep, Robinson.

'When I first retired from boxing I had a little boy, James Damien, who was two when it was discovered he had cerebral palsy, so I got involved with CP and working with charities.

'For most of my life, up until about four years ago, I worked for United Cerebral Palsy. I was the executive director of the Bridgeport branch where I was on the board.

'When I look back on my career I see a young man who was lucky to get a break in boxing but probably didn't take advantage. I only got $15,000 three times. I never got the champion's purse. But the joy of my life has been my wife, Caryl. She's been with me all the way, we've been married 47 years and we have two grown-up daughters [James died of his illness].'

We finished our meals and left the diner. Chico offered me a lift to the station, which I gratefully accepted and outside the restaurant he posed for a couple of pictures, his hands guarding his face, capturing his youth.

There was no doubt he had appreciated the recognition.

He led me to the multi-storey car park and as I followed I saw his face contort with anxiety.

He picked up the pace, then sharply turned and started looking up the aisles of parked cars.

'I'm sure it's here somewhere,' he said, clearly trying not to appear flustered.

Minutes later we were looking on other floors and almost an hour after that we started searching in different car parks.

I was due to get a bus to Hartford in about an hour, but Chico started to get emotional.

Time ticked by and worried Chico stared at me. He was nervously vacant and I was powerless to know what to do.

'I used to be a top contender, but now I can't even find my own car,' he said, close to tears and unnecessarily trying to disguise embarrassment.

He was shaking more violently than earlier, sweating heavily after covering so much ground. His thick blue cardigan looked like a weighted vest as he haunched over more but it remained on like an uncomfortable security blanket.

He urged me to catch my bus, insisting he would be OK. I initially refused and kept trying to help him. We searched high and low, in several car parks until I was close to tears, too.

I never wanted to witness anything like this; I was here to help fighters be remembered for their achievements, not to see how far they had fallen since their fighting primes. I might have seen some sad sights, but this was utterly tragic.

I could do nothing. I wrestled with my conscience and decided I had to go.

I left him looking for his car.

Then that same conscience got the better of me.

I raced back about quarter of a mile with my rucksack in hand.

I hunted everywhere for him and went back to the first multi-storey.

Several more hurried minutes went by and I found the car Chico had described.

It was on the top floor. Now I had the car but no Chico.

I was sweating profusely.

I ran around aimlessly, looking for another half an hour or so, and as I sprinted back to the car park I finally saw Chico speeding out in the vehicle I had seen.

I chased him down the street until he stopped at some lights and caught a glimpse of me in his rear-view mirror.

He wound down the window as I pulled alongside, breathless. 'Get in,' he shouted.

I couldn't turn him down after what he had been through. There would be another bus to Hartford. I threw my bag in the back and jumped in.

Chico seemed to find more confidence in his driving ability as the journey went on and within ten minutes or so we were back at his apartment where I met Caryl.

Chico told her what had happened and she sympathised, offering to take us out to dinner.

After making small talk for a couple of hours we went out to a quiet Italian place. Chico was far more at ease with his wife by his side.

Afterwards, they took me to the Greyhound bus station but I no longer felt Hartford was a good idea.

Reports on Willie Pep's health were always negative and I did not need that now. I doubted Pep wanted it, either.

I didn't want to see the great Pep riddled with Alzheimer's. He was perhaps the finest defensive boxer the world has known. For years the myth circulated that he was the only fighter to win a round without throwing a punch. Now he couldn't look after himself and was being cared for round the clock.

I was on my travels again, but I wasn't going to Hartford. I was going much further and decided to leave Connecticut and retreat to New York.

Chapter 26

PORT Authority bus terminal – a refuge for drunks, addicts and the homeless – felt like home. I knew every corridor, every departure gate and every route in and out of the place. I darted around checking the names of cities I fancied visiting and Toronto stood out. I could be there by the morning, and allowing me a few hours' sleep on the bus really made up my mind. I was exhausted by the Vejar episode.

One last push through the night would be rewarded with a stay in a place with a bed in Canada. The hotel where I'd spent time with Iran Barkley and Larry Holmes before visiting James Scott felt like a long time ago, even if less than four days had gone by.

Tom Jess had given me the number of Marvin Elkind, George Chuvalo's former driver, who went everywhere with the Canadian heavyweight star.

I called him during one of the many stops north and he wasn't sure what to make of the English voice belonging to a youngster who was travelling up on a whim wanting to speak to his friend.

He promptly took my number.

I checked in to a rather grand three-star hotel, the height of luxury for a backpacker on a budget. It was very reasonably priced, and I waited for Marvin or George to call.

It did not take Chuvalo long and he explained that while he would happily meet in central Toronto it would be preferable if I could get out near his home in the suburbs.

I jumped at the chance. After travelling about ten hours and 500 miles from New York an extra ten or 20 was not going to faze me.

The only problem was that he couldn't meet me today.

That was fine, though, as I hadn't given up hope of speaking to Rubin 'Hurricane' Carter.

George gave me directions and told me what public transport I needed.

Get the tube to here, take the bus to here and take another bus to here. It sounded like a well-drilled wild goose chase.

We arranged to meet at an independent coffee and doughnut place near his home. Meanwhile, I pursued Carter and was close after swapping e-mails with his Canadian representatives, but it was not to be.

As the clock to nightfall ticked down, I spent the rest of the day exploring the city and taking in the sights, including a trip up the CN Tower, before enjoying an early night.

Every time I had a half-decent place to stay, as rare as it was, I made sure I was in bed by around 8pm so I could make the most of a bed and the TV. After all, I had no real company other than the fighters I was meeting.

I awoke early and went out for a run around the city.

I returned in time to hand-wash my training gear, enjoyed a free continental breakfast and then set off in pursuit of Chuvalo.

He was right. I did have to go round the houses to meet him and I couldn't help but feel it was a test to see how serious I was, although it probably wasn't.

Finally I patiently stood in the light drizzle outside the cafe. It was cold but not bitterly so and he arrived shortly after I did.

George was a big, burly man still. He wore jeans and his baggy dark shirt utilised several of the buttons, if not the ones at the top or bottom. His hair was greying and there were many lines on a face that had been bashed many times.

I offered to buy him a drink or get him a bite to eat as we walked in through a side door near where he had parked.

He declined and sat on the edge of a plastic bench, apprehensively looking at me. He appeared on guard, suspicious.

Still, when you ask a man with Chuvalo's distressing past how he is doing and he replies, 'Not bad,' you can only assume it's a good day.

The former contender, who twice danced with Muhammad Ali and mixed it up with the likes of Floyd Patterson, Joe Frazier and George Foreman in his 93-fight, 20-year career, encountered far more significant battles outside the ring than he ever had to endure inside.

When even a waitress at the coffee shop, more posh than Dunkin' Donuts but not in the Starbucks league, asked if we wanted anything George declined and despite my hunger so did I.

That was a sign he wanted to keep things brief.

It was often said that his ring career was a metaphor for his life. Despite taking the best shots of some of the hardest hitters in heavyweight boxing he proudly maintained he was never floored. Even though he absorbed more spiteful punishment in life, he was still standing.

To call his story a tragedy does not do his three dead sons or his late wife justice.

We started talking about them first and moments later George walked out into the rain, returning from his car clutching photographs.

'I have four sons. This is Georgie Lee,' he said. 'He's 43 today. I lost three sons. This is him here.'

He handed me the picture of a young man in his prime with muscles on muscles. 'He never lifted a weight outside, in prison he couldn't put the weights down.' Georgie Lee is dead.

'He left two of my three grandchildren and I have another one coming.'

Then he showed me some shots of Steven and Jesse.

'My son Mitchell [alive] is 44, my daughter Vanessa is 35 and I have another son [also dead] who, later this month, would have been 41.'

George, Steven and Jesse were heroin addicts. They stole to feed their habits and served time for robbing drug and convenience stores: ten years for stealing and seven for other offences.

They pinched and sold their dad's boxing memorabilia to pay for drugs. They ended up going to jail because of the lengths they stooped to in order to score heroin. Ultimately, George and Steven died of overdoses. Jesse blew his brains out.

George was a rock and carried on.

His wife of 36 years, Lynne, couldn't cope. She committed suicide after George Jnr's death.

Years later, George set up Fighters Against Drugs. He started talking to youngsters and convicts about the perils of substance abuse.

His message was strong and if it wasn't real it would have been pulled from the schools and groups he told it to for either being too cruel or too brutal.

It is one that is affirmatively hammered home, even between two teary-eyed grown men in a Toronto coffee shop.

'My sons George and Steven would look forward to taking the drugs so much they would shit their pants,' George said. 'They would soil themselves. The one with the muscles and the one that's given me two grandkids, that's him,' he said, pointing to the picture.

'Can you imagine there being something that you covet, that you yearn for so strongly, that you would let your bodily functions go like that? They would inject, feel the effects of the drugs and only then clean themselves up. It's so sad. If you're messing with something you've got to know what you're messing with. You've got to know what kind of pull it's going to have on you. So I'm very graphic and very detailed about things that I talk about. I want people to think, "Holy shit." Call it shock treatment if you will.'

Sensing emotional tension at the table, I can only assume the waiters and waitresses knew not to disturb us.

Here were George and I, in a bustling coffee house with no food and no drinks. The rain was now pouring outside, it was packed inside and we were sat at an empty table with black and white photos of his dead family members in front of us.

But the bigger picture was numb to me by then.

That it was raining outside and paying customers might actually want our seats was neither here nor there.

The only thing I really remember, besides George's heavy words, was that the staff didn't bother us again for the whole hour or so we sat there.

No one came near us.

George elaborated about his mission to save children from the fate his three boys suffered.

'If I don't do it, it's like my kids died in vain,' he added. 'My wife died, too, by the way.'

'Are you OK to talk about it?' I asked, sensing a collapse in one of us, probably me.

'Don't worry about it,' he smiled.

Besides, I knew the story.

I knew that, after the second son died, Lynne went up to her bedroom where they kept pills in a cupboard for the time when hope ran out.

George found her body with a note.

Hope was long gone.

'What do you say when people say, "George, you've led a tragic life?" It must happen, right?' I asked rather bluntly.

'It's true,' he said. 'What can I say?

'I've had more than my fair share. More than the average guy.'

'Not one of these things happens to an average guy?' I pushed.

'I don't know how to explain it,' he replied. 'I guess I have whatever is in a person's make-up that enables them to go through it. I don't know. I only know how I would deal with it. I couldn't tell you how anyone else would because I'm not you and I'm not them.

'All I know is that me, as a person, what enables me to stay alive is my family and whatever family members I have left. I lean on them and they lean on me. I love my son Mitchell, my grandchildren. See this son here?' He raised a black and white image of another of his dead boys.

'He's got two kids. His son's 16, his daughter is 21. She's at university in Ottawa, my granddaughter Rachel and my grandson, Jesse, and I kind of raised them in the early years because their father was in jail all the time. Some people say, "Have you ever thought of doing yourself, committing suicide?" And I say, "How can I do that?" I've got other people relying on me because I'm the figurehead of this family. If I did that, what kind of example would I be setting to everybody else?'

'But has it gone through your mind?'

'Oh yeah. You think of all kinds of weird stuff. Who even in a normal life doesn't think of offing themselves sometimes? But I could never do it because I know there are people who love me, who need me. What kind of example would I be? I have to be there for them. That's the way I look at it. It's as simple as that.'

He had also been married to second wife Joanne for more than ten years.

It was tragic stuff. Had anyone else been in with the likes of Foreman, Frazier, Ali and Patterson then boxing would have been the major talking point of his life. Not with George. Death was the biggest of his.

But we did talk boxing. He recalled his highlights and big fights.

It was in the ring where he was known as a rock-jawed warrior.

While the nimble and fleet-footed Patterson and huge-hitting Jerry Quarry didn't seem to take the same volume of punches George had, they died having suffered long medical histories that were inextricably linked to their fighting careers.

George was incredible, though. He was big, lucid, articulate and intelligent and as we talked he seemed to be more at ease, except for occasional glances at his watch.

He couldn't explain how he had been so fortunate with his health but did say he didn't take as many blows as he appeared to on TV. 'I blocked a lot of those,' he said.

I thought he was joking but my smirk was met with a deadpan glance.

While he was understated about his accomplishments he knew he deserved his place among the best of his time.

That he was never floored was a matter of great pride to George, particularly when you consider the exalted company he kept.

'If you have a neck like a stack of dimes you can know that guy's getting knocked out,' George explained.

'I used to stand on my head a lot. A lot of people don't understand that very few fighters pay scant attention to the punch-absorbing muscles. In football, you do a lot of it in your shoulders. Their muscles are trained to dish out punishment and absorb impact. But very few fighters spend time on muscles to absorb punishment. I used to spend a lot of time on it. It's important.

'I also think physiologically certain people have things that go for them. I have a big jaw and a short neck.'

'It's amazing that you fought all those guys and still talk like you do today,' I interrupted.

'Do you know why? Because one man's meat is another man's poison.

'Before I started fighting I used to stutter and I couldn't remember a God damn thing. Now I remember everything and I don't stutter at all.

'I'm lucky that way. But to be honest with you, there's a very popular misconception.

'That misconception is that I got hit with every punch in the book. I didn't get hit with one-tenth of the punches people thought I did. If I did I would be...'

With that he pretended to stutter and slur.

'By the way,' he continued, 'Chuck Wepner is speaking pretty good and so did Marciano and so did Jack Dempsey in retirement.

'I look at Carl "Bobo" Olson and some of these guys and he never had a mark on him after a fight. He couldn't even talk later in life. But you never know how you are going to be tomorrow. Like today I'm all right – who knows how I'll be tomorrow.

'Look at Floyd Patterson. He was OK until a few years ago. Then, all of a sudden he couldn't remember a thing. Ingemar Johanneson, they tell me his wife had to show him her driving licence so he can recognise her.'

While Chuvalo had a fighter's face, he had come a long way from being the young guy who wanted to box having seen a copy of *The Ring* magazine for the first time. Inspired by the images of the musclebound fighters, he asked his mother to buy him a pair of boxing gloves and, about two years later and after repeatedly pestering her, she relented. He admired Willie Pep, Joe Louis and Rocky Marciano.

At first, he started boxing with friends in his neighbourhood and decided to go to a boxing club once it felt like he knew what he was doing. Big George was not so big then, after all.

'I weighed about 85lb soaking wet, which, to you,' he said, bringing me up to speed, 'is about five or six stone.'

He had around 50 amateur fights and was a prospect for the Melbourne Olympics in 1960 but he could not afford to wait and went professional.

'Everybody who turns pro dances with the idea of being a champion of the world and I thought I had a shot,' he said. 'In my opinion I got screwed when I fought Ernie Terrell. In my opinion I won the fight [for Terrell's WBA title in George's native Toronto]. There's no question in my mind.'

George said Terrell had 'muscle' in the form of Tony Accardo, the feared Chicago Mob boss, and Bernie Glickman, Terrell's manager of note and the front man for the operation.

'Glickman muscled my manager and said, "If Chuvalo wins the fight you will end up in a cement box in Lake Ontario." That's the way it was told to me.

'The same tactics were applied to Herbert Muhammad by Bernie Glickman but he was dealing with a different kettle of fish with Herbert Muhammad and the Black Muslims.

'Herbert Muhammad got some henchmen and, I'm only assuming what he said was, "If Ali doesn't beat Terrell you will end up in a cement box in Lake Michigan."

'With that, two guys go over and they beat the dog shit out of him. They beat Glickman so badly. People don't know this but I know. They beat him so bad he went to hospital. They beat him within an inch of his life. He went straight from the hospital to the looney bin, to the nuthouse, to the insane asylum where he subsequently died. He died in an insane asylum. He was a front man for Tony Accardo who was a big-time mobster and big Mafioso mobster.'

Chuvalo had turned pro in a tournament named after Jack Dempsey, wiping out four opponents in one evening. During a whistle-stop tour through some of the big names on his record he said Buster Mathis was a 'big guy who moved well' and that Ali 'was the best fighter I fought because he had everything. Outside of punching power, which he didn't have a whole lot of, he was extremely fast, good reflexes, hard to hit, took a good punch. He had a lot of heart and a lot of balls.'

George only had 17 days' notice for the Ali rematch.

He said the biggest punchers he faced were Mike DeJohn, Foreman and Mel Turnbow.

'The trouble was,' he conceded, 'I had a manager, Zach Gavin, who was 80 years old. So when you're 80 you don't have much time left, which he didn't. Normally you would be brought along slowly but I was rushed in to fight Bob Baker. I only had a week's sparring, but that's the way it was.'

Chuvalo battled an incredible amount of Olympians including Pete Rademacher, Foreman, Frazier, Ali, Patterson and Mathis (who should have gone to the Olympics but when injured was replaced by Frazier).

'I fought a bunch of them,' he said. 'I never really counted how many.'

He said he 'wasn't in shape for Rademacher' and that Britain's Joe Erskine 'thumbed me a couple of times in the eye'.

George was disqualified against Erskine when they fought in 1961, because of a headbutt.

'He did OK for a feeble puncher,' Chuvalo said.

'If I was smarter, which I wasn't, I wouldn't have done it but I got mad and butted him. I cut him and the referee stopped it. There's a right way and a wrong way to butt a guy. The right way to butt a guy, and I did it with Terrell by the way, as soon as you hit him you do it then and it looks like you're trying to get out of the way.'

George motioned a headbutt in my direction.

'Do you know who taught me that? "Two Ton" Tony Galento. He always said, "There's a right and wrong way to butt."'

Moving on, George said of the 1965 Fight of the Year with Patterson, 'It was a very gruelling pace. It was a very close fight. Some guys thought I won, some guys thought he won.'

Chuvalo lost umpteen times on the scorecards.

'I only won seven decisions,' he said, astonished. 'I had 97 [records say 93] fights; I won seven decisions. I seldom won a decision. Some decisions I won, I had to knock the guy out. I knocked out Mike DeJohn twice in the fight and won a ten-round split decision. I knocked him dead and one time they gave him a five-minute rest and the other time they picked him up and gave him a mandatory eight count.

'I had a couple more like that, too, but this isn't a hard luck story. That's the way it is. This is how it was, because you keep talking about fights I lost.'

He glared at me before his features cracked into a happy smile.

'But I'm glad you asked me about Oscar Bonavena because I outjabbed him, I outboxed him and I beat him easy but I didn't get the decision. Oscar ran like a dog, I swear. Watch the tape, he ran like a dog. But that's just the way it is in life.'

The names we discussed were the stuff of legend but talking to George about his personal life had cast a melancholy shadow over those career highlights.

'When people think of the best heavyweights they think of my era. It was the best era, there's no question,' he said.

'I did not make a million in more than 90 fights. If I told you how much I made clear for Ali you would say, "What happened?"

'After taxes and everything else I made $700 per round. People ask, "How much did you make for fighting Ali? Half a million bucks?"

'"A little lower."'

'"Quarter of a million?"

'"No, a little lower than that."

'"You couldn't have made a hundred thousand, that's nothing."

'"No, lower than that. I made $25,000."

'I made $65,000 gross when I fought him the second time. But all my fights together I would not even have made a million bucks.'

After boxing, George trained and promoted fighters. His relationship with former heavyweight champion Razor Ruddock disintegrated and now he referred to his former charge as 'a bit of an ingrate' before adding 'long story', as if he couldn't be bothered to explain what happened for the umpteenth time.

He had also done what he could to help another family in need. The Hiltons, the fighting Canadian brothers, had called upon him for guidance from time to time through their own troubled lives.

When I asked how they were doing, George said meekly, 'Not too well. I spoke to Davey recently. He called me from prison two months ago in Ontario on a driving charge. The Hiltons are… what can you say? They had all the talent in the world and I like them, they're nice kids.

'I know the father's a nice guy but they couldn't handle the booze. But who the hell can? Looking at them is like looking at my own kids.

'I had three kids who got screwed up with drugs the same way a lot of people get screwed up with drugs – sports stars, actors, actresses, everyday people.

'Now I speak to young people about drugs. I go all over the country. I go to high schools and I speak to communities. I do a lot of speaking at schools and prisons.'

He believed that having the chance to speak to children in school was vital, when they were making decisions about the paths they would take in life.

'Looking back on my career it's hard to believe,' he said. 'I'm not even a fighter no more. I don't even think I'm the same person anymore.'

'How do you hope people remember you years from now?' I asked.

'I just hope they remember me,' he replied, a bashful smile creasing his lips.

'I kind of like, "He was a warrior." Exclamation mark. That's good enough for me. If my great great great great great great great grandchildren say, "He was a warrior!" then that's good enough for me.'

I took a couple of pictures of George in the drizzle outside the coffee shop before he drove off in his big, pale blue, old-school Cadillac.

I stayed outside in the rain, stunned, and stood still for a while.

Rain poured down, covering my forehead and dripping into my eyes. I didn't move. Everything was sinking in.

A couple of minutes passed before I walked to the bus stop and retreated to the hotel.

I stared vacantly out of the train and bus windows, feeling removed from everyone and everything around me.

I was growing up fast.

As I sat on the subway back to the city I looked at a picture George had given me. His face was contorted in pain while in the midst of his fierce war with Floyd Patterson.

Looking at that black and white ten-by-eight it was easy to see why people said his career had paralleled his life.

I asked to stay another night at the hotel and sat on my bed, gazing in to space for around an hour as I chilled down.

It was only the knowledge that I still had to travel thousands of miles that moved me to the shower. There was no way I wanted to do it with man flu. Nor did I want to be interviewing people when I wasn't feeling well.

I gradually snapped out of my trance and spent the rest of the day watching low-budget movies in bed.

I had been out of the hotel for little more than three hours but I was drained. Emotionally I was shattered.

Maybe George had found our chat therapeutic.

I wasn't so sure. If things carried on like this it would be me needing therapy. I was a 20-something kid. I hadn't been trained to encounter raw psychological wounds or the agony I had experienced with Chico.

Chuvalo remained in my thoughts. I wondered about what possibly went through his mind when he was home alone. I was in awe of how he had coped with everything so manfully.

He was exactly what he hoped people thought he was; a warrior.

It had rained almost non-stop in Toronto and the weather was depressing. It may have been November but it was warm in Miami.

So after getting a good night's sleep, I jumped on the Greyhound and decided to take the two-day-plus bus ride south, heading to sunnier climes and, one hoped, brighter tales.

Boxing's foremost historian Hank Kaplan and I had met several times at the International Boxing Hall of Fame. He had always said I would be welcome in Florida if I decided to visit and he was keen to show off his archives.

I called him on the journey south, asking who he thought I might be able to talk to.

Angelo Dundee, he suggested, only for me to say he was too famous.

Not even Hank was sure he could get me 1950s heavyweight contender Roland LaStarza, who lived somewhere in the state, and from an increasingly small pool of names we boiled it down to the old former welterweight champion Johnny Saxton.

Saxton would be perfect. Hank shared a number and just like that I thought I was on the road to the former welterweight star rather than nowhere in particular.

Chapter 27

'WHAT the fuck do you know about Johnny Saxton?' It was a hostility I'd not yet experienced. Paul Spadafora had been unhelpfully aloof. Jake LaMotta shut me down. But the man looking after Saxton wanted my blood.

'What do you wanna talk to Johnny for?' he snapped.

'He's in no shape to do interviews. If you want to know anything about him ask me. You can't talk to him. Your magazine or newspaper or whoever pays for you to come over here should pay me to do an interview with him. I know everything about him.'

With that, he began to quiz me on the fighter.

I got about three out of five right, and the two I didn't get exactly correct were close.

Even if I had nailed five out of five I knew I wasn't going to get near Johnny.

Sure, I had heard from different sources that Johnny was in a bad way but some people had told me the guy I spoke to had taken Saxton off the streets, put him in a home and was paying for his care.

I could hardly be mad at someone for taking a fallen champ under his wing and, after he abruptly hung up, I put the conversation behind me and called Hank again.

He apologised for the chastisement I'd experienced but then almost immediately spilled a name that excited me.

'Florentino Fernandez,' he offered.

'Wow, I thought he was dead,' I said.

'No, are you kidding me?' said Hank. 'He's very much alive and well. The only thing is that you will need a translator,' he said.

That was the condition keeping me from the Spanish-speaking Cuban exile.

Now that was quite a big hitch but I was captivated.

Fernandez was a murderous-punching middleweight who, by chance, had fought some of the men I had already interviewed.

Hank gave me a number for someone he thought could help.

There were countless stops and layovers on the 1,500-mile expedition from Toronto to Florida. Some people who sat next to me would insist on talking, others slept peacefully.

I preferred the latter.

However, before the final drop in Miami a Hispanic guy in his early 20s opened a conversation. Hoping he might be interested in boxing, I brought the subject up. In his Miami childhood he had met a former champion on the seafront shining shoes, although he couldn't remember his name. He said the old fighter had signed an autograph for him.

'Beau Jack?' I asked, knowing that is how and where the former 1930s lightweight king wound up.

'That's it,' he said, before asking me how much I thought he could get if he was to sell the signature now.

I explained my predicament, about needing to find a translator in the Spanish quarter of the city, Hialeah, and then somehow get over to Fernandez's house.

My acquaintance said his mother was collecting him from the station and he would see if she would do the running around for us, picking up Eddie Soler, Hank's bilingual contact, and then taking us to the fighter's home.

I liked the sound of that.

I called Soler and fortunately he said he would be able to help, though he wondered if the stars would align and it would all work out.

We arrived in Miami at around noon, more than 48 hours after I had been in the coffee shop with Chuvalo, and my new pal ran off and embraced his mother. He waved me over and introduced us. She didn't speak English and a look of wide-eyed terror spread across her face. She shouted at her son. She completely lost it.

I had no idea what she was saying but knew it wasn't good.

He tried to reassure me while appeasing her onslaught. Within a couple of minutes we were in the car and she was driving. She was also still ranting and raving.

'Look,' I said, 'if it's a problem just let me out. I'm sure things will be OK.'

'No, she's fine,' the guy shot back, cowering apprehensively from the passenger seat. I knew otherwise.

She stared daggers at me in her rear-view mirror. I sat awkwardly.

'What's wrong?' I asked, confident she wouldn't understand.

'She says we don't know you, that you could be a murderer and she is worried you are going to kill us.'

'How would that get me the interview?' I asked, rather selfishly.

'I know, I know,' he agreed. 'She's just not listening.'

Occasionally she would break out into a scream and at times then she would pray, crossing herself as if I was going to grab her at any second. I was terrified. I reckon we both were.

And although throttling her was the last thing on my mind when we started driving, it wasn't by the time we reached Eddie's house quarter of an hour later.

Picking up innocent translator Eddie kicked the beloved mother in to overdrive. She was truly horrified when this tall, middle-aged white guy with a heavy metal T-shirt talked back to her in Spanish.

Eddie translated her prayers to me, how she hoped we wouldn't kill her or her boy and that if we did we would suffer in the afterlife.

It was so surreal I felt as though I was already there.

As we neared Floro's address, the son gave me his cell number and told me to call when we were finished, saying *he* would come and get us.

I left my warm hooded Nike sweater in the car knowing it would not be needed in the Floridian humidity.

What I didn't know was that I would never see the guy, his mum or my jumper again.

Floro opened the door of his pastel yellow brick bungalow and one could instantly see similarities between how he was in his fighting days and how he looked today. He now sported a Bobby Charlton-style comb-over.

His hair had gone blonde as opposed to grey and although he was clearly above the 160lb middleweight limit he looked stocky and formidable.

He lived in a Mediterranean villa-style home with some friends.

They laughed and joked in Spanish until we took a seat in his spacious yet sparsely furnished front room.

I sat on the sofa while Fernandez and Soler had an armchair each.

One of the ex-fighter's friends stood in the doorway that divided the kitchen and us.

He listened intently, like we all did, when Floro talked.

'You boxed in a tough era,' I started, not knowing if I should look at Fernandez or Soler so quickly glancing at both.

Eddie translated speedily as Florentino responded.

Soler started the process.

'He said, "Back then there were a lot of fighters with a lot of class and talent."'

'And you fought most of them,' I replied, hoping a statement would draw more words.

'Si,' he said, after Soler repeated what I had said.

'I fought several former champions and very good fighters; Ralph Dupas, Jose Torres, Emile Griffith, Dick Tiger. I also fought Gaspar Ortega of Mexico,' he said, naming some of the fighters on his 50–18–1 (43) record.

I told him I had spoken to several of his former opponents including Torres, Giambra and Gene Fullmer.

He enquired about their memories of him.

'They all said you were very tough and they all mentioned how hard you punched,' I responded.

He looked unsurprised.

'That's why some of the fighters did not want to fight me again,' he cut in.

'When I fought Griffith I could not make the welterweight limit and then, when I had to lose a lot of weight before the fight, I felt kind of weak.

'I put Griffith on the canvas but they said it was a slip.

'Griffith was well protected in the New York area.'

Floro, as Soler called him, seemed to have had a number of bad breaks but, like a lot of exciting punchers, he was enjoyable to watch because he could be vulnerable around the whiskers.

He was stopped in ten of his 16 defeats, suffering cut eyes and a badly broken nose against Dick Tiger.

'The reason they gave Gene Fullmer the fight against me was because it was his hometown [Ogden, Utah]. I was the aggressor, Fullmer was backing up all the time. We offered them a rematch but he and his people decided not to take it because he knew he would be in another tough fight.

'I hit him with a right hand and I broke his arm. It was a split decision in favour of Fullmer. I was going to fight his brother Don but his handlers didn't want him to fight me.'

Like so many young Cubans he fell in love with the sport children there are born into.

'I was a very active kid,' he smiled, mischievously.

'I loved sports, so when I was 14 or 15 people were saying I looked strong. That's when I decided to get into it.

'I sparred with a couple of guys and they said that I punched really hard. People would gather together and watch me train and they thought that it looked like the heavy bag was going to explode when I punched it.'

He lost just one of 25 amateur fights and even held an unpaid victory over fellow Cuban Luis Rodriguez. 'And I put him on the canvas, too,' he added.

'I came with a Cuban team of fighters to fight here in Florida as an amateur. I was young and skinny and I fought a Puerto Rican fighter and I lost that fight as I struggled to make the weight. It was very close and I lost by one point. When I went back to Cuba I decided to turn professional and I fought the same guy I boxed in the tournament early in my pro career and knocked him out.'

Organisers thought there was a ringer in town. They couldn't believe how good Fernandez looked.

'Back then they didn't pay that much,' Floro said of turning pro in 1956. 'I was getting $10. Then it was like $40 for four rounds. If I fought six rounds it was $60 and if I fought eight rounds or more they paid me $120.

'Then it was $300 for a ten-rounder, then it was $1,000. Then it would depend on the opponent.'

However, when Fernandez turned professional he had the home comforts of Cuba around him, something he would not have when Fidel Castro revolutionised the sporting landscape and outlawed pro sports.

He had his first 21 fights in Havana, building a growing following with his heavy-hitting style.

So when he was forced to start fighting in America it was back to square one and there was only one decision to make and one place to live if he was going to further his career.

'Was it a hard decision to leave Cuba?' he pondered aloud. 'Oh yes. It was really hard. Cuba was a paradise before Castro. Florida was unknown territory but I had to leave because with Fidel Castro in power things were going from bad to worse.

'I knew I had to get out and into the United States where people would appreciate me as a fighter, see me as a professional and get to know me better.'

His pro ledger was littered with big names and mixed results.

'When I fought [Dick] Tiger I already had an injury to my nose and he caught it with an uppercut. I'm not sure if it was a left or a right but it broke my nose and they had to stop the fight. The doctor checked and said I couldn't fight with the fracture. Up until then I think the fight was even.'

The bout was halted before either fighter could come out for the sixth.

Then Giambra stopped Floro on cuts in seven bloody sessions and Rubin Carter stunned him in just 69 seconds.

'I took him for granted,' Fernandez remembered. 'I put my guard down, got careless and that's why he stopped me so early.

'It coincided with the missile crisis, when the Soviet Union threatened to attack the USA if the USA attacked Cuba so politics was playing heavily on my mind at that time.

'I fought Jose Torres after "Hurricane" had knocked me out so Torres, his people and the Puerto Rican people all thought that I was through. They thought I would be an easy opponent. A lot of people told me Torres would kill me and the people thought I was crazy for fighting him. He was unbeaten and had 39 wins [26 stoppages] and one draw, which was against Benny "Kid" Paret.'

Bold Fernandez dropped Torres twice and stopped him in the fifth – in Puerto Rico.

Florentino's biggest purse was around $25,000, for the Fullmer fight.

He admitted, 'I usually made $5,000 and I would sell out arenas in Puerto Rico every time.'

Nobody was keen to face him or Rocky Rivero so they wound up fighting each other again and again. They boxed twice in 1963, once in 1964 and a final time in 1966.

They stopped each other once and outpointed each other once.

'I didn't really want to fight him because I thought he was a wild animal,' said the man they called 'The Ox', who could punch like a mule.

'But I don't think he really wanted to fight me either.

'Even so, the fights made us good money because they were an attraction and a lot of people showed up to watch. That was guaranteed. We set attendance records with sold-out shows in Puerto Rico.'

I supposed it said a lot that few guys fought Floro again after meeting him the first time. That he had to keep going over old ground with someone as savage as Rivero spoke volumes.

Certainly Floro didn't duck anybody but by 1965 he had been struck by the fighters' curse of thinking he still had it when everyone else could see he did not.

Defeat to the modest Jose Monon Gonzalez was followed by a one-round hammering by up-and-coming Jimmy Lester. Florentino was floored twice and had his jaw broken after just 49 seconds of the second stanza. He then lost five on the bounce, won a couple, told himself he could still do it, lost a couple, told himself he still had it and won a few more, on and off, until 1972.

By August of that year even he knew the game was up. He was 36. Against Vernon McIntosh, who had won nine and lost eight, the Cuban broke his hand with a left hook and was stopped in ten rounds.

He waited for it to heal to carry on but it took too long.

'I retired because I didn't really give my best anymore,' he explained. 'I had fought the best fighters. I beat some of them but there was nothing else I could achieve in boxing. I'm satisfied with what I did. I had accomplished everything I could so I knew when to quit. I did what I wanted in boxing. I missed it but I retired at the right time.

'I had fought for the title. I had fought the best fighters so I don't have any regrets. I missed the training. It was something I did for a long time. I still go to some boxing shows and some people ask me if I'm still retired. They say I look strong and that I can make a comeback but I'm an old guy now.'

Initially he stayed in boxing, training fighters at the famed Fifth Street Gym in Miami where he had been coached by the incomparable Angelo Dundee.

He discovered plenty of fighters didn't share his work ethic and, frustrated, he walked away.

The gym was different then, anyway. The likes of Muhammad Ali and Willie Pastrano were staples of a thriving facility that had long since been demolished.

Floro, a grandfather, had been married for almost 50 years and his wife had three children from a previous marriage. They had one son together. He became an American citizen more than 20 years ago but still saw himself every inch a Cuban.

'I miss Cuba very much,' Fernandez said, thoughtfully, as he shook my hand and surveyed the street he lives on.

He posed for pictures and sighed, 'I miss the family and friends I left behind. I miss the beaches, the beautiful people, seeing Malecon [Havana's famous street]. I miss the Cuba of four decades ago.'

We embraced and Floro's friend dropped me at the Greyhound station before taking Soler home.

I did not have to phone my friend or his crazy mother.

Chapter 28

ACROSS the back four seats in the bus the man had his feet up and snored, oblivious to the misery he was inflicting upon others. I had been in and out of Miami in just a few hours and was trundling north again, a week or so before my flight was due to leave San Francisco.

I had no destination in mind but considered disembarking in Atlanta for Evander Holyfield, and thought about cutting across to Texas for Donald Curry, Roy Harris or Donnie Fleeman, but for some reason carried on. We rolled through the southern states and, despite all of my hunches telling me my efforts would ultimately be futile, I eventually decided to keep going all the way up to Indianapolis. I was in search of my unicorn, Marvin Johnson.

Months had passed since I had tried to contact the three-time light-heavyweight champion. My gritty, stalker-like resolve remained steadfast, however.

Meanwhile, Tom contacted his Minneapolis friend Jim Carlin, who had set up the interview with Ernie Terrell earlier in the year, to warn him I might well make it to snowy Minnesota.

Was Johnson a long shot? Yes. Geographically, he was also well over a thousand miles away from Fernandez. It was another couple of days on the buses, another two days without having to pay for bed or board.

Albert Schweitzer, the German medical missionary, was able to distinguish my schools of thought when he said, 'An optimist is a person who sees a green light everywhere, while the pessimist sees only the red stop-light. The truly wise person is colour blind.'

Clearly I was neither Schweitzer's pessimist, nor was I truly wise.

It was late in Indianapolis and unsurprisingly I had failed to contact Johnson in several attempts at various bus stations.

I dropped my bag on to the floor in a quiet corner of the station, near the smelly toilets, and put on the remaining jumper that had been around my waist.

I took a baggy T-shirt from my bag, crumpling it into a pillow, and tried to sleep on the cold, hard floor with moderate success.

Busloads of people came and left. Queues formed and dispersed. I dozed and hallucinated. I hadn't had more than three hours of consecutive sleep in a while. My eating was starting to form a habitual non-existence. I was so hungry but managed to drink water from fountains.

I spent most of the night counting the second hand on my watch until I lost concentration, waiting for a decent hour to make my call.

When it finally came, the answer machine kicked in at Marvin's work.

I left a message, as I had done before. I then telephoned his sister's home and was given his home number, which I promptly called. I tried and tried.

Then, after several hours and following many efforts, I spoke to a lady who I assumed was Marvin's wife. I asked to talk to Marvin.

She said she would see if he would come to the phone. I tried to listen to some whispers, could hear the receiver changing hands and then heard his gruff voice.

'Hello,' he bellowed.

I made my flimsy introduction.

'Where are you?' he asked.

I told him.

'You're in Indianapolis? Now?' he said, in shock.

'Are you the guy that came here a while ago?'

I conceded it was me.

'Well,' he considered, pausing and leaving me hanging tentatively on his every syllable. 'I don't do this anymore but seeing as you have made so much of an effort we should talk.'

The sigh of relief reverberated around the bustling terminal.

'Give me about ten minutes and meet me outside,' he said. The phone went dead.

I brushed my teeth, shaved and waited patiently outside. Marvin drove slowly by on the other side of the road. His window was down.

He shouted at me from across the road, 'I'll turn around and come down that side.'

His saloon car was spotless.

At first glance it looked like Marvin Johnson was doing very well, thank you very much. His voice was gravelly, sure, even a touch slurred, but he was well dressed in smart cream trousers and he wore a shirt beneath a woolly jumper.

'I'm going to take you to my mother's house,' he said.

'Our family gets together on Sundays. We can go there and you can meet my sisters and my mom.'

I hadn't been invited to meet anyone's parents in a while.

I was just pleased I had found him.

He drove steadily, telling me the house was only five minutes away.

Before long, and I suppose it was approaching lunchtime, he pulled up in front of a smart clapboard house.

Neighbourhood kids were out putting up lights and decorations, although I thought it early for Christmas.

It was real middle America.

This wasn't a ghetto. It wasn't a mansion. It was somewhere in between.

It did not look like a place where you would expect to find a three-time world champion either.

Perhaps that was why he talked about his past with regret and resentment.

Going into the pro ranks, the 1972 Olympic bronze medallist had promised himself he would make a cool million dollars, retire and never have to work again.

He didn't manage to do it and so, despite the achievements crammed into his 43–6 (35 knockouts) record, he felt he should never have bothered in the first place. Now, aged 50, he was working at the Sheriff's Department and was still some years from retiring.

'Federal law says prisoners are entitled to one hour of outdoor activities per day and my job is to ensure that the inmates are offered recreation,' he said.

He never imagined it would be like this.

He was a noble champion who had faced the top champions and challengers of his era in a ferocious 14-year career.

The physical signs of life in sport's hardest game had added to his bitterness. He didn't move as freely as a man who hadn't been involved in barbaric wars.

That's always been a problem for fighters, that when they are so immersed in boxing they never give life after the sport a second thought; not out of carelessness but because they are so fixated on the immediate goal they do not look beyond it for fear of losing focus.

'I didn't think about life after boxing from the point of view of having to work like I'm working,' he sadly confessed.

'My thinking was, I'm going to get a million dollars from this fight game and I would have enough money to invest it right and never have to work. That didn't work out.

'I thought that if I'm gonna be successful in boxing then I want to make sure that I did everything I was supposed to do. I needed to give my full and undivided attention to the fight game.'

Marvin admitted he had 'never been much of a self-publicist', which is why he had shied away from interview requests and media attention for the best part of a decade before I arrived.

However, because of his proud championship history, people in the city knew who he was and what he had done.

That explains why, when letters were mailed to the city with Marvin Johnson, three-time world champion on, or Marvin Johnson – Police officer, or Marvin Johnson – Indiana County jail, they invariably made it to him.

He showed me one that was addressed:

Marvin Johnson

Former light-heavyweight champion

Indianapolis.

And he said it, like most of them, was a request for an autograph.

Another reason people knew him locally was because of the car commercials he did for Chrysler which involved him being filmed with gloves saying their vehicles are sold at knockout prices, that sort of thing.

He didn't do it for the money or the recognition but to help his nephew, the same one I had spoken to, who worked there.

Unlike many others, it took Marvin a while to warm to talking about boxing.

Eventually he spoke of how he broke Victor Galindez's jaw en route to winning his first championship.

When he floored the Argentine I asked if he thought Galindez would get up.

'I knew he was going to,' Marvin smiled, almost reluctantly.

Although Johnson did not shirk any questions, he seemed overwhelmingly negative when it came to the sport.

He didn't watch it anymore and had no interest in any of the fighters in the multi-million-dollar pay-per-view world it had become, where the boxers who wore his belt made more for one fight against modest opposition than he did in his career.

He became a little emotional. It was tough going for both of us.

It wasn't his fault I showed up in his city wanting to rake through a past he wasn't happy talking about. I knew he felt obligated to talk to me because of my unnatural persistence.

But, as the afternoon slid by and the evening approached Marvin asked what I was doing to celebrate tonight.

'Celebrate what?' I asked.

'Thanksgiving,' he said. 'It's Thanksgiving today.'

I apologised wholeheartedly for intruding on what I knew was a family day and he insisted it wasn't a problem. In fact, as we took a tour of his mum's house he sent out his sister to get us some takeaway turkey from a nearby restaurant. That broke any atmosphere that had previously existed. And the Johnson family began to embrace me.

Marvin's relatives, his mum and sisters, had all seemed pleased to see me and I think they thought my visit would perhaps make Marvin realise his past should be treasured, not swept under the carpet.

From the looks they gave me, I think they thought Marvin was flattered that someone had taken so much trouble to meet him. He might even have been quite embarrassed. I reckoned it was a confidence boost for him.

We talked about some of the fighters from his era and the ones I had already seen.

Still, unusually, he didn't ask after them. He didn't seem to care. They were in his past, not his future.

We talked about his two wars with Saad Muhammad, who took his NABF title in their first fight and the WBC crown in the second. They were both epic, bloody slugfests.

I asked him what he would do if he saw Saad walking past his house.

'Being honest with you,' he said, looking into thin air, 'I'd just let him walk right on by.'

The reason for this, he explained, was not only because Saad had been his history and should stay there, but because Saad had beaten him and Marvin was as competitive now as he was in his fighting days. And that was saying something.

'It's over now, you've got to go on with life,' Marvin said of why he would let Saad go.

And there was another reason.

'I didn't make the money he made,' he added, with us both knowing full well that Matthew had squandered millions. 'His world changed financially, everything changed for him. It didn't change for me. Nothing changed for me.'

He carefully probed more about who I had seen and I told him about my Northern State Prison visit.

'I thought he was out,' he said of Scott in disbelief. 'Oh man, you mean he did not get out?'

Marvin was shocked.

There had been talk of Johnson fighting Scott in Rahway but it never happened and Marvin, having boxed exhibitions in prisons as an amateur, said he wouldn't have been overawed by the hostile confines of the New Jersey jail.

In his words, 'The only question I had about James Scott was, "Can I whup him?" I heard about all those press-ups he was doing and I could barely do 100.'

Marvin lost his second world title to another old acquaintance, Eddie Mustafa Muhammad.

He and Eddie went back to the amateur days and hadn't spoken in years, unsurprisingly.

Marvin was stopped with body shots in 11 rounds.

'Eddie hit me with a rib punch and every time I put my elbow back he still managed to land it and I haven't been able to figure out how he did it yet,' Marvin smiled, ever-so-slightly warming to the task.

'All I know is every time he reached around with that hook he hit me right there.

'Even if we fought today he could hit me with that punch and I wouldn't know how to avoid it.'

After two big championship wins and subsequent losses Johnson was written off as being over the hill before he stepped in with young Jamaican Leslie Stewart.

By now Marvin had already been given the fighting nickname 'Pops' because he was getting on and his bushy moustache and receding hairline made him look even older.

Pulling off the upset, Johnson became the first three-time light-heavyweight champ and that, he said, was his most satisfying win.

Was it because he proved the doubters wrong?

No.

Because he still had it?

Nope.

It was because it was all about getting closer to that million-dollar mark and it would guarantee him a career-high purse.

He was moving in the right direction, towards his million. He dreamed of fighting Sugar Ray Leonard at 175lb, earning the job Donny Lalonde eventually cashed in on. A year later Stewart had won a rematch and Marvin's hopes were dashed.

He reckons he over-trained.

'Instead of running four miles I ran eight. Instead of sparring ten rounds I sparred 20, instead of doing 50 press-ups I did 100.

'When we got there two days before the fight I was drained and I didn't feel right in the fight. Three days after I was like Superman.'

A cloned 175-pounder, Marvin could never become a candidate to enter the heavyweight division, boxing's flagship weight class and the one in which the millions could be made.

He didn't earn anything like the amount Saad had, let alone Michael Spinks whom Marvin thought hit the top at the right time when most of his decorated colleagues had little left after bashing and bludgeoning one another for several years. And Marvin had a point when he said Spinks wasn't even really from his era.

Johnson turned pro after the 1972 Games and Spinks won gold as part of the USA's famous 1976 Montreal team when Marvin was already boxing at championship level.

'Being part of the era with Matthew, Eddie Mustafa and all those guys, I was the only guy to win the title three times,' he said, finally with some pride.

However, his desire to put himself down was becoming frustrating to someone who had admired him. So the point was driven home that Marvin had been a success, that people did remember his achievements and that he was a force to be reckoned with.

It gave him food for thought if little else but it didn't surprise me when he said his championship belts were in storage somewhere.

I didn't doubt him. They were probably collecting dust in an attic and when it was suggested they should be on display he knocked that idea, insisting they were in the past and he needed to concentrate on his future, his family and his job.

How times had changed.

Marvin was a shaven-headed bad boy in his day. There was still no hair, only a faint moustache with a grey flicker breaking out from within.

He was married to his childhood sweetheart, Delores, and they had four kids, three boys and one girl. They were in their 20s and late teens. His huge extended family included dozens of cousins and grandkids. Now, of his career, he said he had 'sacrificed a few things I wish I hadn't sacrificed'.

Despite that, he insisted he would do it all again.

'I would,' he said, thinking long and hard, stroking his moustache. 'But I would change a lot.'

And although he hit the heights as a professional his fondest memories were as an innocent amateur, inspired by the hopes of making a fortune and realising his ambitions.

Back then he fought the best in the world in something like 65 bouts. But, because of his failed attempts to earn financial security, he did not get what he wanted from boxing. He failed in his mission.

That made him the nine-to-five guy he had become. It meant the man, a former king of the world, took orders from people for a living. He did what he was told to do, when he was told to do it.

Is there a harder way to bring somebody down to earth with a bump than, having been called a world champion, for them to be bossed around in the workplace by people who were fans and others who don't even know who they are talking to?

'If you can think pretty rationally then you can qualify for a better job,' Marvin said, of his prospects. 'Where I'm working right now, there's a couple of positions in the department that I would like but I just don't qualify for. I just have to accept that.

'I'd like to retire, but I would need to hit the lottery to do that.'

I threatened that I would stay in touch and said I was determined he should not forget his proud past. Surprisingly he encouraged me to do so. Something seemed to be changing in him the longer I stayed and the more we talked.

Something had been triggered.

I hoped it was something I said and that I made Marvin feel accomplished because he had clearly been trying to forget everything.

I told him he should embrace his legacy, not hide from it.

When he dropped me back at the Greyhound station late that night he finally admitted that maybe, just maybe, I was right.

His cold eyes looked at me.

I still don't think he could believe he had let me into his world.

He helped me with my bag to the station door.

I turned to shake his hand but he embraced me with a bear hug.

I had finally found Marvin. Not just the fighter, but the man. There was something deep beneath his hostile exterior. He had complexities I couldn't begin to understand.

He had been scarred, hurt, battered, bruised and disappointed but here he was, and he had a new friend.

It was a defining moment in my travels and would become a turning point in his life.

When I started I hoped I could make a difference in one fighter's life.

I felt I had just done that.

Chapter 29

THE T-shirt was pressed against the window of the Greyhound again. My head rested against it. I had become a dab hand at sleeping on buses. Even the layovers weren't so bad anymore and on the nights when I hardly had a wink I could always refer to AE Housman, the English scholar and poet, who wrote, 'Up, lad: when the journey's over there'll be time enough to sleep.'

The snow was thick in freezing Minneapolis and Jim Carlin, who met me at the station, had arranged dinner at his home with former heavyweight contender Duane Bobick.

He did not live far from the bus station, maybe 20 minutes, and he was keen to find out where I had spent the last couple of weeks.

Like just about everyone else he thought I was crazy, although he seemed to enjoy the tales nonetheless.

His home was spectacular, a mansion.

It had three levels, underfloor heating, massive rooms, views over a picturesque lake and mod cons on the mod cons.

The basement – the equivalent of a large self-contained bungalow – was mine for the night.

Jim's wife cooked a sumptuous feast that evoked a silence from the four of us while the hosts, Duane and I tucked in.

Bobick was polite and unobtrusive. He behaved like a house guest rather than an invited celebrity. He was another fighter who had experienced troughs of despair while enjoying smatterings of success.

Like Chuvalo in a way but so different in others, he took me on a teary journey through his career as a 1970s heavyweight contender. You never really know what happens to a man who vanishes from the public eye after the final bell tolls on his career.

Some of them go on to live in the shadows and turn out to be successes in life. Others fade into poverty and obscurity, trying to survive a struggle that rapidly becomes their toughest fight.

When Duane said he 'dropped off the end of the world' one wondered just how far he had fallen. However, he was dressed smartly – a cream shirt tucked in to dark trousers – and spoke well.

He was intense and precise, keen to impart as much information as he could.

His short sleeves shared with us an injury I knew about before my visit. He had been involved in an industrial accident and the scars on his misshapen right hand indicated it was serious. A finger was all-but missing.

'When you fell off the end of the earth, where did you fall?' I enquired.

He sighed and looked up.

'Did you work?' I pressed.

'No. I looked for work,' he said. 'My ex-father-in-law had got me into the construction business. I tried sales but I couldn't really do that because I did not see what I was trying to sell. I hadn't been there and seen it applied to tell you if it was good and from that aspect it had to be something I believed in and it had to work and, if it did, I would sell it, or find a way to sell it. It might take me a while to do but I'll do it. They were the early days at the end of the world.

'Basically, I'm on disability after my accident. I work part-time in the health industry as a personal trainer with older people and I've found something I had forgotten.'

Duane had a lot of training knowledge having been coached by the best in the US Navy and American Olympic teams.

He also knew about determination, having overcome an extensive rehabilitation programme on his arms that lesser men would not have coped with.

The accident happened during a stint working in a paper mill in 1997.

His vaunted right arm, the same one that put future heavyweight champion Larry Holmes on the deck in the amateurs, became trapped in a machine and started reeling him in.

He struggled, trying to pull his arm free with his left only for that one to be dragged in too.

The blood drained out of his arms, flesh and muscle was shredded and churned out across the workshop and into Duane's face. Crushed bones remained on show but there was not much else.

'I was laying on the floor except for a little bit of muscle here,' he said, pointing to the back of his forearm. 'From my elbow down to the wrist it was all bare bone. My skin had been twisted off and there was muscle laying all over the floor.

'I was conscious and God said to me, "You're going to be all right." And I don't know if I said "Yes" or thanked Him right then and there but I've been thanking Him ever since. Amen.'

Jim and his wife joined in with the chorus. Amen.

Bobick was in his physical prime when he joined the Navy. He had been serving as part of the National Guard until the accident but they no longer wanted him because of his disability.

'It was a wake-up call,' he said.

But things got worse.

He was initially told it would not only be a fight to use his arms again but it was going to take a minor miracle for him to actually keep the limbs.

'It basically turned my world upside down,' Duane recalled. 'At the time, I was still only 46 and I had three or four years getting back together and I went over the 50 mark and then no one wants to hire because it costs too much for their insurance regardless of the fact that, you know, I have some restrictions on this arm, too. So that comes into play. But, erm, basically it's put me out of the workforce and other than that I'm not sure why or where or what I'm supposed to be doing.

'You deal with it. I'm trying to work it out and I'm doing the best I can.'

If in doubt, boxers will always go back to what they know, and Duane knew boxing. He had been away for years but was contemplating a return to the sport in some capacity and had recently attended some National Golden Gloves fights. The buzz was coming back.

'What you're looking at is part of you,' he said. 'It took up the greatest share of my life and it was a part I enjoyed. I had fun, I made some money and there isn't a great deal I would change.'

Sure, he now liked writing and reciting poetry and he had been happily married to his third wife for nearly 20 years, but more than three decades ago Duane was a fearsome puncher who was going places, including the fateful 1972 Munich Olympics. He was a team-mate of my new friend Marvin Johnson.

Duane was a star amateur who beat the likes of Teofilo Stevenson, the Cuban legend, and Larry Holmes, eventually becoming a solid if over-hyped pro who won 47 times and who was arguably defined by one of just four defeats.

It was the individuality of the sport that drew him to boxing. He did not want to rely upon anybody else for success, intending for the buck to stop with him.

'It was a personal thing, me against whoever. Let's give it a shot,' he said.

He started fighting near his Little Falls home in Bouler, not too far from Minneapolis.

In his initial amateur contest he was almost knocked out in the first round but survived only to lose on points.

In a rematch, a week later, Duane was again spattered in blood, only this time it was not his.

'I just kept jabbing,' Duane recalled proudly.

He enjoyed the notoriety boxing gave him and 'became a bit of a rebel'.

But before he could get too sidetracked he joined the Navy and the rebellion was soon over.

He thrived and loved life on the boxing team.

He would spar more than 20 rounds each day.

'I was training to the point where you get to the end of the road and you can't do any more. Then you add some on. It was 24/7.

'Three three-minute rounds doesn't seem a lot unless you're in there going balls to the wall. That's what I did.'

His dedication paid off.

He beat the great Stevenson in the Pan Am Games.

He knocked Holmes out of the Olympic trials.

'I had him on the deck but basically, again, it comes to focus. I was going to Munich. Larry Holmes, forget it, you ain't going. I'm going.

'It was that kind of attitude I brought. I know he's going to hit me but I'm going to hit him harder. If he's going to hit me ten times I'm going to hit him 20 times and basically I was very mobile and every time I hit him after the right hand that put him down [in round one] he was back-pedalling and I think, at that time, and I don't know what his thoughts were, at that time he was telling me, "I give up the fight".

Holmes was disqualified for excessive holding in the third session and critics confined him to the gutless category for years afterwards, until he proved otherwise by becoming one of the great heavyweight champions.

'The Olympic style of boxing is about being up straight and the sportsmanship you've got to show at all times. In the pros you don't have to deal with sportsmanship at all,' said Duane. 'Whatever fight I was in I was a sportsman.'

Stating the obvious, he was also a white heavyweight which, in the seventies, was real currency. It didn't take long for reporters to get wind of the promising white hope as the Munich Olympics neared.

'Well, prior to getting over there in Bear Mountain [where Bobick trained for the Olympics] there was a guy who came in from Poland. He heard I was of Polish descent and came and did a little article on me. What you're dealing with in heavyweights, for so long, most of them in the United States were black and all of a sudden there is a white heavyweight representing the United States, which I think was a bit of a novelty. I can remember walking through the Olympic Village and I could hear my name "Blah, blah, blah, Bobick," and I couldn't understand a word they were saying but so many people recognised me.

'I had a lot of people, you know, just, how can I say it… it was just fun.

'But when we got there I only sparred with people on the team, Marvin Johnson and Raymond Russell, and the gym was kind of chaotic.

'There were two fights in my life when I had totally no focus, they were in Germany, in Munich, against Stevenson and my fight with Ken Norton at Madison Square Garden.

'I woke up at 5am in Munich and I felt something was dreadfully wrong. I didn't know what it was but I couldn't think of anything so I went back to sleep. Then I got up and went for the weigh-in at 8am and after we got done with that we heard the Games had been cancelled because of the terrorism [the terrorist siege had taken place that morning].

'Then, about an hour later, we got the schedule for the day and it was going to go on. When you're strung up here like this and then it's cancelled you're like boom, all deflated, and you go down to the bottom.

'When you find out it's back on you go back up but only so far. You don't go back up to where you were.

'The US Olympic Committee didn't think about me at all because nobody came up to me and said anything.

'But for Stevenson, the Cubans moved their athletes out of the village so they could keep their focus on what was coming up.'

The legendary Stevenson halted Duane in the second round.

'I think I had decided way before to go professional and I was hoping for a gold medal because that would have meant a lot of money.

'As it was, it brought in not a lot.

'My professional debut, I was paid around $2,000 and while that sounded good, part of it was because I was a Minnesota kid working out in New York who came back here [to Minnesota] for my debut.

'I thought by the time I was 30 years old I would be able to do anything I wanted to and not have to worry about work.'

He laughed laconically.

Yet his pro career got off to a flying start, partly through good matchmaking and partly because Duane could fight.

He was named Rookie of the Year in 1973 by winning 15 times in his first year. All were knockouts but he was finding out the two codes were completely different.

'I didn't do as much sparring but I would train for fighters with different styles,' he said. 'That makes you change the way you do things because the reality of it is they are two totally different sports.'

He did well, spurred on by a friendly rivalry with brother Rodney, who was also a pro heavyweight.

Duane was Joe Frazier's chief sparring partner while, at the same time, Rodney was Muhammad Ali's.

That's an indication of how good the brothers were and how highly they were regarded in the business.

'I didn't work with Rodney a lot because when I joined the Navy I was away for four years,' Duane continued. 'I was home once in a while but then I went pro and I went out to New York. Basically, after I got out of high school I was gone.

'But Rodney and I did have one fight together. It was a bar fight but we didn't fight in the bar, we fought out on the street. He was giving me some abuse and he was drunk. I'd had a couple but I was nowhere near drunk and, you know, we went outside on the street, there was snow all over the place. It was slippery as hell and he was running his mouth about how he was going to beat the crap out of me and how he's rated number three in America and I was number two. He was younger than me but I ruled the roost and there was just a little bit of a sibling rivalry.

'The guy actually was scary. I really don't think I would have wanted to fight him because he was bigger, stronger and he could take an awesome, awesome punch. But we went outside and I caught him a couple of times and we fell down. It was right at that time, I was just getting ready to boot him in the head because he was talking so much smack, that I stopped and thought, "This is my brother. Hold on, that's not Rodney."'

Duane's kid brother couldn't hold his drink.

'The difference was talent-wise, Rodney had as much or more than me, but his focus was not like mine. His priorities at the time were drinking and partying. He did a lot of that after his fights.

'We got along good. What drew us a little closer was when I was training for Norton in San Bernardino he came out and was working with me. I had a rib injury initially which postponed the fight a little bit, and then he came out and he saw the seriousness of the camp. Having been in all these camps with Ali he had seen how he worked and what he didn't see is, when Ali had a tough fight coming, he didn't see him really put the nose to the stone like you gotta do.

'Then, all of a sudden at this camp, he started getting his life back together. He got custody of his daughter and he was in the process of putting things right and getting serious and maybe going to some school or something. He talked about that. Then erm,' Duane continued, slowing down and pinching the bridge of his nose to fight back tears.

'Then, erm,' he tried again.

'Two weeks after the Norton fight he got killed in a car accident.'

Rodney was just 25.

Duane's other brother, Leroy, still lived nearby in St Paul and worked in real estate.

'He is OK,' Duane said, happily enough. 'But when he was in the Marine Corps he had a couple of guys jump him and kicked him and hit him and stuff so he's got a plate in his head and stuff. He's got two daughters and he's doing pretty well, I think.'

One former Bobick victim was my old Atlantic City ally Chuck Wepner.

'I tell you,' Duane smirked, as I told him that I had recently been with Chuck. 'He's a diamond in the rough and he's always going to stay in the rough. He's not going to get polished up. Here was a guy who, when it came to dirty tactics, he had them all, and he tried them all on me. But I knew enough about him that I was ready for every one of them and when he tried them I made him pay. He's a great guy, though. He could take a lot and he could knock you out.'

We talked about the case Chuck was tackling Stallone with and Bobick was another fighter who had a spurious claim to being an inspiration behind scenes in the *Rocky* films.

'Prior to Stallone's movie coming out, a lady came down from Canada and did a little article on me for *People* magazine,' he went on. 'That was where they picked up running up the museum steps in Philadelphia because that's what I did. I was the one running up the steps because I lived less than half a mile away from there and running up there was part of my training.'

After around 25 fights, Duane had moved to the home of the fictional fighter, Philadelphia, to train under his former sparring boss Frazier.

Top trainer George Benton also worked with him, notably improving his left hook, and Duane said Frazier was 'a great plus' for his career.

'We were buddies,' said Bobick. 'We weren't the same colour but we were buddies and we got along good. I always had a lot of respect for Joe.'

And while the trainer–fighter relationship was a decent fit, a match with Norton all but ended the high hopes people had for Duane Bobick.

In 48 brutal seconds at New York's Madison Square Garden, he went from bona fide contender to Great White Hype and he was never viewed in the same light again.

Talking of the Norton nightmare, he said, 'I agreed with Eddie Futch, who was also helping train me, and said I wouldn't go out in the crowd before the fight but that's what pumped me up. I would go and speak to the guys in the nosebleeds because that was where I came from. I was a man of the people and we took that away and that was the first time I walked into the ring without butterflies and I knew that, without butterflies, something was wrong.

'It was the same when I woke up that morning in Munich, I knew something was wrong.

'The stoppage was right against Norton because the legs weren't there. I would go after him because I was the hunter, right, and boom, the legs wobbled, they weren't there. But something in my head said do the rope-a-dope.

'I don't do the rope-a-dope,' he exclaimed, with disbelief.

'I think what might have hurt me a little bit is the referee we had, Arthur Mercante, who I had met a few times. We had chatted and we got along good. He didn't want to see me hurt and I think, maybe in some aspects, some of the other referees might have just waited a little bit longer to say the fight was over.

'But that's OK with me. It's gone. It's history.

'After the Norton fight my wife at the time let me know she didn't like boxing and it blew me away a little bit. It really did.'

'Were you close to fighting Ali?'

'Well, the Norton fight, had I beat Norton I would have fought Ali.

'I would like to have fought Ali, not even just for the payday but I think I could have beaten him. I was like Frazier and I was like Ali and I shifted between the two depending on who I was fighting. I had the best of both worlds going for me and he only had what he could do. Yeah, he had tricks to stop the punches and stuff but I probably would have done more physical damage to him than a lot of other guys out there.'

'If you could have had Norton again would it have been different?'

'Oh yes. Hindsight is 20/20 but then you don't have glasses on your butt either. There's no point looking back.'

Duane had been suffering with bursitis when he decided to haul the curtain down on his career. He had promised himself that if he could not be 100 per cent physically fit he would not fight.

Like a fair few ex-boxers, Bobick found himself on the big screen, playing a part in the film *Billy Boy* in South Africa. But, post-Norton his fame levels were never the same again.

They eroded by the year and little was heard of him until his accident in 1997. Then all went quiet again.

He asked me for Marvin Johnson's phone number and said he and his former Olympic room-mate had some catching up to do. I hoped it might do Marvin some good.

'If I could take the information I know now back 30 years things would be a bit different,' Duane said, as we enjoyed post-dinner coffee.

'Would you do it again?'

He let out a huge sigh.

'That's a hard one.

'I have no regrets whatsoever about boxing. I've been to Australia, I've been to South America, I've been to Europe, I've been to Asia.

'I travelled.

'I looked up to Joe Louis. I was Joe Louis, I was Rocky Marciano [when I was young], but honestly, when we were kids, I was [baseball legend] Mickey Mantle. That's where I was going to be and that was my focus.

'I think back to being a 15- or 16-year-old kid on the banks of the Mississippi River and then getting to see the world. I wanted to get out of here. I wanted to see the world.

'I did it.'

After the meal, Duane posed for pictures with his hands up, guarding his face in a fighting pose. He was clearly bothered about raising his mangled right paw into the camera's viewfinder.

'Don't worry about that,' I said, reassuring him.

Moments later he was gone.

Duane was one of those men who fell into the all-too-human category. The Superman cape fighters wear was long gone and Clark Kent had been revealed.

America's one-time great hope, Olympic prospect and heavyweight contender was ordinary. He was just a man.

Chapter 30

THE Carlin residence was five-star luxury and the sleeping was good. It was much-needed, too. After a night there, the final leg of the journey to the West Coast would be confronted but Jim Carlin insisted on lunch out, and we would be joined by a guest.

He knew Jim Beattie, a giant white heavyweight contender from the 1960s, and he'd arranged for us to meet.

Now Beattie was not a great fighter but he had come close to a title fight and, like Bobick had claimed, was only one bout or so from facing Ali.

Jim Carlin and I sat at a table waiting for him in a smart Minnesota restaurant. I would occasionally look up excitedly, hoping to catch a glimpse of Beattie walking in. At 6ft 8in I would have a job mistaking him for someone else.

We sipped drinks for all of five minutes before the doorway, through which light had been pouring, was filled and a shadow darkened the room.

People looked up from their tables as a colossus ducked under the frame.

'This must be him,' I said.

Jim looked up and smiled.

He waved over to Beattie who, in turn, waved a rolled-up copy of today's paper, clasped firmly in his left hand.

His hair was thin on top and he had a grey, woolly beard disguising rosy cheeks.

He moved heavily between the tables as more people looked up.

He shook Jim's hand warmly and reached out for mine with a smile. I had felt a lot of firm handshakes on my travels but his topped the lot. His palm seemed to paralyse my arm.

Even when he sat down he looked all of six foot.

I asked if I could start recording the interview as we ate but he said with the gentle, kind voice of a children's doctor, 'Let me interview you first.

'What have you been doing? Where are you going? Why have you been doing it?'

They were just some of the questions he fired my way as Carlin smiled.

It wasn't long before I turned the tables, though.

Beattie spoke with an incisive, articulate honesty, the type you might expect from a successful gold broker.

He looked nothing like the New York sideshow act the Mob portrayed him as when he was fighting.

Sure he was tall, but that aside he looked every inch the businessman.

He was passive, not aggressive.

We ordered our food; Beattie didn't order enormous quantities of anything as I assumed a man of his size might have.

Big Jim was now a vegetarian, too. After fighting lung cancer in 1984 and 1985 he became clinically depressed and wanted to lose weight. He couldn't get beneath 265lb despite 'running and running' and, by giving up meat, his weight plummeted from 305lb to 'a firm and fit 229lb'.

As a kid, like many fighters, he came from rough beginnings.

'I was one of the children that were kind of like ping-pong balls and I finally realised I didn't want to be picked on anymore,' he said. 'I didn't want to be beaten up anymore so at the age of 13, when I started training, I was 5ft 9in and weighed 145lb. I was a welterweight and at 14 I had my first Golden Gloves match.

'I fought this youngster for three rounds and survived and I thought, "This is all right." I finally felt like I belonged some place.

'I went to a boxing gymnasium at a police gym in St Paul and I started in 1957 or 1958 when I was still a kid. There was a man there who was very nice to me and he taught me how to box. He was like my surrogate father. I came from a very dysfunctional family; so much so that they took all the "fun" out of dysfunctional.'

From 56 amateur fights, Big Jim enjoyed 51 wins. 'A lot of them were knockouts,' he pointed out.

'My two brothers, one older and one younger, were excellent baseball players and my father had been a baseball player and I was tired of sitting on the bench with my mother and the girls. So I quit going to the ball games and finally found something that I could put my time into. Little by little I started to build up my self-respect and my self-esteem by boxing.'

He grew into the man I saw before me and emotionally into an individual who could take care of himself.

He now seemed so confident it was almost difficult to envisage how he could be scared before a fight.

Every boxer experiences pre-fight fear, it's far worse than plain old nerves, and despite his immense physical advantages Jim was no different.

'No, I was never nervous,' he said. 'I was scared to death. I was terrified; particularly when I turned pro because I had a breathing disorder. I didn't realise it but I was asthmatic and as a youngster I had a lot of bouts with pneumonia. I was very weak so I knew it was going to be tough to go past three rounds.

'Amateur boxing was just the limit I could go. I would have been a great amateur forever. But then I went into my first pro fight, a four-rounder. My second was a six-rounder and because I was very colourful in those wins I was boosted to eight- and ten-rounders right away. I soon learned that after about four or five rounds my asthma started to kick in and I was virtually disabled after five or six rounds, so I was almost just fighting with my heart.

'My first two fights were here for a local manager but he had started a relationship with my family and it was getting very uncomfortable so, after the AAU tournament that I came second in – I lost to a guy I had already knocked out – I had several more fights and got some overtures from New York to come out there and fight as a professional. So I chose that. I was 19 and I went into the gyms where there were guys that I had only read about, such as Nino Valdez, Willie Besmanoff, Zora Folley, Eddie Machen, Sonny Liston and I boxed with them.

'The first trainer I met that impressed me was Ray Arcel. He wanted to work with me, but because of the managerial arrangement I had a trainer already. He was Freddie Fierro and he had trained quite a few world champions; Billy Conn, Joey Maxim, Fritzie Zivic and he trained the tallest heavyweight in boxing, Ben Moroz, who was 7ft 2in [record books give several heights starting at 6ft 8in]. So I thought he would know something about training big men.

'I was 6ft 8in, but never ever taken seriously as a fighter because I was so skinny but as soon as they got in the ring with me they saw I could hit like hell. I wasn't a great boxer but the man who trained me here in Minnesota as an amateur, Roger Twigg, trained me in preparation for a professional career. He was from Washington DC, he was a Secret Service man who had protected Presidents Truman, Eisenhower and Kennedy. He came to Minnesota after he trained a very good middleweight in Washington named Holly Mims.

'He taught me basically all the tricks; how to throw a certain hook to the belly called a shovel hook, not a conventional or traditional shot but because of my southpaw stance I could throw it right from my hip straight into someone's liver, which was right where it was supposed to hit.

'When you catch a punch from a guy with my latitude and leverage you would just see these big guys collapsing.'

Jim was taken on in the big city by what he called 'a consortium of New York gangsters'.

'Did you know Blinky Palermo and Frankie Carbo?' I asked.

'Well, yes, but the man I spent most of my time with, the main one of note, was Frank Costello and he was probably the original Godfather.

'Blinky was very crude but Frank Costello was a fine man and I don't know how many people met their inevitable end at his hand or his word but he was always nice to me.'

In New York, Beattie lived in Manhattan, 65th Street and Central Park West, an exclusive area where Bobby Kennedy's personal staff were neighbours.

'It was non-stop action and non-stop partying. It was alive with excitement,' he recalled of 1960s New York. 'People were breaking out of the repressive 1950s mentality and just starting to explore their own ability to relate to this very sophisticated and highly politicised world.'

One person who did not welcome Beattie into professional boxing was occasional sparring partner Liston.

'Our gym workouts were wars,' said Jim. 'He tried to intimidate me in the gym. I was just a kid, 21 years old.'

'And one of the only guys he had to look up to a little bit,' Carlin added, explaining why Sonny might have been a little tough on the raw Minnesotan.

'The reason he banged me around so much was I got so much publicity everywhere I went,' Beattie went on. 'I was in *Life* magazine three times.'

But Jim wasn't in New York for fun. He had some heavy individuals pushing him and he didn't want to let them down, even though he seemed to lack the self-belief to get to the very top.

Because of his unique appearance, even a fifth-round stoppage loss in his fifth contest against average Canadian Johnny Barazza did not set him back.

'Actually, because I was such an oddity, promoters were looking for an excuse to use me. They weren't looking for an excuse not to use me.

'I will be honest with you, I never really gave myself a shot at winning the title. I figured, "What the hell, if there's a chance I could fight for the heavyweight title it'd be fine." I had no master plan. I was a big dumb kid who didn't know shit from apple sauce. I was just out there trying to have some fun. But I happened to be unusually tall and was also quite handsome for a young guy. Don't let this beat-up image in front of you fool you. When I was 20, 21 years old… In fact at Christmas in 1964 I busted my left hand throwing a left hook. I broke it and I was living with an actress who was on Broadway at the time and she said, "Now you've got a broken hand, you're not going to be training and you're not sitting around the house all day while I'm out working so why don't you get to work with me acting. There's a theatre two blocks from me and they are looking for a tall white man, you can do tall and white as good as anybody."

'I was 6ft 8in, I was a big white guy with a big dumb smile. "They are looking for a guy just like you,"' she insisted.

'I said, "No kidding?" I auditioned and I got the role.'

Just like that, Beattie was in *Flora the Red Menace*, Liza Minelli's first Broadway show.

For nine months, while his hand healed, he took to the stage every night – he was also running to stay in shape – and by the time the show's stint came to an end he was ready to get back in the ring.

But he still lacked the composure, quality and class to crack the top level.

Jim said he over-trained for a fight with Buster Mathis, evident by his lighter than usual weight of 238lb.

'I had boxed him as an amateur. He was faster than I thought he was going to be. I was spearing him with my jab pretty effectively but he hit me in the second round with two big right hands and I can't remember too much after that.

'Has anybody else told you about fighting a fight semi-conscious?' he enquired politely.

'I've done it,' I laughed.

'Tom McNeeley was a rough, tough guy. I saw him fight Floyd Patterson for the title and he did extremely well because Patterson was underrated as a fighter. He was one of the most dangerous heavyweights that ever lived. He could be halfway across the ring from you and throw this flying left hook and tear your brains out without even seeing him, he was that fast. McNeeley did very well against him but as usual my managers had done their homework. McNeeley had slipped a little bit and his dedication to boxing wasn't what it had been. He was still good, but he wasn't the same guy when I fought him.'

Regardless, the Minnesota press gang thought their giant would be slain by the more experienced McNeeley.

Hometown papers said, 'Poor Jim Beattie, he's going to be fed to the wolves' and that he would 'get chewed up like all those kids that go to New York'.

'Well, I almost killed him,' said Beattie. 'I hit him so hard with a left hook in the fifth round he couldn't move for about five minutes.

'I was on a roll. Then I had a couple of good wins. I fought Mel Turnbow. Many men wouldn't fight him because he hit so hard and in the first round of our fight at the Boston Garden he knocked two molars off my gumline, he burst my eardrum, he broke my nose and smashed my cheekbone with a right hand.'

Turnbow, Beattie said, left on a stretcher after losing in the sixth.

'Then I fought a guy called Orville Qualls back here and he was undefeated [records say he was 9–1–1 when he met Beattie]. He had good wins, many knockouts and Angelo Dundee called me and said, "What the hell are you doing fighting Orville

Qualls? He's been down here [training in Dundee's Miami gym] fighting champions.'"

He warned Beattie he might lose his top ten spot and a possible fight with Ali.

'I beat him real bad. In fact, I knocked him out twice. They had this rule that the bell can save you and I knocked him dead in the third round and they dragged him back to his corner and fixed him up using stuff that today they would put you in jail for. They sent him back out and he got knocked out again. It almost brought a tear to my eye. I didn't have to beat him like that.'

Beattie, the very personification of a gentle giant, cut a figure more like Lennie from *Of Mice and Men*, but as soon as he talked that image left one's thoughts. He was clearly umpteen academical notches above hapless Lennie.

'So I had some good wins,' he went on. 'Now let's talk about a guy named Jim Woody.

'The second time I lost to him I was just careless.

'My manager, Charlie Bower, had just died and I lost something; part of my commitment, part of my fearlessness, because boxing on a professional level – particularly with the heavyweights – if you watch the damage that can be done with one heavyweight punch you become extremely respectful of heavyweights.

'I almost fought Ali in 1966 and if I had not been beaten by Woody I would have. It sounds strange to say this but Ali was always afraid of me. Now I don't think he was exactly shaking in his boots but he would rather fight someone else than fight me.

'To start with, he had an extremely difficult time with southpaws and he also had a very difficult time with tall boxers.'

Despite the said damage that can be caused by the fists of a heavyweight, the punches don't appear to have affected Jim and he was still doing some acting work. In fact, he had recently finished filming for a movie although he modestly added, 'It was the smallest part ever written for an actor.'.

He wasn't sure who played the lead in the film, he just went in, did his bit and went home.

But Jim's claim to fame wasn't really his boxing. It wasn't even his Broadway stint or a cameo role. It was his co-starring position as *The Great White Hope* in the film of the same name starring James Earl Jones as Jack Johnson.

But it almost didn't happen.

Although he had the obvious tools for the job, he drove such a hard bargain the producer had second thoughts about using him.

'If you had pushed any harder you would have lost the whole deal,' Jim was told.

After what has gone down in film history as a mild success, Beattie was, at the time, advised that if he stayed in Hollywood he would make a 'very, very good living'. The catch was he would never be a leading man.

He thought there was more chance of him becoming a leading man in boxing because he believed in his power.

It didn't work out that way. Beattie turned his back on the sport in 1970 without officially retiring. That allowed him to make a comeback five years later, even though financially he wanted for nothing.

'I was living very well,' he said. 'I had made some very good investments with the money I had and in about 1975 I discovered I was bored to tears and was going to start getting into trouble. You know, when you put your life on the line and then you go to work and sell life insurance for some guy it's a noble act but having had my experiences I couldn't deal with it.

'I went back to training.'

Jim's career fizzled once again and a firm, permanent retirement followed.

'What do you see when you look back on your career?'

'A lot of mistakes,' he said so quickly he had to repeat it.

'A lot of things I wish I hadn't done. There were things I wish I had done. But I spend very little of my time looking back. The only area of life I get any enjoyment out of is right here and right now and I enjoy what I'm doing.'

'But aren't you pleased with your accomplishments in boxing?'

'Sure. But I'm pleased with my accomplishments as a father. Now a couple of women might say I haven't got a lot of accomplishments from being a husband but that's just their opinion.'

Beattie was on to his fourth wife. 'When did you last get married?'

'Saturday,' he joked. 'I'm with the right woman now.'

333

He had been with Peggy for ten years and she worked as a counsellor, helping couples with problems and mediating between industrial companies to help their relationships.

Although he continued with some acting, Jim was successful after boxing.

'I'm a gold dealer,' he said proudly.

'Gold digger?' I asked, thinking he was cracking another joke.

'No, not a gold digger, a gold dealer. A gold broker, I've been doing it for five years. It's very satisfying. I work with very nice people and my customers are all very pleasant. It's a very good business. They are the ones who have got the money to buy it, wealthy people that you build up some kind of allegiance with.'

Although he didn't strike gold in boxing, he had in his retirement.

Carlin drove me to the Greyhound bus station where he had met me just 24 hours earlier. He supplied me with an enormous bag of pistachio nuts for my onward journey. From his home, I had managed to set up my next interview. I was going on to Stockton in California and had 48 hours left.

I had enjoyed the wintry climes of Minneapolis. There was little doubt Bobick was a superior fighter to Beattie but I felt as though he, with so much sadness, had been abandoned on boxing's wastelands.

Yet in the same city, another ex-fighter, Big Jim, had refused to rely on boxing. He had stability in his life. They were both working hard and lived firmly in the real world where their achievements in boxing had no relevance.

Although I felt Jim had left boxing behind, Duane had been left behind by boxing. Two different fighters were moving in different directions, living different lives in the same city.

And I was leaving them both.

The near-2,000-mile bus ride through the nights to Stockton was an entertaining one. The Greyhound was filled with students going back to university and college after the Thanksgiving holidays and the driver, Bob (he said 'Baaab'), sang campfire songs and told stories over the speaker system. The sun disappeared behind the Midwest mountains and the party continued into the night.

Chapter 31

DESPITE five attempts at world titles, former light-heavyweight contender Yaqui Lopez had all but vanished from the subconscious of fight fans. I had managed to obtain a phone number for Yaqui's former manager Jack Cruz.

He told me to call him, letting him know when I arrived in Stockton, California, while guaranteeing Yaqui's participation at the same time.

Lopez was one of the few remaining fighters from the light-heavyweight era I had spent so much time researching that I hadn't spoken to.

Yet my enthusiasm was accompanied by a sprinkling of trepidation because he had been in umpteen brutal battles in his 50-fight career.

I had seen what those same wars had done to Matthew Saad Muhammad and Marvin Johnson, who had been left suffering with varying levels of post-fight trauma.

I wondered if I had not heard about Yaqui because boxing might have neglected him, the same way I thought it had poor Jimmy Young and Duane Bobick.

I had not seen any recent pictures of Lopez, either, which aroused suspicion that I would not like what I found.

Maybe I would meet a mumbling, fumbling man who was at least supported by a strong family, proud of his achievements and his legacy as one of the best fighters never to be crowned champion.

Upon arrival at Sacramento I took a local bus ride, about 45 minutes to an hour, to Stockton.

There was, however, a problem. I didn't have any tapes left for my dictaphone and my notepads were full.

So my first port of call was a stationery shop in the town centre, which I found, and then I waited for it to open at 9am.

Stockton was unlike anywhere else I had been. It was a largely Hispanic town in terms of architecture and population and so it was surprising when a British lady served me in the store.

She had married an American GI and had moved to the city years ago.

With new tapes and a fresh notebook in hand, I returned to the bus terminal to call Jack Cruz. He told me to sit tight. He would send someone to come and get me.

These little things were so greatly appreciated.

While I loved the hunt – tracking down old fighters – kind gestures like this made everything so much easier.

I thanked him and he replied, almost sounding offended, that it was the least he could do.

I knew I was in good hands.

Jack was Yaqui's father-in-law and had been his promoter and trainer and, after waiting for about an hour, a man approached me immediately guessing that the big, hungry and unshaven blonde Englishman with a rucksack was the man he had been sent to chauffeur.

Benny Casing, a featherweight from 1958 to 1972 with a 20–5–4 record, had also been Yaqui's cutman.

He didn't talk much, gently skimming over the fact he fought and that he had a long association with Yaqui. I think he was initially apprehensive and wanted to know what the hell I was doing in Stockton, about 5,500 miles from home, to meet a fighter who had never held a major title and who had been firmly off the boxing radar.

We chatted but he seemed to be concentrating on the road more than our conversation. I couldn't criticise him for that.

He drove us to Jack's bungalow and while I didn't want to go round the houses and make too many stops before chatting with Yaqui, I was happy to meet Jack.

He was clearly in poor health. He wore a dressing gown and was overweight. He used a frame to get around, breathed heavily and took medication throughout our conversation.

The three of us talked for an hour or so and I enjoyed spending time with them but, with all the respect in the world for the kind strangers, I was growing anxious.

Spending time with Casing and Cruz was kind of like sitting through the undercard to get to the main event. It's not that it wasn't a good undercard, interesting and fun; it's just not why I bought the ticket.

We drank iced tea and conversed some more while Jack, who had also trained Casing, gushed over his two charges, telling me what good boxers they were and what fine men they had become.

Coming up to lunchtime, Jack said he would call Yaqui.

He said, 'Follow me.'

I assumed we were going to wherever he kept the phone, but we went to the front gate and he called out, 'Yaqui, Yaqui. Get over here you lazy so and so.'

A man emerged from the house across the street.

It was Lopez, vaguely similar to how he used to look.

I couldn't believe what I was seeing.

He appeared to be almost in his fighting shape.

I needn't have worried.

His rugged features had only gently eroded.

A previously thick mop of jet-black hair was now a tidy grey parcel that he occasionally ran his fingers through.

His muscles didn't bulge like they once did but they did not appear softer, just leaner.

The scar tissue around his eyes remained but it was relaxed now he didn't have the same sharp facial ridges as when he was boiling down to make 175lb.

He looked like an older, Mexican version of the French footballer David Ginola, not entirely unattractive, particularly when you consider those slamming straight rights he ate flush from Saad Muhammad. The last time I had seen him, he was getting off the deck against Saad on tape in their second crimson-stained classic more than 20 years ago.

Then his face was puffy and blood-filled. He walked like a drunk around the ring having been decked four times in the 14th in one of boxing's most savage battles.

It was a give-and-take affair, one of the ones where Saad said he could only see shadows in the ring as he and Lopez hurled punches recklessly towards each another. They both borrowed against their futures in that one. Yaqui's investment now seemed sounder than the winner's.

It was certainly one of the fights that contributed to Saad being in the state I found him in. It was the sort of fight that had filled me with unnecessary dread that Lopez would be in a similar way to Matthew.

He appeared to have wrecked Saad, it would only make sense if the loser was worse off.

I told Yaqui I had formed an alliance with his old rival and updated him about Saad's condition. He was moved but had heard Matthew was the worse for wear.

'Before our fights I just knew we were going to go to war,' Yaqui said.

That was light years away from Yaqui's humble beginnings. His real name is Alvaro and he was born and raised in Mexico.

'I wanted to be a bull-fighter but I got injured,' he said.

'Then, my mother and father sent for me and I left Mexico. I was actually born underneath a bullring but when I was young I was with a bull, fighting, and its horn came through my ankle and destroyed it.

'I liked the excitement when it was me and the bull and everyone would clap. It was a great atmosphere.'

With his first dream over, there was another sport young Lopez could hear calling.

'I loved watching boxing and then I met Jack's daughter and found out her father was a boxing promoter. I asked her to introduce me so I could learn how to box.

'She looked at me funny but she did it,' he pointed at Cruz, who raised his hands in recognition, 'and he looked me up and down and said, "Are you sure? Really?"'

Jack explained, 'I took him down to the YMCA and he didn't know how to walk let alone box but I could tell he would go places because he always worked so hard. He had a great work ethic.'

He lost just one of 16 fights, his first. He was due to meet an equally green novice in his amateur debut until an eleventh-hour switch of opponent. Across the ring stood a cocky old-hand with more than a hundred fights on his card.

Jack remembered, 'It was still a close fight and afterwards the fans followed Albert [the American for Alvaro] asking for his hand wraps, autograph and gloves believing they had just seen something special. I guess that was a sign of things to come.'

Yaqui cut in, 'I had a really brave manager, he'd make *me* fight anybody.'

Team Lopez would drive one hour each way from Stockton to Oakland to train, becoming a tight, close-knit unit.

'At first everyone wanted to spar Yaqui,' Cruz recalled. They'd lie in wait for him. Four months later he'd arrive and there was no one there. No one wanted to spar him anymore.'

Lopez had become a handful. He was often avoided, not just because he had a shot at beating the top fighters but because they were concerned about the type of battle they would find themselves in. He would make them work for three minutes of each round and they would be taking more than their fair share of punches.

Having repeatedly heard Cruz call Yaqui by his American name, Albert, he explained how his Yaqui nickname came about.

With enthusiasm in his voice, Jack took the story on.

'The organisers of an amateur card were waiting for an Indian but the guy hadn't shown up. The guy we were supposed to be fighting didn't show up either so we were going to go home empty-handed.

'I said, "My guy's Indian."

'They looked at Yaqui and said, "Are you sure?"'

Jack answered for him, 'I said, "Hell yeah he's an Indian."

'They looked at Yaqui and said, "Are you sure? What tribe's he from?"

'All I could think of from Mexico was Yaqui Indians so I said, "He's a Yaqui."

'From then on the crowd started cheering "Come on, Yaqui" and that's how we got his name.'

Lopez turned professional in 1972, aged 21.

He was pitched in tough.

He fought prospect Jesse Burnett in his opening contest, losing an eight-round tear-up on points. It was the first of four bouts they would have but they had bigger names and were better fighters when they renewed acquaintances, twice in 1975 and finally in 1978. Burnett won the first two, Lopez the final two. All were decided on points and were close, hard-fought affairs.

Out of nowhere, Benny suddenly talked without being spoken to.

'I learned how to be a cutman in those fights,' he said, shaking his head. He pointed to the skin around Yaqui's eyes while holding his thumb and finger the distance apart, replicating the lengths of some of Yaqui's gruesome wounds.

Cruz added, 'He could have filled a couple of buckets of blood from the Burnett fights alone.

'In one of them, when Yaqui went back to the corner, Benny said to him, "He's tired, go get him."

'Do you know what Yaqui said to him? "Me too, I'm tired too, what about me?"

'Right after that fight Yaqui started picking up on his roadwork and his training.'

Further stiff tests awaited and critics raised eyebrows when he was matched with American banger Andy Kendall.

'He was the biggest puncher I ever faced,' Yaqui said.

'He was No.4 in the world [No.3 in *The Ring*'s US ratings]. When I signed the contract I didn't know anything about him. I told my friends I was going to fight Kendall and they showed me a copy of *The Ring,* where he was rated and I was shocked.'

Cruz had a story for every Yaqui Lopez moment and they started discussing his 1976 WBC title fight with Liverpudlian star John Conteh in Copenhagen. Lopez, as normal, was the underdog.

'I knew he was a good fighter,' Yaqui said. 'I'd heard that he was a good, scientific boxer but I was young, too, and at the time pretty good also.

'We went to Copenhagen three days before the fight and we were jet-lagged. I'd left my training stuff at home and George Francis [Conteh's manager] had booked us a route to Copenhagen that took us 19 hours.'

'We went everywhere but Copenhagen,' interjected Cruz.

'It was a hard fight but he didn't hurt me,' Lopez started again.

'If we'd gone over there 15 days earlier things would have been different but I learned a lot from fighting Conteh.'

Boxing News called the contest 'hard fought but decisive', saying it was 'thoroughly absorbing and entertaining'.

While Yaqui shook him in the sixth, Conteh said afterwards that he had not been under extreme duress.

Lopez fought as many top names as anyone during that era. He lists Galindez, Saad Muhammad, Conteh, Rossman, Gary

Summerhays, Tony Mundine and Lonnie Bennett among the best opponents.

'When we fought Galindez the first time they had a press conference in Rome and we were late. When we got there Galindez just stood there staring at me.

'It was an evil stare. I went up to him laughing and said, "Don't get mad at me now, wait until we are in the ring. Then you can get mad."

'He tried to out-psyche me.'

It didn't work and Yaqui gave him hell.

An 8,000-strong crowd voiced their displeasure at the verdict. 'Galindez has such a tough time with Lopez' headlined *Boxing News*. The Argentine with attitude edged all three cards, 147–146, 146–145 and 148–146 but the magazine called it a 'spectacular struggle'.

It got better before it got worse for Lopez who, after two quick wins, secured a shot at Mike Rossman in order to get back into the mix.

'I applied a lot of pressure and he didn't know what to do,' remembered Yaqui. 'I caught him pretty good in the sixth and at the end of the round he was out on his feet.

'They had to stop the fight.'

Yaqui was ahead on two cards while the other judge had them level. He had earned his biggest win and another shot at Galindez.

Their second fight, also for the South American's WBA crown, proved more conclusive for everyone apart from Lopez who disputed the loss.

'I know I've won. I don't know what I have got to do to beat Galindez,' he told the media afterwards.

It was a tactical fight with few dramatic moments and this time the consensus was Victor was a worthy winner.

Yaqui won a tough 12-rounder against Burnett in July 1978 but rumbled from one war into another when he fought Matt Franklin, latterly Saad, for the NABF light-heavyweight title.

Ringsiders praised Yaqui's guts for standing up to a fierce beating for 11 rounds. The Philadelphia orphan was on a roll and hit Lopez with everything. Yaqui wasn't without his own success, however.

'It was a tough fight,' he recalled. 'They stopped it on a cut. I felt I was ahead and learned a lot.'

He had been out on his feet in the third when a jarring right catapulted him across the ring and into the ropes. He would have gone even further had the strands not been there but, resilient and game as ever, he battled back and established a firm foothold in the middle rounds.

'Matthew told me after that one, "I'm going to be a world champion and when I am I'll give you a rematch."

Cruz stepped in, 'And he did. It was very good of him.'

Often bloodied in his fights, and fighting through thick and sticky crimson, Lopez became a cult hero via terrestrial TV, which beamed fights into living rooms across America on Saturday afternoons.

He was also one of the brave few who experienced the hostile confines of Rahway.

'I was kind of scared going in there,' admitted Yaqui, who fought James Scott in the prison sports hall. 'I went there with my wife and my little boy and people called my hotel the night before saying "you better be careful" and then they'd hang up.

'That happened several times.

'Scott was tough but before the fight you were supposed to take a drug test. I had to pee in a cup and he didn't, so right then I was suspicious.'

'You couldn't hurt him,' said Cruz, who thought Scott's brutal training regimen alone was not enough for him to stand up to Lopez's tenacious onslaught for the full ten rounds.

He extravagantly surmised that Scott, who won widely on two cards, was on 'angel dust or something'.

Two routine eight-round stoppages followed for Yaqui, who earned a rematch with Saad, partly because the champion had given him his word years earlier.

'My best performance had to be the second fight with Saad Muhammad,' Lopez recollected of the night he left his name in the record books and defined his career. Before the fight I just knew we were going to go to war.

'They gave it Fight of the Year, Round of the Year [the eighth] and some people called it the Fight of the Decade.'

'Action. Non-stop riveting action,' added Cruz.

In the eighth, Saad somehow stood firm and smiled after taking almost 30 unanswered punches.

He covered up, grinning through his guard, and then responded once he thought Yaqui had punched himself out.

'In that round he caught me good and I could feel blood running down my face and I thought "uh oh",' Lopez said.

'I remembered our last fight was stopped on cuts so I had to go for broke. I hit him with everything. He was hurt. Even though he was smiling I knew he was hurt.

'Jersey Joe Walcott was the commissioner and he was telling the referee to stop the fight. The referee had his back to him and the crowd was going so crazy there was no way he could hear him.'

Cruz carried on as was becoming customary, filling any gaps in Yaqui's stories.

Lopez did the same when the occasion required.

'The commission told us there would be no smelling salts. If you used smelling salts you'd be disqualified,' said Cruz.

'We didn't use any but after round eight in his corner about 12 of those little capsule things had been emptied and we could smell them from our corner. I haven't seen him but I bet Matthew's in bad shape now because he took an awful beating that night.

'Afterwards they had a press conference and it took him over an hour to get ready. When he did show he had two guys holding him up and he could only whisper.'

Yaqui wasn't in great shape himself, but it was true there was a chance the fight had taken something out of Saad he would never get back. It was that wicked.

Saad had used another of his nine lives.

'I went down four times,' said Yaqui, of the heartbreaking 14th.

'I wasn't hurt, it was exhaustion. He got his second wind but I never got mine.

'After that fight I thought my career was all over but after going back to California and resting a while I decided I had one more big fight left in me.'

Jack interrupted. 'I kept trying to get him to quit but he said, "One more fight, one more fight."'

Surely still reeling from the Saad war, Lopez was back in action just three months later when he lost to 1976 Olympic hero Michael Spinks.

'Spinks was beat in that fight,' Jack shouted. 'Yaqui had him beat and that brother of his, Leon, was running around the ring saying, "Hang in there. Hang in there."'

Now Yaqui interjected. 'But then he caught me with a left hook on the temple and I was hurt. I couldn't recover.'

Boxing News said at the start of the fight it looked like Spinks had 'bitten off more than he could chew' as Yaqui dominated.

Spinks, with his career in front of him and Yaqui's in decline, won in the seventh, scoring two knockdowns.

It seemed Lopez's title window had slammed shut.

He had lost valiant efforts to Saad, twice to Galindez and Conteh. Defeats to the lesser-known John Davis and ST Gordon followed.

And while Jack wanted his son-in-law to quit, Lopez had that misplaced boxer's optimism that he could salvage a championship shot, another decent payday and produce one last grandstand performance.

His persistence was rewarded, to a degree, when he stepped up in weight to challenge Carlos De Leon for the WBC cruiserweight title.

He wasn't surprised he had a fifth attempt. He felt he had earned it.

'To tell you the truth, I always worked hard and every fight I had on TV or even off TV the people liked to watch.'

'He was a crowd pleaser,' Jack smiled with paternal pride.

Still, he did not deserve the beating he took against De Leon.

Yaqui was stopped in the fourth, cut severely above his right eye.

He was never really in the fight, having been dropped in the first 40 seconds. Rather patronisingly, *Boxing News* said he 'put up his usual brave effort' but the wound meant the fight couldn't continue.

It was getting to the stage where someone had to intervene to get him out of the sport but ultimately fate had its say and, at 33, he knew he had to find another job.

'I won against Bash Ali but the judges gave it to him. They wanted me to quit,' he concluded of the split decision defeat that rounded off a career of 39 wins and 15 defeats over 12 years.

He had dominated Bash five years earlier, winning every round of ten, but after an era of wars it wasn't the same Lopez who met an improved Ali.

Despite fighting the best he missed out on the life-changing purses afforded to the likes of champions, such as Spinks and

Saad. He reckoned his best payday was around $50,000 before deductions, still a vast improvement on the $35 he made for his debut.

In retirement Lopez was employed in construction and as a garbage man but years of lifting heavy bins caused arthritic problems in his lower back, meaning he no longer worked.

There was, however, no escaping from how he'd be remembered and he knew his place in boxing folklore.

'I like it that people remember me as a tough warrior,' he said, clearly still thinking back. 'I'd never give up. I would bleed, I would go down and get backed up but never give up. It's an honour to be remembered alongside such tough fighters in such a tough era and it's an honour that you have travelled so many miles to meet me.

'Even when I die, the record with Saad Muhammad is still there. It was one of the greatest light-heavyweight fights in history and that means a lot to me.

'I have no regrets. I always tried my best and worked hard.

'We got to travel all over the world,' he said, looking at the others.

Emotion entered his voice for the first time.

'I took you guys everywhere,' he then quickly joked.

'No, we took you,' Cruz fired back swiftly, not letting Yaqui get away with his light-hearted insolence.

Yaqui left the house with a smile and told me to come across the street once I had finished talking to Jack and Benny.

Jack waved me in close and said softly after the door closed behind Yaqui, 'Albert takes care of me now. I can't do it anymore. I'm 80 years old. He comes over and he cleans my house, does my washing and brings me my medicine. He may cuss me out while he's doing it but he does it!

'I don't know what I'd do without this guy. He could have been a doctor he's so smart. I don't like to tell him that, of course, but he is.

'You can't beat this guy at dominoes or cards. He's very sharp.'

That is how they passed the time each day. They played board games and reminisced. They all enjoyed it. They had spent their lives together and planned on doing so until the very end.

I made the 30-yard walk across to Yaqui's house where I took some pictures of the fighter.

His home was similar to Jack's. It was another small bungalow.

Contrary to a lot of fighters' homes I had been in, where there was hardly any memorabilia on show, Yaqui's walls were plastered in fight posters from his biggest nights.

They were in immaculate condition.

Names like Saad, Spinks, Rossman, Galindez and many others stood out in a nostalgic haze.

Yaqui's wife Beatrice, Jack's daughter, came home from work just as I was leaving and said she was happy I had come to see her husband.

Back at Jack's he asked where my next stop would be.

I knew my travels were coming to an end.

Time was ticking and I needed to get to San Francisco before my flight home in the morning.

Jack implored me to say at his for the night.

I had arrived on his doorstep with nothing to offer and favours to ask and he wanted to help me further still.

But Benny drove me to the station and I took the bus to Sacramento, waited for an evening connection to San Francisco, scoffed a big bag of soft-baked Pepperidge Farm cookies and slept in the station when I arrived.

I took a local bus out to the airport where I waited patiently and retraced the footsteps of an incredible trip that had started in Newark less than 30 days earlier.

The journey through boxing's wastelands was over.

Epilogue

I HAD discovered that victory in life after boxing led in survival rather than success. Maybe the most remarkable journey I made came when Matthew Saad Muhammad and I took that beaten-up old Cadillac to Madison Square Garden.

Perhaps most heartbreaking, as the final pages of this book were being written in May 2014, Matthew died. It turned out he'd been fighting Lou Gehrig's disease, which had launched an all-out assault on his nervous system. He had a stroke and passed away a week later. He was just 59. The Philadelphia orphan, who'd spent years homeless after we had been roughing it in Atlantic City, was buried in the city where he'd been abandoned. Former foe Richie Kates was at the funeral, among around 250 mourners. So was Yaqui Lopez, who flew in from Stockton, and Dwight Qawi, sporting a long, grey beard and walking with a cane, was also there.

There had never been a light at the end of a long, tragic tunnel for 'Miracle' Matthew. I still have my Team Saad T-shirt. It's priceless.

I was back in the Garden the week of his funeral to watch Miguel Cotto and Sergio Martinez do battle for the same middleweight crown Saad and I had seen another Puerto Rican, Felix Trinidad, fight Bernard Hopkins for 13 years earlier.

Ring announcer Michael Buffer ordered silence while they chimed ten bells for Matthew, the fallen warrior.

The place he had not been able to get into for free all those years ago came to a standstill in his name.

The next day, back at the Hall of Fame, 14 years after we first met there, I listened to a further sombre ten bells for my old friend. I spoke to Marvin Johnson several times after we finally met. He had been so negative when we finally got together but I think a phone call from Duane Bobick and perhaps my persistence changed his outlook.

Marvin had told me he wasn't interested in going to any boxing events so when my friend Larry Tornambe, a ring announcer from Philadelphia, asked if I could get him to attend Matthew Saad Muhammad's induction at the Pennsylvania Boxing Hall of Fame in 2006 I informed him not to get his hopes up.

I told Marvin to expect a call from Larry and, surprisingly, he agreed to go. I also rallied round Yaqui and Eddie who guaranteed their attendance. They had a fantastic time. They were hugging one another, laughing and smiling.

When Saad and Yaqui saw each other they embraced and wept.

Phone calls to the four light-heavyweight stars in the days that followed were the most rewarding I had made.

Saad was honoured they had come from Nevada, California and Indiana to share his special night.

Yaqui and Eddie loved it. Marvin was thrilled to be involved.

Still buzzing at his first taste of a new world – where his achievements would be appreciated – he said, 'It was great that we all came. I tell you it was so great, it was a much different atmosphere to when we were fighting because then it was all about business. This time it was just a happy occasion and a time of celebration. We were all there to celebrate Saad Muhammad and it felt really good. I hadn't seen those guys in so many years. I'm glad I went.'

Possibly the hardest fighter to track down, Marvin was the most gratifying. I felt like I had made a significant difference.

Of the reunion, Eddie Mustafa said, 'It was magical. Everyone was teary-eyed.'

Sadly, Jack Cruz, Yaqui's kind manager who offered this weary Englishman a place to rest his head and who felt offended when I didn't accept, died. He lost his long battle with illness and passed away in 2005 where he hoped he would, with his loved ones, Yaqui included, around him. He'd recently written of Lopez, 'I don't know what I did to deserve him.'

I stayed in touch with poor Jimmy Young on the phone for a while after I returned home from travelling. His mood would alter and, as with many boxers, his number would frequently change. Sometimes he would be bright and perky, on other occasions he sounded too depressed to even talk. If that was the case I would try to cheer him up by initiating a conversation about his victories and his achievements as I had done in the fast-food joint a couple of years earlier. Sometimes I put the phone down thinking I had made a difference, that I had lifted his spirits.

One February night in 2005, back in England, I woke with a start and for some unexplainable reason fired up my laptop and checked my e-mails.

It was about 3am and Tom Jess had just sent me an emotional message. Jimmy had died. Heart problems.

I continued to call Harold Johnson once in a while. Sure, he had no idea who I was but I thought the odd phone call here or there would have broken up his everyday monotony.

As for Jeff Chandler, I was always tempted to retrace my footsteps and show up on his doorstep just to see that complete look of amazement again. He eventually moved into a nicer neighbourhood in Delaware.

I joined the staff at *Boxing News* in 2007, five years after that first interview with Micky Ward ran, and in 2008 had to write Joey Giardello's obituary. I left the office with a heavy heart that day and vacantly surfed the Internet on the train home only to discover Rocky Castellani had also passed away less than a week earlier.

Eddie Mustafa has become an ally in Vegas, a good place to have friends in boxing while Joey Giambra was still trying to get Jack Nicholson on board for the movie. I wondered if Jose Torres, who returned to live in Puerto Rico, read Giambra's book before he died of a heart attack at the age of 72 in 2009.

On a later trip to the States I was in Madison Square Garden to cover Chris Byrd–Andrew Golota and John Ruiz–Fres Oquendo for different heavyweight titles. Jose was ringside and signing autographs before we saw one another. He recognised me but wasn't sure from where or when.

'You,' he said, pointing at me. I lit up with pride that he recalled who I was. 'You were in my house.'

'Holy shit,' I thought, as members of the press section turned to look at me. 'People will think I'm a burglar.'

I did not see him again. He died in 2009. People will remember him for his two books and light-heavyweight title winning career. I'll remember him for shadowboxing on his balcony in his underwear.

I exchanged Christmas cards with Chico Vejar and the Fullmers, seeing Don a couple more times at different functions. I was sad to learn of his passing in 2012. The man who'd been the pride of Salt Lake City's fire department and sporting community, who'd gone out of his way to bring me a bag of cherries, died from leukaemia while Gene fought on against Parkinson's.

I didn't hear anything else about Florentino Fernandez until news spread of his passing in 2013 from a heart attack.

I called Boogaloo Watts every so often and remained in contact with Buster Drayton for a while.

George Chuvalo is still battling on. He's still sharp, too. We have met up on a few occasions and neither of us have forgotten the day that tears filled the coffee shop as the rain beat down outside. Aaron and Frankie Pryor and I exchanged e-mails and sometimes traded pictures of my children and their grandchildren and Dwight Qawi was eventually inducted into the International Boxing Hall of Fame. He said his induction gave him closure and that it was the final chapter of his life in boxing. I wasn't so sure.

There's rarely closure in this sport. A few months later I heard he was training fighters.

Big Ernie Terrell's business continued to boom, as did Big Jim Beattie's, but as the years ticked by Ernie's health began to falter and he could no longer do interviews. Jim Carlin protected him from anyone who might have been able to take advantage of him.

Hedgemon Lewis and Richard Steele could still be found in the searing climes of Nevada, but no longer at the defunct Nevada Partners gym.

Duane Bobick fell in love with boxing again after we talked. I know he called Marvin Johnson several times to reminisce and Marvin thoroughly enjoyed their chats. Bobick was only dipping his toes back into the sport when I found him and he went on to become the deputy commissioner of the Minnesota boxing commission.

His health faltered, however, and recently he was forced to move into a care home.

Buster Douglas and Vonzell Johnson aren't on good terms any longer. Buster's landscaping efforts are still paying hefty dividends and Artie and BJ are grown up.

Chuck Wepner eventually settled out of court with Stallone, which is what he wanted to do all along.

I wrote to James Scott a couple of times. I heard he was paroled a few years after my visit, then he was in a halfway house in New Jersey, taking his vital first steps back into the community he had been absent from for 30 years. Later, Sammy Goss – the US bantamweight at the 1968 Olympics – took him on as a trainer at the Goss and Goss Gym in Trenton. 'He's great with the kids,' Sammy told me in May 2010.

By 2014, Scott's health deteriorated and the man who spent more than half of his life in prison was fighting dementia in a rest home.

Richie Kates and Marvin Johnson were still working to uphold law and order. In many ways it had all started with Micky Ward, of course, and those trips to Lowell.

In 2009 his friend Arturo Gatti died while holidaying in Brazil with his fiancée. It was termed suicide but deemed a mystery by those who knew him best.

Micky and I continued to speak every once in a while.

In 2010 a film called *The Fighter*, based on Micky's life and starring Mark Wahlberg as my old friend, was released. An Oscar-winner, it was huge. We chatted after I'd become the editor of *Boxing News*. 'We both did good,' he joked. 'Micky, they just made a movie of your life,' I replied.

There was an emptiness in his voice, though. Gatti had completed him and now he was gone. 'We were supposed to grow old together, telling war stories,' Micky lamented.

Without Saad, Atlantic City just isn't the same.

A couple of years ago I went back to see Leavander Johnson.

He towered over me, his bronze features staring happily in the sunshine. He held his hands aloft in a victorious pose with the world title proudly around his waist.

The statue erected in his memory did him justice.

Leavander did fulfil what he always considered his destiny, finally winning the IBF world lightweight title at his fourth attempt.

His was a story of perseverance, determination and dreams.

I watched his first title defence, in Vegas in September 2005, from a hotel room in Orlando and Leavander lost his title to Jesus Chavez.

It was a brutal fight. He took consistent, booming head shots throughout the contest. His legs often looked rubbery. It was hard to watch. All I thought about was how sorry I was that he would lose his title in the initial defence.

He was battered. I thought Bill could have pulled him out before Leavander's game resistance was eventually crushed in the 11th. I was disappointed for him, though pleased he'd lived his dream. Later that night he was in hospital, fighting for his life having been rushed to a medical facility in Nevada with a blood clot on the brain.

I followed his progress for several days until it was sadly announced that the sparkly smiled, determined young man whose dreams had come true had died doing what he loved.

It was always a gamble to take a non-digital camera but I couldn't afford one. I had no idea if I was capturing the guys well or even if I was getting then in the pictures at all with my ancient APS Canon. The only thing I could do was try to make sure they were in the viewfinder, click and hope they were there when the photos were developed.

They came out OK except for one, the picture I had taken of the beaming Saad Muhammad, Bill Johnson and his Leavander as they laughed, hugged and smiled. As much as any other, however, that image will stay with me.

I called Bill, my old pad man, the day he buried Leavander.

He seemed detached; sounded like he was in a trance. He said he didn't blame Chavez and that it could have been the other way round.

Jesus Chavez, along with about 1,000 people including numerous boxing luminaries and New Jersey dignitaries, was at the funeral.

'I wouldn't change a thing' was engraved on Leavander's headstone.

His older sibling, Craig, told me he couldn't have wished for a nicer brother, trying to stay strong as his voice quivered.

'I was so lucky,' he said quietly. 'He'll live on, but it was a privilege to ride on his wings.'

I, too, was grateful to Leavander for that.

Spending time with him and the fighters, whether they were contenders or champions, whether it was crying, laughing, joking or talking about their pasts or their futures, I was lucky, too, that they had allowed me to fly on their wings, if only for a brief moment of their remarkable journeys.